Malte Liesner

Greek Historical Phonology Workbook

Reichert Verlag Wiesbaden 2015

Greek Historical Phonology Workbook

Malte Liesner

Reichert Verlag Wiesbaden 2015

Bibliografische Information der Deutschen Nationalbibliothek

Die Deutsche Nationalbibliothek verzeichnet diese Publikation in der Deutschen Nationalbibliografie; detaillierte bibliografische Daten sind im Internet über http://dnb.dnb.de abrufbar.

ISBN: 978-3-95490-105-0
www.reichert-verlag.de

Printed in Germany

Preface

While I am writing these lines thousands of immigrants are pouring into Germany fleeing from war and terror. For this weekend alone, the local government of Munich is expecting 40,000 people arriving mostly from Syria, Afghanistan and countries in Africa carrying their children, babies and all the rest they have in their hands. They are desperate for a new life, a better life without war and terror. And while I am thinking about g's and k's and how they change into each other, the biggest refugee crisis since World War II is on the way and getting worse day by day.

I strongly believe that Christians, Muslims, Jews, Buddhists and the supporters of other religions worship one and the same God which is the universal energy found in the universe called love. We humans have a direct and intimate contact to and also a certain kind of control over this energy and are therefore directly linked to what we call God. But as long as we do not manage to establish harmony in our hearts and in the world directly surrounding us, my hope of a peaceful world remains a distant dream.

Education is one of the key tools for development but education is much more than the mere transportation of information. It is about having contact with people and acting as an example for others. Education is also not the single responsibility of teachers but it starts in the family with the parents being the first teachers of their children and likewise the children being the teachers of their parents showing them how to focus and live in the moment.

Christian Morgenstern, a German poet, teacher and writer who lived from 1871–1914 once said: *As they can only afford to pay teachers 600 marks, the peoples stay so dumb that they must afford wars which cost 6 billion marks.*

Königsberg, Germany. September 2015
Malte Liesner

Contents

Consonant Changes

Appendices

1 Greek in Space and Time

Ancient Greek is one of the major branches of the Indo-European language family and subdivided into several dialects whose exact subclassification is disputed (cf. the overview in appendix 3). Due to systematic grammatical and lexical correspondences, the Indo-European languages enable us to reconstruct a proto-language out of which the individual Indo-European languages developed. This common ancestor of all Indo-European languages is known as Proto-Indo-European whose reconstruction is based on the systematic comparison of correspondences between the individual attested Indo-European languages. Proto-Indo-European is, however, not an attested but a reconstructed language. This workbook traces the phonological development from Proto-Indo-European to Attic Greek, the dialect which was spoken in the Attica region, whose variant of the 5th century BC is known as Classical Ancient Greek. The famous works of the philosophers Plato and Aristotle, the historians Xenophon, Thucydides as well as of the playwrights Aeschylus, Sophocles, Euripides and Aristophanes were written in Attic. Due to the political and cultural importance of Athens at that time, a modified Attic variant became the basis of the transregional lingua franca known as Koine Greek which developed as a consequence of the conquests of Alexander the Great in the 4th century BC and was spoken until the 3rd century AD.

Sociolects as Language Variants

Classical Attic Greek was a language of prestige and subjected to the norms of conservative orthography which did not display sound changes which were ongoing or had already taken place. It is very common that the spelling of a language lags far behind the actual development, as it can also be seen in the word *night* [nai̯t] whose spelling represents the pronunciation [niçt] which was in use about 600 years ago. Important indications of the actual pronunciation of ancient languages are therefore phonetic misspellings, inscriptions and non-official letters of semi-educated writers who often wrote the way they spoke. In contrast to Attic, the phonologically progressive dialect Boeotian was never subjected to standardized orthography so that many writers spelled its actual pronunciation. Many Boeotian developments of the 5th century BC anticipate later Attic developments so that it is possible that in the 5th century BC already the Attic variant of the uneducated population differed strongly from the language of the educated elite on which the reconstruction of the phonological system of the Attic dialect is based. This situation is similar to the coexistence of Classical Latin and Vulgar Latin which became the ancestor of the Romance languages and must have exhibited in classical times already many sound changed which were not spelled due to standardized Latin orthography.

This contrast of everyday language and an artificially heightened language norm based on Classical Attic is to some extent typical for Greek still today. The modern Greek vernacular, which is known as Demotic Greek or Demotiki, stands in opposition to the artificially archaic Katharevousa, which is based on Classical Attic and was the official standard language until 1976. Katharevousa is, however, still important in medical and judicary terminology as well as for the official communication of the Greek Orthodox Church but most speakers do not use it for writing anymore. Such a coexistence of two complementary languages in one language system is known as diglossia. The linguistic difference between the speakers of the two languages is referred to as diastratic difference. **Cf.** Teodorsson 1978:94–6; Horrocks 2010:163–165; Wilms 2013:73.

Diachronic Language Change

The phonology and morphology of languages are always subjected to changes. The change from one state of language to the next state is known as **diachronic language change** and constitutes the main subject of this book in which the phonological development of Attic is traced from reconstructed PIE. As languages change gradually and mostly unnoticed, the classification of Greek language epochs given in the following table must therefore not be regarded as separate entities of the development of Greek. Classifications like this one are often composed not from the linguistic but rather historical aspect.

Stages of Greek Diachronic Development

Language	Timeframe
Proto-Indo-European = PIE	ca. 3500 BC
Proto-Greek	ca. 2000 BC
Mycenaean Greek	ca. 1400–1100 BC
Classical Ancient Greek	ca. 800–300 BC
Koine Greek	ca. 300 BC–300 AD
Late Antique Greek	ca. 300–600 AD
Medieval Greek	ca. 600–1500 AD
Modern Greek	since ca. 1500 AD

PIE as the common ancerstor of all the IE languages was spoken probably around 3500 BC in the vicinity of the Black Sea. Proto-Greek, which is the reconstructable predecessor of all Greek dialects, was probably not a homogenous language anymore but rather subdivided into dialects already. The first attestation of Mycenaean, which is the most ancient attested form of the Greek language, dates back to the 14th century BC. The syllabic spelling of the Mycenaean Linear B clay tablets, which are a corpus of texts of the royal court administration, was deciphered in 1952. Mycenaean was, however, not the predecessor of the other Greek dialects but rather an individual dialect besides the unattested prestages of the other dialects. Between the collaps of the Mycenaean culture and the start of the Ancient Greek alphabetic tradition come the so-called dark ages about which only little to nothing is known.

The Homeric epics Iliad and Odyssey, which deal with the destruction of Troy and Ulysses's odyssey back home, are dated to the starting time of alphabetic Ancient Greek. They are of high linguistic and cultural importance and composed in an artificial literary language which contains elements from several Ancient Greek dialects. The Attic variant of the 5th century BC, which is known is Ancient Classical Greek, was superseded by Koine Greek in the Hellenistic period which eventually led to Medieval and Modern Greek. Koine Greek is also the language of the New Testament which is the central collection of texts which proclaim Jesus Christ as the Son of God. **Cf.** SI §12–15; Wilms 2013:85–146.

2 Spelling and Transcription

In the early Greek times, there existed many different alphabets which also included letters such as digamma Ϝ, koppa Ϟ or sampi ϡ. These letters are absent in the following Ionic alphabet which was introduced as the official alphabet in Athens in 403 BC with slight modifications in order to adapt it to the Attic dialect. Originally, only capital letters known as majuscules were used for writing before a cursive writing was developed, out of which the minuscules developed. In the early times, the direction of writing was from right to left similar to the Phoenecian alphabet out of which the Old Greek alphabet was derived.

Majuskel	Minuskel	Transkription
Α	α / (ᾱ)	[a] / [ā]
Β	β	[b]
Γ	γ	[g] / [ŋ]
Δ	δ	[d]
Ε	ε	[e]
Ζ	ζ	[zd]
Η	η	[ę̄]
Θ	θ	[t^h]
Ι	ι / (ῑ)	[i] / [ī] / [i̯]
Κ	κ	[k]
Λ	λ	[l]
Μ	μ	[m]
Ν	ν	[n]
Ξ	ξ	[ks]
Ο	ο	[o]
Π	π	[p]
Ρ	ρ	[r] / [r^h]
Σ	σ, ς	[s] / [z]
Τ	τ	[t]
Υ	υ / (ῡ)	[y] / [ȳ] / [u̯]
Φ	φ	[p^h]
Χ	χ	[k^h]
Ψ	ψ	[ps]
Ω	ω	[ǭ]
ʿ		[h]

Vowels

The accent signs ά, ὰ, ᾶ are transcribed [á à ã]. The short vowels α, ε, ι, ο, υ are transcribed [a e i o y]: **ἀ**ντί [**a**ntí] 'against'; δ**έ**κα [d**é**ka] 'ten'; **ἵ**να [h**í**na] 'in order to'; π**ό**λις [p**ó**lis] 'city'; λ**ύ**κος [l**ý**kos] 'wolf'. The long vowels ᾱ, η, ῑ, ω, ῡ, ει, ου are transcribed with a macron [ā ę̄ ī ǭ ȳ ę̄ ū] and accent signs are placed above the macron: τρ**ᾱ**χύς [tr**ā**k^{h}ýs] 'rough'; ζ**η**τέω [zd**ę̄**téǭ] 'I search'; π**ῑ́**νω [p**ī́**nǭ] 'I drink'; **ὠ**μός [**ǭ**mós] 'raw'; λ**ῡ**γρός [l**ȳ**grós] 'sad'; λ**εί**πω [l**ę̄́**pǭ] 'I leave'; ἐξ**ου**σίᾱ [eks**ū**síā] 'permit'.
As the second element of diphthongs, ι and υ are transcribed [i̯] and [u̯]: τρα**υ**ματίζω [tra**u̯**matízdǭ] 'I wound'; σπε**υ**στικός [spe**u̯**stikós] 'in a hurry'; α**ἱ** βίβλο**ι** [ha**i̯** bíblo**i̯**] 'the books'. Accent signs are placed on the first element of a diphthong: τρα**ῦ**μα [trãu̯ma] 'wound'; **αἷ**μα [**hãi̯**ma] 'blood'; σπε**ύ**δω [spéu̯dǭ] 'I hurry up'.
The iota subscript of long diphthongs is transcribed [i̯] after the long vowel: dat. sg. δώρ**ῳ** [dǭ́r**ǭi̯**] 'present'; κλ**ῇ**σις [kl**ę̄̃i̯**sis] 'closure'. A trema represents the discrete pronunciation of two vowels: Hom. π**άϊ**ς [p**ái**s] 'child'; Hom. dat. sg. κέρ**αϊ** [kér**ai**] 'horn'.

Consonants

The stops voiced β, δ, γ are transcribed [b d g]: **β**ιάζω [**b**iázdǭ] 'zwinge'; **δ**ῶμα [**d**ǭ̃ma] 'house', **γ**λίσχρος [**g**lísk^{h}ros] 'sticky'. The voiceless stops π, τ, κ are transcribed [p t k]: **π**νεῦμα [**p**nẽu̯ma] 'wind'; **τ**είρω [**t**ę̄́rǭ] 'I weaken'; **κ**ύ**κ**λος [**k**ý**k**los] 'circle'. The voiceless aspirated stops φ, θ, χ are transcribed [p^h t^h k^h]: **φ**αίνω [**p^h**ái̯nǭ] 'I show'; **θ**ᾶκος [**t^h**ãkós] 'seat'; **χ**εῖρ [**k^h**ę̄̃r] 'hand'.
The resonants μ, ν, ρ, λ are transcribed [m n r l] and initial ῥ is transcribed [r^h]: **μ**οχλός [**m**ok^{h}lós] 'lever'; **ν**ῦ**ν** [**n**ȳ̃**n**] 'now'; ἱδ**ρ**ώς [hid**r**ǭ́s] 'sweat'; **λ**ά**λ**ος [**l**á**l**os] 'talkative'; **ῥ**εῦμα [**r^h**ẽu̯ma] 'current'.
The letters ξ [ks], ψ [ps] and ζ [zd] stand for two sounds: **ξ**υρόν [**ks**yrón] 'cutting blade'; **ψ**ῦχω [**ps**ȳ́k^{h}ǭ] 'I breathe', **ζ**ώνη [**zd**ǭ́nę̄] 'belt'. The sound [s] is noted σ in the initial and medial position and ς in the final position: νό**σ**το**ς** [nó**s**to**s**] 'return'. Before β, δ, γ, the letter σ is transcribed [z]: πρέ**σ**βυς [pré**z**bys] 'old', **ζ**ώνη [**zd**ǭ́nę̄] 'belt', μί**σ**γω [mí**z**gǭ] 'I mix'. Before γ, κ, χ, ν, μ, the letter γ denotes the velar nasal [ŋ]: ἐ**γ**γύς [e**ŋ**gýs] 'near'; ἐ**γ**κύκλιος [e**ŋ**kýklios] 'round'; λα**γ**χάνω [la**ŋ**k^{h}ánǭ] 'I forget'. The spiritus asper ʿ is transcribed [h]: **ἁ**ρμονίᾱ [**h**armoníā] 'harmony'. The spiritus lenis ʾ is not transcribed.

Exercises

E1 Easy Transcriptions

A λόγος [lógos] 'word' **B** πόνος [__________] 'effort' **C** τόνος [__________] 'tension' **D** κλῑ́νω [__________] 'I lean' **E** κλέπτω [__________] 'I steal' **F** μῑκρός [__________] 'small'

E2 Transcription of φ, θ, χ as [p^h], [t^h], [k^h]

A τίθημι [títʰēmi] 'I put' **B** φημί [__________] 'I say' **C** χώρᾱ [__________] 'space' **D** συμφορᾱ́ [__________] 'occurence' **E** συχνός [__________] 'frequently' **F** λόχος [__________] 'ambush'

E3 Transcription of ι and υ as [i̯] and [u̯] in Diphthongs

A καυλός [__________] 'stalk' **B** αἱρέω [__________] 'I take' **C** σπεύδω [__________] 'I hurry up'

E4 Transcription of ψ, ξ, ζ as [ps], [ks], [zd]

A ξένος [ksénos] 'foreigner' **B** ξύλον [__________] 'wood' **C** ψεύδειν [__________] 'to lie' **D** ψυχή [__________] 'soul' **E** ψέγειν [__________] 'to criticize' **F** νίζω [__________] 'I wash'

E5 Transcription of Inital ῥ as [r^h] and Transcription of Iota-Subscript as [i̯]

A ῥῆμα [__________] 'word' **B** ῥίπτειν [__________] 'to throw' **C** ῥήτωρ [__________] 'speaker' **D** dat. λόγῳ [__________] 'word' **E** dat. τῑμῇ [__________] 'honor' **F** dat. θεᾷ [__________] 'goddess'

E6 Transcription of γ [ŋ] Before γ, κ, χ, μ, ν

A ἄγγελος [__________] 'messenger' **B** ἀγμός [__________] 'abyss' **C** ὄγμος [__________] 'furrow'

E7 The Symbols *ϝ and *i̯ Can Be Used for [u̯] and [i̯]

A *κλέϝος [kleu̯s] 'honor' **B** *ὄϝις [__________] 'sheep' **C** *καλϝός [__________] 'beautiful' **D** *τένι̯ω [__________] 'I stretch' **E** *μάνι̯ω [__________] 'I am furious' **F** *δαι̯ϝήρ [__________] 'brother-in-law'

3 Basics of Phonetics

Phonetics is the study of the production and properties of human speech sounds. One of the most important classification of sounds is that according to the place of articulation, which describes where a sound is produced, and the manner of articulation, which describes how a sound is produced.

Fundamental Places of Articulation

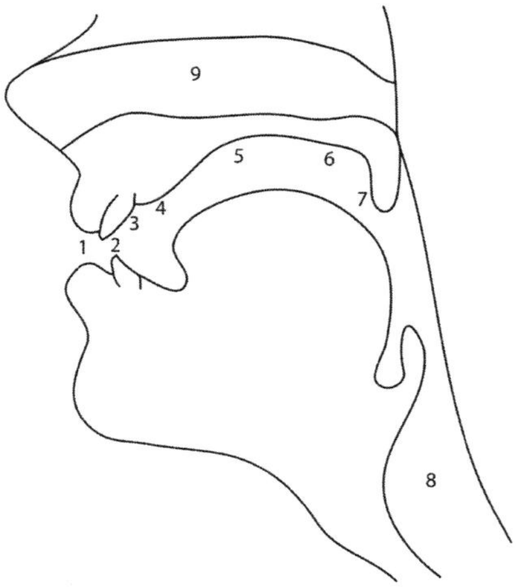

Place of Articulation		Description
1	labial	With the lips
2	interdental	Between the teeth
3	dental	At the teeth
4	alveolar	At the teeth-ridge
5	palatal	At the hard palate
6	velar	At the soft palate
7	uvular	At the uvula
8	glottal	At the vocal folds
9	nasal	In the nasal cavity

Fundamental Manners of Articulation

Vowel	Vowels are articulated with an open vocal tract. The airflow passes out of the mouth unconstrictedly.
Consonant	Consonants are articulated with a complete or partial occlusion of the vocal tract.
Stop	The airflow stops completely due to an occlusion of the oral vocal tract. All languages have stop consonants, the most common are [p], [t], [k] and their voiced counterparts [b], [d], [g].
Nasal	The airflow passes through the nose while there is an occlusion of the oral vocal tract, which determines the resonant cavity of the consonant and therefore produces the sound of e.g. dental [n], labial [m] or velar [ŋ].
Fricative	A partial closure of the vowel tract causes the airflow to become turbulent which produces fricative consonants like [s], [f], [h]. Fricatives are also called spirants or stridents.
Lateral	During the articulation of the alveolar lateral /l/, the airflow escapes along the sides of the tongue while the tongue blocks the airflow in the middle. /l/ and /r/ are traditionally known as liquids.
Voiced Sounds	The vocal cords vibrate while articulating a voiced sound. All the vowels and the consonants [b d g u̯ i̯ r l m n ŋ] are voiced sounds.
Approximant	The approximant consonants [w] and [j], which are also called semivowels, have an intermediate articulation between vowels and fricative consonants.
Trill	The alveolar trill consonant /r/ is articulated while the tongue vibrates against the teeth-ridge. In the Initial position, it had a voiceless aspirated allophone [r^h]. /l/ and /r/ are traditionally known as liquids.
Resonants	Due to their similar phonological behavior, the trill [r], the lateral [l] and the nasals are grouped together as resonants.

Basics of Phonology

Human beings can produce a broad variety of sounds with their innate articulation organs but languages only use a choice of these sounds for contrasting words from each other. This choice is known as the **phoneme inventory** of a language and the individual sounds, which are used for contrasting words, are known as **phonemes**.

Change of Meaning through the Interchange of Phonemes

Phonemes are determined by the so-called minimal pair analysis in which words are contrasted which differ in one feature or one sound only, as it is the case in the English minimal pair *night* and *light*, in which the interchange of the two English phonemes /n/ and /l/ changes the meaning of the words. Greek examples are the comparison of πόρος [póros] 'ford' and φόρος [pʰóros] 'tax' on the one hand as well as πάτος [pátos] 'path' and πάθος [pátʰos] 'suffering' one the other hand. Therefore, the sounds [p], [pʰ], [t], [tʰ] can be classified as phonemes /p/, /pʰ/, /t/, /tʰ/. Independent of their phonological function within a language system, sounds are generally noted in [square] brackets. If one wants to assert their phonological function of being able to change the meaning of words, these sounds are classified as phonemes and noted in /slashes/. The Attic vowel and consonant phonemes are determined in the next chapter by searching for minimal pairs.
In this book, sounds like *ā*, *p*, *pʰ* are generally noted in *italic* print and only furnished with slashes if their phonemic status is spoken about explicitly. Phonetic transcriptions like [pátos] are noted in square bracket although the exact phonetic nature of old languages can only be determined with approximation. More detailed information can be found in the book *Vox Graeca* (Allen 1974).

Allophonic Variants

The frequent prefix ἐν- 'in, into' preserved or changed its form depending on the consonant following. Before vowels or the dental consonants δ, τ, θ, ν, it remained such as in ἐν-δύω 'I go into', ἐν-τίθημι 'I put into', ἐν-θρῴσκω 'I jump into' and ἐν-νοέω 'I have in mind'. Before the labial consonants β, π, φ, μ, the prefix ἐν- changed to ἐμ- such as in ἐμ-βαίνω 'I walk into', ἐμ-πίπτω 'I fall into', ἐμ-φύω 'I plant into', ἐμ-μένω 'I stay within', and before the velar consonants γ, κ, χ, the prefix ἐν- changed to ἐγ- [eŋ] such as in ἐγ-γράφω 'I write into', ἐγ-κλείω 'I enclose' and ἐγ-χέω 'I pour into'. These changes are due to the assimilation of the place of articulation of the nasal to the consonant following. Before dental consonants, dental ν remained, before labial consonants it became labial μ, and before velar consonants it became velar γ [ŋ] (cf. SC 24). The meaning 'into', however, does not change regardless of whether the prefix is pronounced ἐν-, ἐμ- or ἐγ- [eŋ]. The nasal /n/ has therefore different phonetic realizations depending on its phonological environment. If the interchange of sounds does not change the meaning of a word, these variant realizations are known as **allophones,** and in this case, the allophones [m], [n], [ŋ] are assigned to the phoneme /n/.

Unclear Phoneme Status

Due to the phonological opposition *g* :: *ŋ* in the minimal pair *ἐκ-γράφειν > (30.3) ἐγ-γράφειν [eggráphẹ̄n] 'to copy, to delete' :: *ἐν-γράφειν (24.2) > ἐγ-γράφειν [eŋgrápʰẹ̄n] 'to write into', it is theoretically possible to derive a phoneme /ŋ/. This opposition is however so rare that the sound [ŋ] could be regarded to have no more than a marginal phoneme status. This example shows that in some cases it can be problematic to determine the exact phoneme status. **Cf.** Allen 1974:36–37; Sommerstein 1973:2; Kümmel 2007:449.

4 Defining Attic Consonant Phonemes

Search the following jumbled list for minimal pairs and write them at the according place in the table. Cross out used words in the list. **Cf.** Lupaş 1972:110–114.

~~βάθος 'depth'~~, τέρας 'omen', ἔτος 'year', βόλος 'throw', χόρτος 'fodder', ~~πάθος 'misery'~~, κέρας 'horn', δόλος 'trick', φόρτος 'burden', τόμος 'a piece cut off', ὕπνος 'sleep', μαίνω 'I am furious', ἔπος 'word', βαίνω 'I go', τόνος 'tension', τρέφω 'I nourish', ὕμνος 'song', τρέμω 'I tremble', ὅλος 'whole', πόσις 'husband', ῥύμη 'force', νεώς 'temple', δῶμα 'house', πόλος 'pole', λεώς 'people', σορός 'urn', λῦμη 'insult', σῶμα 'body', πόλις 'city', τορός 'piercing'

Opposition	**Minimal Pairs**
p :: *b*	πάθος 'misery' :: βάθος 'depth'
p :: *t*	::
p :: *m*	::
p :: *h*	::
p^h :: k^h	::
p^h :: *m*	::
b :: *d*	::
b :: *m*	::
t :: *k*	::
n :: *m*	::
n :: *l*	::
r :: *l*	::
s :: *l*	::
s :: *t*	::
s :: *d*	::

Defining Attic Vowel Phonemes

Search the following jumbled list for minimal pairs and write them at the according place in the table. Cross out used words in the list. **Cf.** Lupaş 1972:126–131.

~~ᾰ̓́κων ‘spear’~~, gen. sg. νίκης ‘of the victory’, δασμός ‘tax’, δεσμός ‘fetter’, ὄχος ‘carriage’, ~~ᾱ̓́κων ‘involuntary’~~, ἄχος ‘pain’, acc. pl. νίκᾱς ‘the Siege’, 3. sg. imp. ἔστω ‘he shall be’, ptc. prs. νικῶν ‘winning’, λέγω ‘I speak’, 1. pl. ipf. εἴχομεν ‘we had’, λόχος ‘hideout’, inf. prs. λῡπεῖν ‘to mourn’, λέχος ‘bed’, λήγω ‘I stop’, ἦμος ‘when’, 1. pl. prs. ἔχομεν ‘we have’, 3. sg. imp. ῐ̓́στω ‘he shall know’, inf. prs. νικᾶν ‘to win’, τόκος ‘birth’, λῡ́πη ‘a mourning’, ὦμος ‘shoulder’, 1. pl. prs. ῐ̔κετεύομεν ‘we beg’, λῡ́πει ‘mourn!’, πύστις ‘investigation’, 1. pl. ipf. ῑ̔κετεύομεν ‘we begged’, πίστις ‘trust’, ptc. prs. nt. λῡποῦν ‘mourning’, τύκος ‘mallet’

Opposition	**Minimal Pairs**
a :: *ā*	ᾰ̓́κων ‘spear’ :: ᾱ̓́κων ‘involuntary’
a :: *e*	::
a :: *o*	::
ā :: *ę̄*	::
ā :: *ǭ*	::
e :: *ę̄*	::
e :: *ẹ̄*	::
e :: *o*	::
e :: *i*	::
ę̄ :: *ẹ̄*	::
ę̄ :: *ǭ*	::
ẹ̄ :: *ū*	::
i :: *u*	::
i :: *ī*	::
o :: *u*	::

FUNDAMENTALS

5 Feature Structure of Attic Vowels

Short and Long Vowels

		Front		Back
		Rounded	Unrounded	Rounded
Close	Short	ι /i/	υ /y/	
	Long	ῑ /ī/	ῡ /ȳ/	ου /ū/
Close-mid		ει /ẹ̄/		ο /o/
Central		ε /e/		
Open-mid		η /ę̄/		ω /ǭ/
Open		α /a/ – ᾱ /ā/		

Additional Remarks for Individual Sounds

- The vowels /a/, /e/, /i/, /o/, /y/ could be short or long but the long vowels /ā/, /ī/, /ȳ/ were not explicitly noted in Greek spelling and are deduced by metrical or etymological analysis. In post-classical times, the phonemic feature of vowel length was lost and became a purely allophonic side effect of stressed vowels in open syllables.
- Short ε /e/ was neither the exact counterpart to /ẹ̄/ nor to /ę̄/ but was probably pronounced between these sounds (Allen 1974:84).
- The vowels /y/ and /ȳ/ developed from PIE /u/ and /ū/ in preclassical times. Initial υ /y/ was always aspirated ὑ /hy/. An example is **údōr* > (12) **ýdōr* > (x14.5) ὕδωρ [hýdǭr] 'water' in comparison to Lat. *unda* 'wave' without initial /h/.
- Long close-mid ει /ẹ̄/ orginated through monophthongization of the preclassical diphthong [ei̯] such as in *λείπω [léi̯pǭ] > (14.2) λείπω [lẹ̄́pǭ] 'I leave', through vowel contractions such as in the 2. pl. *αἰτέ-ε-τε [ai̯téete] > (7.2) αἰτεῖτε [ai̯tẹ̄̂te] 'you ask for', and through compensatory lengthening of short ε such as in the aor. *ἔδερσα [édersa] > (2.1) *ἔδειρα [édẹ̄ra] 'skinned'.
- ου /ū/ orginated out of long close-mid /ọ̄/. Sources of /ọ̄/ were the preclassical diphthong *[ou̯] such as in *σπουδή [spou̯dę̄́] > (14.1) *σπọ̄δή > (15) σπουδή [spūdę̄́] 'hurry', vowel contractions such as in the 1. pl. *δηλό-ομεν > (7.3) *δηλọ̄̂μεν > (15) δηλοῦμεν [dę̄lū̃men] 'we reveal' and compensatory lengthening such as in the acc. pl. *φίλονς > (4.2) *φίλọ̄ς > (15) φίλους 'friends'. **Cf.** Rix §52, 56, 67; LJ 192; Allen 1974.

Monophthongs / Diphthongs / Long Diphthongs / Monophthongization

A single vowel is also known as a **monophthong** to differentiate it from the junction of two vowels within one syllable which is known as a **diphthong**. As there can be only one syllabic nucleus within a syllable, the vowel which is not the nucleus is allophonically articulated as a semivowel. The sequence of the two phonemes /a/ and /i/ is most often pronounced as a diphthong [ai̯] in which /i/ is allophonically articulated as its semivowel [i̯]. A disyllabic realization [ai] is also possible in which case the two vowels constitute a hiatus. These two realizations explain the difference of Hom. ὄϊς [óis] 'sheep' to Att. οἶς [õi̯s], whereby the Homeric disyllabic sequence [oi] is realized as a diphthong [oi̯] in Attic (cf. chapter 14).

The sequence of a long vowel plus a semivowel is known as a **long diphthong** and the development of a diphthong to a monophthong is known as **monophthongization**. In this book, diphthongs are not considered to be individual phonemes. **Cf.** LJ §194–197.

Feature Structure of Attic Diphthongs

Diphthongs and Long Diphthongs

	Front		Back
	Unrounded	**Rounded**	**Rounded**
Close		υι [yi̯]	
Close-mid	ευ [eu̯]		οι [oi̯]
Open-mid	ῃ [ēi̯] / ηυ [ēu̯]		ῳ [ǭi̯] / ωυ [ǭu̯]
Open	αι [ai̯] / ᾳ [āi̯] / αυ [au̯] / ᾱυ [āu̯]		

Additional Remarks about the Diphthongs

- υι [yi̯] before a consonant had monophthongized to [ȳ] in preclassical times already: *ἰχθυ-ίδιον > ἰχθῡ́διον 'small fish'. Also in the position before a vowel, the diphthong [yi̯] monophthongized to [ȳ] at an early date: υἱός [hyi̯ós] > ὑός [hȳós] 'son'.
- Before a vowel, the semi-vocalic element of the diphthongs was doubled: αι [ai̯i̯], αυ [au̯u̯], οι [oi̯i̯], ευ [eu̯u̯], υι [yi̯i̯]. **Cf.** Allen 1974:78.

Additional Remarks about the Long Diphthongs

- The long diphthongs ᾳ [āi̯], ῃ [ēi̯], ῳ [ǭi̯] with the second element [i̯] were relatively frequent because they appeared in the endings of the dat. sg. -ῃ and -ῳ. The long diphthongs ᾱυ [āu̯], ηυ [ēu̯] and ωυ [ǭu̯] with the second element [u̯] were however very rare and examples such as τᾱὐτό [tāu̯tó] < τὸ αὐτό 'the same', aor. pass. ηὑρέθην [hēu̯réthēn] 'I was found' from εὑρίσκω 'I find', πρωὐδᾱν [prǭu̯dā̃n] 'to proclaim' < (10.2) *προ-αὐδᾱν from αὐδάω 'I speak' are hard to find.
- In postclassical or eventually during the classical times, the semi-vocalic element of the long diphthongs was lost as it can be seen in Greek loanwords in Latin which were borrowed before and after the loss of the semi-vocalic element. The words τραγῳδός [tragǭi̯dós] 'tragedian' and κωμῳδός [kǭmǭi̯dós] 'comedian' were borrowed before the loss of [i̯] because Lat. tragoedus and comoedus have the spelling <oe>, which is the Latin continuation of former [oi̯]. The words μελῳδός [melǭi̯dós] 'singing songs' and ῥαψῳδός [rhapsǭi̯dós] 'rhapsodist' were borrowed after the loss of [i̯] as the the spelling <o> of Lat. melōdus and rhapsōdus indicates.
- The long diphthongs ᾳ [āi̯], ῃ [ēi̯], ῳ [ǭi̯], which are written with iota subscript in modern text editions, were originally written ωι, ηι, ᾱι with iota adscript because the semivowel was actually still spoken during the classical period. The iota subscript was an invention of Byzantine grammarians after the semi-vocalic element [i̯] had vanished.
- The rare PIE long diphthongs with the second element [u̯] had become short diphthongs in the medial position by Osthoff's law (SC 1.3) such as in **di̯ēu̯s* > Ζεύς [zdéu̯s] in Proto-Greek times already. In the final position, long diphthongs remained until Classical Attic before they became long vowels by the loss of the final semivowel in post-classical times (cf. chapter 10/14). In the medial position, the long diphthong ηι had merged with ει [ẹ̄] by 400 BC already as it can be seen in λειτουργία 'service' and κλείς 'key' for older ληιτουργία and κληίς. New long diphthongs were formed in Attic due to vowel contractions (cf. chapter 14).

6 Feature Structure of Attic Consonants

Consonant Phonemes and Important Allophones

		Labial	Alveolar	Velar	Glottal
Stop	Voiceless	π /p/	τ /t/	κ /k/	
	Voiceless aspirated	φ /p^h/	θ /t^h/	χ /k^h/	
	Voiced	β /b/	δ /d/	γ /g/	
Fricative			σ /s/ ~ [z]		ʽ/h/
Nasal		μ /m/	ν /n/	γ [ŋ]	
Lateral			λ /l/		
Trill			ϱ /r/ ~ [r^h]		

Additional Remarks about Individual Sounds

- The graphemes φ, θ, χ represented the aspirated stops /p^h/, /t^h/, /k^h/ which became the fricatives /f/, /θ/, /x/ in post classical times. This sound change explains why in Latin the common Greek male name Φίλιππος was first spelled *Pilipus* and in later times *Philippus* or *Filippus*.
- The alveolar trill /r/ had a voiceless aspirated allophone [r^h] in the initial position such as in ῥέζω [r^{h}ézdǭ] 'I color', as a geminate in the medial position such as in συρρέω [syrr^{h}éǭ] 'I flow together', which is also attested as συῤῥεω, as well as after the tenuis aspiratae φ, θ, χ such as in τάφρος [táp^{h}r^{h}os] 'ditch', τέθριππος [tét^{h}r^{h}ippos] 'four-in-hand' and χρῆμα [k^{h}r^{h}ę̃ma] 'thing'. Normally, a voiceless [r] is phonetically noted as [r̥]. This notation is in this book reserved for syllabic [r̥] so that the notation [r^h] stands for voiceless aspirated /r/ without further indicating the feature of voicelessness.
- In preclassical times, the resonants /l/, /m/, n/ had voiceless aspirated allophones [l^h], [m^h], [n^h] in the initial position, which can can be seen in inscriptional attestations such as λhάβετος, λhέōν, μhεγάλō. In Attic, only [r^h] remained while the allophones of the other resonants were dismissed. **Cf.** Rix §86; Sturtevant 1940:67–70.
- The alveolar fricative /s/ had a voiced allophone [z] before voiced stops such as in μίσγω [mízgǭ] 'I mix', κτίζω [ktízdǭ] 'I settle' and πρέσβυς [prézbys] 'old', which can be seen in Hellenistic spellings such πρεζβευτᾶς, in which ζ must be interpreted as [z]. **Cf.** Rix §87.
- The letter ζ was pronounced [zd] and originated out of the two sounds *sd, which had probably been pronounced [zd] in PIE times already, as well as out of the metathesis of **dz*, which itself originated from the palatalization of **gi̯*, **di̯* and **i̯* (cf. chapter 28).
- The glottal fricative *h* was restricted to the initial position and was lost in Attic in postclassical times. This sound change is known as psilosis and happened in other dialects such as Ionic in classical times already.
- The labial nasal μ constitutes the phoneme /m/, or it can be the allophone [m] of the phoneme /n/ before labial sounds such as in *ἐν-πίπτω > (24.1) ἐμπίπτω [empíptǭ] 'I fall into'. The velar nasal [ŋ] is the allophone of the phoneme /n/ before velar sounds such as in *ἐν-γράφω > (24.2) ἐγγράφω [eŋgráp^{h}ǭ] 'I write into' as well as the allophone of /g/ before nasals such as in ὄγμος [óŋmos] 'furrow'. The sound [ŋ] is also known as *agma*.

Exercises for Chapters 5 and 6

E1 Complete the Feature Structures of the Following Sounds:

r^h [trill, ____________ , ____________]

n [____________ , ____________ , ____________]

h [____________ , ____________]

i [____________ , ____________ , ____________ , ____________]

y [____________ , ____________ , ____________ , ____________]

ę̄ [____________ , ____________ , ____________]

ẹ̄ [____________ , ____________ , ____________]

ǭ [____________ , ____________ , ____________]

ȳ [____________ , ____________ , ____________ , ____________]

E2 Which Feature Separates the Following Minimal Pairs?

p ~ p^h : ____________________ **ŋ ~ n** : ____________________

g ~ k : ____________________ **r ~ r^h** : ____________________ / ____________________

E3 Complete the Binary Features of the Following Consonants:

	Labial				Alveolar								Velar				Glottal
	p	p^h	b	m	s	t	t^h	d	n	l	r	[r^h]	k	k^h	g	[ŋ]	h
Stop	+																
Nasal	-																
Fricative	-																
Lateral	-																
Voiced	-																
Aspirated	-																
Approxim.	-																
Trill	-																

7 Methodology of Historical Comparative Linguistics

Comparative linguistics is based on the comparison of related word forms and the explanation of found similarities and differences. If one compares the root √ἀγ- which is the derivation base of **ἄγω** 'I lead', ἀγός 'leader' and ἀγών 'meeting place' to its form ἀκ- in the related PPP ἀκ-τός 'led', the difference ἀγ- :: ἀκ- calls for an explanation. In this case, the voiceless τ of ἀκτός caused the preceding voiced γ to become voiceless κ. The form ἀκτός [aktós] can therefore be traced back to a preform *ἀγτός [agtós], which is furnished with an asterisk to indicate that this form is reconstructed and not attested. This correlation is noted as: *ἀγτός > ἀκτός and read as: "the preform *ἀγτός became the attested form ἀκτός". This rule did, however, not transform every Greek γ into κ, and must therefore be restricted to the position before τ, which is written: γ > κ / _τ and read "g becomes k before t". The positional restriction is noted to the right of the slash whereby the underscore represents the position of the sound noted to the left of the derivational operator >. The sound change γ > κ / _τ is listed in the index with the number 29.10. This number is then put in parentheses between the input form and the output form: *ἀγτός > (29.10) ἀκτός. Phonetic transcriptions may be optionally added: *ἀγτός [agtós] > (29.10) ἀκτός [aktós].
The derivation *ἀγτός > (29.10) ἀκτός states input and output form of the sound change but not the form ἄγω which enables to trace ἀκτός back to its preform *ἀγτός. This form ἄγω is therefore put to the left of the comparation operator: ἄγω :: *ἀγτός > (29.10) ἀκτός. The element to the left of the comparation operator always illustrates the phonological feature which undergoes a change in the following chain of derivations. In the case of gen. sg. γέροντ-ος 'of the old man' :: voc. *γέροντ > (x12.2) γέρον 'old man!', different case forms are compared to show that the consonant τ, which is seen in the gen. sg. to the left of the comparation operator, existed in the preform of the voc. *γέροντ but was lost in the development to the attested form γέρον. In the case of σέλας 'glance' :: *σελάσνᾱ > (2.2) *σελᾱ́νᾱ > (13) σελήνη 'moon', different derivations of the same root are compared to illustrate the loss of *σ before ν with compensatory lengthening of the preceding vowel in *σελάσνᾱ, which is derived from σέλας with the suffix νᾱ. In the case of prs. γαμέω 'I marry' :: aor. *ἔγαμσε > (2.1) *ἔγᾱμε > (13) ἔγημε 'I married', different tense forms of a verb are compared to illustrate that the vowel η of ἔγημε goes back to α which can be seen in the prs. γαμέω. Translations are put into 'inverted commas'. If the two words to the left and right of the comparation operator have the same meaning, only the right word is translated at the end of the derivation chain.

- **Word Comparison involving Words from other IE Languages**

Sometimes, Greek data alone does not exhibit the feature or the sound which shall be illustrated. Therefore, also words from other languages appear to the left of the comparation operator e.g. Lat. *mōns, montis* 'mountain' :: *μόντι̯α > (x19.2) *μόνσσα > (45.4) *μόνσα > (4.1) *μο̣̃σα > (15) μοῦσα [mū̃sa] 'muse'. In this case, the Latin word *mōns* was chosen because its gen. *montis* shows the formant *-nt-* which can be attributed to the preform *μόντι̯α. The literal meaning of μοῦσα was therefore something like 'dwelling at the foot of a mountain' or 'related to a mountain'. The words from other languages were chosen to exhibit clearly the feature in question but when in comes to more difficult etymologies, it might not be visible at first glance.

Exercises

E1 Complete the Missing Formula or the Description:

SC	Formula		Description
25.3	$p^h > p$ / _m	*φμ > πμ	p^h becomes *p* before *m*.
29.2		*βτ > πτ	
31.1	*p* > *b* / _*m*		
32.2		*βμ > μμ	
35.1	*n* > *r* / _*r*		
35.2	*u̯ > *r* / _*r*		
42.1		*τκ > κτ	
47.4		*μλ > μβλ	
x16.1	*i̯ > Ø / *V*_*V*		

E2 Fill in the Sound Change Formula According to the Sound Change Number:

A *πάλϝᾱ > (13) *πάλϝη > (x21.3) πάλη 'flour'

*πάλϝᾱ > (__________) *πάλϝη > (__________) πάλη 'flour'

B *$ág^w nos$ > (x24.3) *ἄβνος > (32.1) ἄμνος 'lamb'

*$ág^w nos$ > (__________) *ἄβνος > (__________) ἄμνος 'lamb'

C *Δι̯ηύς > (1.3) *Δι̯εύς > (x18.2) Ζεύς 'Zeus'

*Δι̯ηύς > (__________) *Δι̯εύς > (__________) Ζεύς 'Zeus'

E3 Complete the Gap:

A ἁγνός 'holy' :: prs. *ἅγι̯ω > (x18.1) __________ 'I revere'

B λέγω 'I speak' :: perf. *λέλεγται > (29.10) __________ 'has spoken'

C κῆρυξ, κήρυκος 'herald' :: aor. pass. *ἐκηρύκθη > (26.3) __________ 'was proclaimed'

D φλέγω 'I burn' :: nom. sg. *φλόγ-ς > (29.9) __________ 'flame'

8 Accentuation of Attic Words

Position and Nature of the Accent

The accent position of many Greek words was inherited from PIE and corresponds therefore to the accent position of Sanskrit words as it can be seen from comparing Skr. *pitā́* 'father' and *bhrā́tā* 'brother' to πατήρ and φράτηρ. The Greek accent position can also be an innovation such as in μήτηρ. In this case, the accent position of Skr. *mātā́* 'mother' is different but the accent position of both languages agrees in the vocative μῆτερ and *mā́tā*. Therefore, the accent position of the Greek nom. can be regarded as an innovation in analogy to the vocative μῆτερ. The original accent position of the nominative μήτηρ can be therefore traced back to *μητήρ. Both, the accent position as well as the nature of the accent had a distinctive function in Greek as it can be seen from the comparison of the 2. sg. imp. aor. midd. παίδευσαι, 3. sg. opt. aor. act. παιδεύσαι and inf. aor. act. παιδεῦσαι whose meaning was differentiated by the accent only. In the minimal pair φόρος 'fee' :: φορός 'carrying', the change of accent position caused a change of the word class.
In contrast to English, the accent position was not primarily marked by in increase in air pressure (= stress accent) but by a change of pitch (= pitch accent). The acute ά designated a rising pitch, the gravis ὰ designated a falling pitch and the circumflex designated a rising pitch followed by a falling pitch. **Cf.** Probert 2003; SI §243–245.

Syllable Types

Open Syllables end in a short vowel (**φί**-λος, **χο**-ρός) while closed syllables end in a consonants (φί-**λος**, χο-**ρός**). If an open syllable ends in a vowel, it is called a short or light syllable. If an open syllable ends in a long vowel or a diphthong, it is called long by position. All closed syllables and those which are long by position are heavy syllables. A long syllable may therefore also contain a short vowel if the syllable is closed by a consonant (φί-**λος**).

Accentuation Rules

1. The acute may be placed only on one of the last three syllables.
2. The acute is placed on a short or long final syllable: ἀγών, χορός.
3 The acute is placed on a short penultimate syllable: φίλος.
4-. The acute is placed on a long penultimate syllable if the last syllable is long: παιδεύω 'I educate', ἀνθρώπους.
5. The acute is placed on a short or long antepenultimate syllable if the last syllable is long: ἄνθρωπος.
6. The grave accent replaces the acute on the last syllable if another accentuated word follows: πολλὰ βιβλία.
7. The circumflex can be placed only on the last or penultimate syllable if it is long by nature.
8. The circumflex can be placed on a long last syllable: gen. sg. ἀρετῆς, γενεᾶς.
9. The circumflex is placed on a long penultimate syllable if the last syllable is short: δῆμος, Κῦρος.
10. αι and οι mostly count as short in the final position which mainly affects the nom. pl. of the *a*-stems and *o*-stems.

Word Classification Scheme by Position and Nature of the Accent

	Antepenultimate Syllable	Penultimate Syllable	Last Syllable
Oxytona (acute / grave accent)			ἀγών / χορός
Paroxytona (acute)		πόλις / φίλος	
Proparoxytona (acute)	Μενέλεως / ἄνθρωπος		
Perispomena (circumflex)			ἀρετῆς / γενεᾶς
Properispomena (circumflex)		δῆμος / Κῦρος	

Exercises

E1 Fill in the Table:

~~θήρ~~ / ναῦς / Περικλῆς / θυγάτηρ / δαίμων / ~~φερόμενος~~ / ἀνήρ / πτῶμα / θήρατρον / κρατήρ / ῥήτωρ / δοῦλος / δῶρον / ἰχθῦς

	Antepenultimate Syllable	Penultimate Syllable	Last Syllable
Oxytona			θήρ /
Paroxytona			
Proparoxytona	φερόμενος /		
Perispomena			
Properispomena			

E2 Accentuate the Word Forms:

The accent position may vary within a paradigm. The nom. sg. ἄνθρωπος, the acc. sg. ἄνθρωπον and the nom. pl. ἄνθρωποι have the acute on the antepenultimate syllable because the last syllable is short (accentuation rule 5). If the final syllable becomes long like in the gen. sg. ἀνθρώπου or the acc. pl. ἀνθρώπους, the acute must be transferred onto the penultimate syllable (accentuation rule 4). The only exceptions to this rule are forms like the gen. sg. πόλεως whose final syllable originated through the interchange of vowel quantities (cf. SC 1.2 as well as chapter 10).

Nominative	δοῦλος	δῆμος	δῶρον	πόλεμος	ἄνθρωπος	υἱός
Genitive	δουλου	δημου	δωρου	πολεμου	ἀνθρωπου	υἱου
Dative	δουλῳ	δημῳ	δωρῳ	πολεμῳ	ἀνθρωπῳ	υἱῳ
Accusative	δουλον	δημον	δωρον	πολεμον	ἀνθρωπον	υἱον

Wheeler's Law

This rule describes the retraction of the accent in dactylic words, which are characterized by the sequence of one long and two short syllables (x̄x̆x̆). This rule is valid for all Greek dialects. The comparison of Skr. *peśalá-* 'colorful' to ποικίλος 'colorful' leads to PIE **poi̯kelós* with the additional suffix change *-elos* -> *-ilos* in Greek. The original place of accent was retained in **poik̂eló-* > *peśalá-* whereas it was retracted in **poi̯k̂ilós* > (x1.1) ποικίλος. This also applies to dactylic words like ἡδύλος < *ἡδυλός 'sweet' and βουκόλος < *βουκολός 'herdsman' in contrast to non-dactylic words like παχυλός 'thickish' and ὑψηλός 'high' in which the original place of accent was retained. The new accent position of ποικίλος was subsequently analogically generalized in all forms of the paradigm. This is the reason for the accentuation of the gen. ποκίλου in which there is no dactylic structure. **Cf.** Rix §49; SI §244.

Vendryes' Law

Vendryes' law, which is also known as the ἔγωγε-law, describes a retraction of the accent position in Attic words which consisted of a short syllable plus a long accented syllable plus a short syllable. In these words, the accent position was placed onto the first syllable. In this way, Old-Att. τροπαῖον developed to the classical form τρόπαιον 'victory monument'. Likewise, common Greek ἑτοῖμος became Att. ἕτοιμος and ἐπ'εῖτα became Att. ἔπειτα. Hom. ἐγώγε, which is composed of ἐγώ and enclitic γε, should have become *ἐγῶγε according to accentuation rule 9 but is attested as Att. ἔγωγε. **Cf.** Vendryes 1938.

9 Apophony in Attic Greek

The characteristic pattern of vowel change of the Englisch verb *sing*, *sang*, *sung* is known as apophony or ablaut and goes back to different vowel grades of PIE roots. Also Greek exhibits an inherited vowel change as a fundamental pattern of verbal and nominal formation and derivation.There is a regular connection between words which differ by the change of the vowels ε, η, ο, ω as well as the absence of a vowel. These so-called ablaut grades are known as *e*-grade, *o*-grade, *ō*-grade and zero-grade, which describes the absence of a vowel. Lexical root are conventionally stated in the *e*-grade.

The two words λέγ-ειν 'to speak' and λ**ό**γ-ος 'word' are both based on the same root appearing in the two ablaut variants √λεγ- and √λ**ο**γ-. The root √πετ- 'to fly' exhibits the *e*-grade in πέτ-ομαι 'I fly', the *o*-grade in ποτ-ή 'flight' and the zero-grade in **πτ**-ερόν 'wing'. Likewise, the root √φερ- 'to carry' exhibits the *e*-grade in φέρ-ειν 'to carry', the *o*-grade in φ**ό**ρ-ος 'tax', the *ō*-grade in φώρ 'thief' and the zero-grade in δί-**φρ**-ος 'chariot-board'. Usually, not all ablaut grades are found in the forms built from one root as it is the case in words related to πα-τ**ή**ρ 'father'. The *e*-grade is found in the nom. pl. πα-τέρ-ες, the *ē*-grade in the nom. sg. πα-τ**ή**ρ, the zero-grade in the dat. pl. πα-**τρ**ά-σιν, the *o*-grade in εὐπά-τ**ο**ρ-ες 'of noble descent', and the *ō*-grade in ἀπά-τωρ 'without a father'.

In addition to this from PIE inherited ablaut pattern, another systematic vowel change is found in the interchange of long and a short vowels of the suffix in δείκ-νῡ-μι 'I show' :: δείκ-νῠ-μεν 'we show'. This vowel change does, however, not continue a PIE ablaut pattern but was created anew by Greek speakers.

Regular Development of PIE Ablaut Grades in Greek

The root √δερκ- exhibits the *e*-grade in prs. δέρκ-ομαι 'I look' and the *o*-grade in perf. δέ-δ**ο**ρκ-α 'I have looked'. In the inf. aor. δ**ρα**κεῖν, one finds δρακ- is the regular development of an original zero-grade **dr̥k̂-*, whereby **r* was articulated as syllabic **r̥* between consonants and resulted in ρα or αρ (cf. SC x25; chapter 32). The root √φθερ- 'to destroy' exhibits the *o*-grade in φθ**ο**ρ-ά 'destruction' and the zero-grade in φθ**αρ**τός 'destructible'. The corresponding prs. φθ**εί**ρω [p^ht^hẹ́rǭ] < *φθέρ-i̯ω 'I destroy' is the regular development of an original *e*-grade because it goes back to the preform *φθέρ-i̯ω [p^ht^héri̯ǭ] which developed to φθείρω due to the loss of *i̯ with compensatory lengthening of ε [e] > (3) ει [ẹ̄]. Likewise, the verb τείνω 'I stretch' goes back to *τένi̯ω with an original *e*-grade, and the corresponding noun τόνος 'tension' exhibits the *o*-grade. In the case of the PPP τ**α**τός 'stretched', one finds α as the continuant of **n*, as this was articulated as syllabic **n̥* between consonants and resulted in α or αν. Nouns often exhibit the *o*-grade (τρ**ό**πος, φ**ό**ρος, στ**ό**λος) and present infinitives the *e*-grade (τρέπειν, φέρειν, στέλλειν) whereas the zero-grade is regularly found in the strong aorist (ἐτ**ρά**πην, ἐστ**άλ**ην) and in the PPP (τ**α**τός, δ**αρ**τός).

Apophony and the Laryngeal Theory

The vowel change *a* :: *o* in pairs like ἄγω 'I lead' :: ὄγμος 'furrow' and ἀκμή 'peak' :: ὀξύς 'sharp' can likewise be integrated into the original PIE ablaut pattern by means of the laryngeal theory (cf. chapter 34–35). The vowel *a* of these formations was originally an **e* and became *a* through an adjacent laryngeal *h_2. In this way, ἄγω is traced back to *h_2*eĝō* with a normal *e*-grade of the root *h_2*eĝ-* 'to impel' which stands in a regular relation to the *o*-grade seen in *h_2*oĝmos* > ὄγμος. Likewise, ἀκμή < *h_2*ek̂meh*$_2$ and ὀξύς < *h_2*ok̂sus* continue the *e*-grade and the *o*-grade of the root *h_2*ek̂-* 'to be sharp'.

Exercises

Complete the Table According to Ablaut Grades. The Ablaut Vowel is Underlined. Fields Marked with – Remain Empty.

δέρκομαι - ἐγενόμην - πείθω - κύων - δρακεῖν - πατέρες - πέποιθα - δέδορκα - κύον - πατήρ - τρέπειν - ἔπιθον - κυνός - τρόπος - ἀπάτωρ - γίγνομαι - εὐπάτορες - ἔθος - εἴ-ωθα - οἶδα - τρωπάω - ἦθος - πατράσιν - λοιπός - στέλλω - ἔσταλκα - φώρ - γέγονα - πτέσθαι - εἰδέναι - ἔτραπον - λιπεῖν - στόλος - σπουδή - φέρω - ἐλήλουθα - φυγεῖν - ἔλυθον - σπεύδω - ἰδεῖν - λείπω - ποτέομαι - φόρος - τίθεμεν - πέτομαι - πωτήεις - τίθημι - ἐλεύθερος - φεύγω - δίφρος

***e*-grade**	***o*-grade**	***ē*-grade**	***ō*-grade**	**zero-grade**
δέρκομαι		-	-	
		-	-	ἔπιθον
-	κύον	-		
		πατήρ		
	τρόπος	-		
	γέγονα	-	-	
	-		εἴ-ωθα	-
εἰδέναι		-	-	
	λοιπός	-	-	
στέλλω		-	-	
	σπουδή	-	-	-
		-	φώρ	
		-		πτέσθαι
	-	τίθημι	-	-
		-	-	ἔλυθον
φεύγω	-	-	-	

10 Vowel Shortening

SC 1.1 A Long Vowel is Shortened Before a Vowel

The rule *vocalis ante vocalem corripitur* 'a vowel before a vowel is shortened', which is known from Latin grammar, was also active in Attic and explains the vowel length difference of Hom. ἠώς [ẹ̄ǭs] and Att. ἕως [héǭs] 'dawn' as well as of Hom. ζωός [zdǭós] and Attic ζοός [zdoós] 'alive'. Two vowels often came together by the loss of one of the intervocalic consonants *ι̯, *σ, or *ϝ which can be seen in the above examples as ἠώς goes back to *ἠϝώς [ẹ̄u̯ǭs] and ζωός to *ζωϝός [zdǭu̯ós]. Furthermore, the verbal root of the present φύομαι [pʰýomai̯] 'I become' can be identified as √φῡ- with long ῡ by comparing it to its future φῡσομαι [pʰȳsomai̯] 'I will become'. The development of the present form was therefore *φῡομαι > (1.1) φύομαι, in which case the two vowels joined due to the morphological formation of the present tense whereby the vowel *o* was directly attached to the root √φῡ- in contrast to the future form which exhibits intervocalic σ between the two vowels which was retained in analogy to verbs such as λέξω 'I will read', in which the future morpheme was retained. **Cf.** Rix §64, 81b; LJ §279–282; Footnote 2.

SC 1.2 Quantitative Metathesis

The Attic dialect used another possibility of resolving the sequence of long vowel plus short vowel, which was the metathesis of the two sequences ηα and ηο to εᾱ and εω whereby in addition to the shortening of the first vowel a lengthening of the second vowel took place. By the comparison to Homeric acc. sg. βασιλῆα and gen. sg. πόληος, Attic βασιλέᾱ [basiléā] 'king' and πόλεως [póleǭs] 'city' can be traced back to *βασιλῆα and *πόληος and even further to *βασιλῆϝα and *πόληι̯ος by considering their stem formation. First, intervocalic *ϝ and *ι̯ were lost bevore ηα and ηο were changed to εᾱ and εω. According to the Attic accentuation rules, the expected form would be πολέως* rather than πόλεως because normally the acute could not be placed on the antepentultimate syllable if the final syllable was long (cf. chapter 8). However, the long ω in the final syllable, which is due to quantitative metathesis, did not influence the accentuation pattern because the previous sequence of sounds continued to have an effect on the accentuation pattern of the word. **Cf.** Rix §65; SI §79; LJ §283–284.

SC 1.3 Shortening of a Long Vowel Before Resonant + Consonant

Older than both described vowel shortenings is the so-called Osthoff's law which states that a long vowel is shortened before μ, ν, ϱ, λ, ι̯, ϝ plus another consonant. By the comparison with Skr. *gaus* < **gāu̯s* 'cow' and *naus* < **nāu̯s* 'ship', the diphthongs of βοῦς [bōu̯s] and ναῦς [nāu̯s] can be traced back to long diphthongs and the words therefore to [bǒu̯s] and [nā̆u̯s]. This sound change affected the *nt*-participles of verbal roots ending in a long vowel such as √γνω- 'to know' whose ptc. aor. nom. pl. m. *γνώ-ντ-ες is attested as γνόντες. It furthermore explains the forms of the aor. pass. nom. pl. παιδευθέντες, which goes back to *παιδευ-θή-ντ-ες because the aor. pass morpheme can be determined as -θη- through forms like 2. sg. ἐ-παιδεύ-θη-ς 'you were educated'. Secondary medial ηι [ẹ̄i̯] was also shortened early to [ei̯] which subsequently developed to [ẹ̄] like original [ei̯] (cf. chapt. 15) as it can be seen from the comparison of Hom. κληΐς [klẹ̄ís] und Att. κλείς [klẹ̄́s] 'lock' which both go back to *κλᾱϝίς and are related to Lat. *clāvis* 'key'. At first, ᾱ was raised to η before intervocalic *ϝ was lost: *κλᾱϝίς > (13) *κληϝίς > (x21.2) Hom. κληΐς [klẹ̄ís]. The vowel hiatus of Hom. κληΐς was resolved in Attic κλείς before vowel shortening according to Osthoff's law and the monophthongization of [ei̯] > [ẹ̄] took place: Hom. κληΐς [klẹ̄ís] > (23.1) [klẹ̄́i̯s] > (1.3) [kléi̯s] > (14.2) Attic κλείς [klẹ̄́s]. **Cf.** Rix §64; SI §79; LJ §225.

Exercises

E1 Vowel Before Vowel is Shortened

A aor. ἔδρᾱσα 'I did' :: prs. *δρᾱ́ω > (1.1) ___________ 'I do' **B** Hom. ζωή :: *ζωή > (1.1) ___________ 'life' **C** fut. δῡ́σομαι 'I will immerse' :: *δῡ́ομαι > (1.1) ___________ 'I immerse' **D** nom. sg. σῦς 'pig' :: gen. sg. *σῡός > (1.1) ___________ 'of the pig' **E** nom. sg. ἰχθῦς 'fish' :: gen. sg. *ἰχθῡ́ος > (1.1) ___________ 'of the fish' **F** ναῦς 'ship' :: gen. pl. *νᾱϝῶν > (13) *___________ > (x21.2) *___________ > (1.1) ___________ 'of the ships' **G** gen. pl. Hom. βασιλήων :: *βασιλῆϝων > (x21.2) *___________ > (1.1) ___________ 'of the kings' **H** Hom. αἰετός :: ἀετός > (1.1) ___________ 'eagle' **I** Hom. αἰεί :: ἀεί > (1.1) ___________ 'always'

E2 Quantitative Methesis

A ἄστυ 'city' :: gen. sg. *ἄστηϝος > (x21.2) *___________ > (1.2) ___________ 'of the city' **B** Hom. νηός :: gen. sg. *νᾱϝός > (13) *___________ > (x21.2) *___________ > (1.2) ___________ 'of the ship' **C** βασιλεύς 'king' :: gen. sg. βασιλῆϝος > (x21.2) Hom. ___________ > (1.2) ___________ 'of the king'

E3 Osthoff's Law

A √βᾰ- 'to go one step' :: ptc. aor.*βᾱ́ντες > (1.3) ___________ 'going' **B** √στᾰ- 'to stand' :: ptc. aor. *στᾱ́-ντ-ες > (1.3) ___________ 'standing' **C** √φῡ- 'to become' :: ptc. aor. *φῡ́-ντ-ες > (1.3) ___________ 'being' **D** φαίνω 'I shine' :: ptc. aor. *φανή-ντ-ες > (1.3) ___________ 'shining' **E** Ion. Πήρσαι :: *Πᾱ́ρσαι > (13) *___________ > (1.3) ___________ 'Persians' **F** nom. sg. *βασιληύς > (1.3) ___________ 'king' **G** Skr. *dyaús* 'sky' :: *Ζηύς > (1.3) ___________ 'Zeus' **H** Av. *snāvarə* :: *νηῦρον > (1.3) ___________ 'tendon' **I** Av. *dāiš* :: *ἔδηιξα [édē̜i̯ksa] > (1.3) [___________] > (14.2) ___________ [___________] 'I showed'

1.1:	*V̄ > V̆/ _V*	**13:**	**ā > ē̜*	**x16.1:**	**i̯ > Ø / V_V*
1.2:	*V̄V̆ > V̆V̄*	**14.2:**	**ei̯ > ẹ̄*	**x21.1:**	**u̯ > Ø / V_V*
1.3:	*V̄ > V̆ / _RC*				

11 Compensatory Lengthening I

SC 2 Compensatory Lengthening in Primary Sequences of Sigma plus Resonant

In all primary sequences consisting of *σ plus a resonant ν, μ, ϱ, λ, the fricative *σ was lost with compensatory lengthening of the preceding vowel. By the comparison with σέλας 'shininess', Att.-Ion. σελήνη 'moon' can be traced back to *σελάσνᾱ, whereby *σ in the sequence *σν was lost with compensatory lengthening before *ᾱ was raised to η: *σελάσνᾱ > (2.2) *σελᾱ́νᾱ > (13) σελήνη. The opposite sequence of sounds *νσ exhibits the same result, which can be seen in φαίνω 'I show' and its derived aorist *ἔφανσα which first became *ἔφᾱνα by compensatory lengthening and then Att.-Ion. ἔφηνα 'I showed' by the raising of ᾱ > η. Further examples are the aor. *ἔνεμσα [énemsa] > (2.1) ἔνειμα [énẹma] 'I distributed' derived from the root √νεμ-, as well as the aor. *ἔστελσα [éstelsa] > (2.1) ἔστειλα [éstẹla] 'I equipped' derived from the root √στελ-. The Attic sequence of long vowel plus single consonant corresponds to a sequence of short vowel plus double consonant in the respective Aeol. forms σελάννα, ἔφαννα, ἔνεμμα, ἔστελλα. After a long vowel or a diphthong, the loss of *σ did not have any consequences as can be seen in *αὔσϱιον > αὔϱιον 'tomorrow'. The ᾱ, which originated out of α, was further raised to η because SC 2 happened before the raising of ᾱ > η. **Cf.** Rix §63a; SI §228; LJ §114–117, 123.

SC x15.2 Assimilation Instead of Compensatory Lengthening

Cases like Hom. ταϱσός 'torrefyer' and κόϱση 'temple' show the retention of the sequence *ϱσ, whereas it assimilated to Att. ϱϱ in ταϱϱός and κόϱϱη. The sequence *ϱσ also assimilated to ϱϱ at a morpheme boundary consisting of preverb and verb or adjective. Therefore, the verb ἐπι-ϱϱέει 'he flows hither', which is derived from ῥέω 'I flow', can be traced back to *ἐπι-σϱέϝει because the verbal root can be determined as √σϱεϝ- due to Skr. *sráv-ati* 'he flows'. Likewise, the adjective ἄ-λληκτον 'endless', which is derived from λήγω 'I stop', goes back to *ἄ-σληκτον because the vebal root can be determined as √σληγ- due to Oscan *slaagí-* 'border'. Formations such as *ζώσνῡμι > (37.1) ζώννῡμι 'I girdle' as well as *σβέσνῡμι > (37.1) σβέννῡμι 'I extinguish' also exhibit the respective sound change in which cases the σ assimilated to the first sound of the verbal morpheme -νῡ-. **Cf.** chapters 21 and 25; Rix §70c; SI §229; LJ §117, 119–120.

SC 4 Compensatory Lengthening after Nasal-Loss

If the sequence *νσ was in the final position or originated anew due to Greek sound changes, it was the nasal ν which disappeared with compensatory lengthening in contrast to the above described loss of *σ before ν. This explains the development of the acc. pl. of the *o-* and *a-stems* such as acc. pl. *ἀϱετάνς [aretáns] > (4.2) ἀϱετᾱ́ς [aretā́s], which is derived from ἀϱετή [aretẹ̄́] 'virtue', or the acc. pl. *φίλονς > (4.2) *φίλο̄ς > (15) φίλους [pʰílūs], which is derived from φίλος [pʰílos] 'friend', in which [ọ̄] was raised to [ū] after it had originated through compensatory lengthening. The sequence *νσ also originated via *νσσ out of *ντι̯ or *ντσ (cf. chapter 19) as it was the case in nom. sg. f. *πάνσα > (4.1) πᾶσα 'whole' which corresponds to Arc. πάνσα in which ν before σ is preserved. An *nt*-stem can be identified in the gen. sg. m. παντός which enables to trace πᾶσα back to *πάντι̯α. The development was: *πάντι̯α > (x19.2) *πάνσσα > (45.4) *πάνσα > (4.1) πᾶσα. Examples for the development of *ντσ are supplied by the dat. pl. of the *nt*-stems such as γίγᾱς 'giant' :: dat. pl. *γίγαντ-σι > (33) *γίγανσ-σι > (45.4) *γίγανσι > (4.1) γίγᾱσι. The newly formed ᾱ was not raised to η because SC 4 happened after the raising of ᾱ > η. **Cf.** Rix §63b; SI §228.4; LJ §124/125.

Exercises

E1 Resonant plus Fricative *σ

A prs. κραίνω 'I finish' :: aor. *ἔκρανσα > (2.1) ___________ 'I finished' **B** prs. περαίνω 'I finish' :: *ἐπέρανσα > (2.1) ___________ 'I finished' **C** καθαρός 'pure' :: *ἐκάθαρσα > (2.1) *___________ > (13) ___________ 'I cleaned' **D** prs. γαμέω 'I marry' :: aor. *ἔγαμσα > (2.1) *___________ > (13) ___________ 'I married' **E** σφάλμα 'fall' :: *ἔσφαλσα > (2.1) *___________ > (13) ___________ 'I deceived' **F** fut. κλινῶ 'I will lean' :: aor. *ἔκλινσα > (2.1) ___________ 'I leaned' **G** prs. ἀγγέλλω 'I proclaim' :: aor. *ἤγγελσα > (2.1) ___________ 'I proclaimed' **H** fut. κρινῶ 'I will judge' :: aor. *ἔκρινσα > (2.1) ___________ 'I judged' **I** fut. κτενῶ 'I will kill' :: aor. *ἔκτενσα > (2.1) ___________ 'I killed' **J** prs. δέρω 'I skin' :: aor. *ἔδερσα > (2.1) ___________ 'I skinned' **K** fut. σπερῶ 'I will sow' :: aor. *ἔσπερσα > (2.1) ___________ 'I sowed' **L** fut. φθερῶ 'I will destroy' :: aor. *ἔφθερσα > (2.1) ___________ 'I destroyed'

E2 Fricative *σ plus Resonant

A κάρᾱ 'head' :: *κάρασνος > (2.2) ___________ 'chief' **B** 2. pl. ἐστέ 'you are' :: 1. sg. *ἐσμί > (2.2) ___________ 'I am' **C** ναῦς 'ship' :: *ναύ-κρασρος > (2.2) ___________ 'captain' **D** κρύσταλλος 'ice' :: *κρυσμός > (2.2) ___________ 'frost'

E3 Loss of Resonant in the Final Position

A nom. sg. nt. μέλαν :: nom. sg. m. *μέλανς > (4.2) ___________ 'black' **B** acc. pl. f. *τάνς > (4.2) ___________ 'those' **C** Lat. *sim-plex* 'simple' :: *σένς > (x13.1) *___________ > (4.2) ___________ 'one' **D** Skr. *mā́s-* :: *μήνς > (1.3) *___________ > (4.2) Ion. ___________ 'month' **E** φίλος 'friend' :: acc. pl. *φίλονς > (4.2) *___________ > (15) ___________ 'friends'

LWP 1.3:	*V̄ > V̆ / _RC*	**LWP 4.2:**	**Vns# > V̄s#*	**LWP x13.1:**	**s > h / #_V*
LWP 2.1:	**VRs > V̄R*	**LWP 13:**	**ā > ę̄*		
LWP 2.2:	**VsR > V̄R*	**LWP 15:**	**ǭ > ū*		

12 Compensatory Lengthening II

SC 3 Compensatory Lengthening of ε, ι, υ after Loss of the Semivowel *ι̯

In sequences consisting of a vowel ε, ι, υ plus a resonant ν, ϱ, ϝ plus iota *ι̯, the semivowel *ι̯ was lost with compensatory lengthening of the vowel before the resonant. In this way, φθείϱω [pʰtʰẹ̄rọ̄] 'I destroy', κϱῑ́νω [krī́nọ̄] 'I determine' and πλῡ́νω [plū́nọ̄] 'I wash' can be traced back to *φθέϱ-ι̯ω, *κϱίν-ι̯ω and *πλύν-ι̯ω whereby the Attic sequence of long vowel plus single consonant corresponds to the sequence of long vowel plus double consonant in Aeolic φθέϱϱω, κϱίννω, πλύννω. This sound change also affected the sequence *ϝι̯ such as in f. sg. *ὠκέϝι̯α [ọ̄kéu̯i̯a] which is derived from ὠκύς 'fast'. The preform [ọ̄kéu̯i̯a] became [ọ̄kẹ̄u̯a] through the iota-loss with compensatory lengthening, before *ϝ was lost between vowels, which resulted in ὠκεῖα [ọ̄kẹ̄a]. This form is also attested as ὠκέα [ọ̄kéa] with vowel shortening according to SC 1.1. Eventually, the loss of *σ and the loss of *ι̯ could lead to similar results on the surface as it was the case in the prs. *κτένι̯ω > (3.1) κτείνω 'I kill' and its corrresponding aor. *ἔκτενσα > (2.1) ἔκτεινα 'I killed'. **Cf.** Rix §70b, 88; SI §203, 205; §227.

SC x17 Iota-Epenthesis before α and ο after Loss of the Semivowel *ι̯

In sequences consisting of a vowel α, o plus a resonant ν, ϱ, ϝ plus iota *ι̯, the semivowel *ι̯ was lost, and between the vowel and the resonant an additional ι̯ was inserted, which looks like a metathesis of the resonant and iota on the surface. In this case, however, the ι̯ is an inserted palatal transitional consonant before a previously palatalized sequence, which process is known as iota-epenthesis. This analysis enables to connect etymologically the words φανεϱός 'visible' and *φάνι̯ω > (x17) φαίνω 'I show', the words καθαϱός 'clean' and *καθάϱι̯ω > (x17) καθαίϱω 'I clean' and the words μόϱος 'fate' and *μόϱι̯α > (x17) μοῖϱα 'part'. An example for the sequence *ϝι̯ is the derivation *κάϝι̯ω > (x17) καίω 'I burn' which is built from the root √καϝ- which can be seen in its aorist ἔ-καυ-σα 'I burned' and the noun καῦμα 'heat'. The process can be modelled as: *κάϝι̯ω > (x17) *κάι̯ϝω > (x21.3) καίω whereby the iota-epenthesis took place before *ϝ was lost. **Cf.** Rix §70a; SI §203; LJ §155; Footnote 6.

SC 36.4 Assimilation of Iota after λ

In sequences consisting of a vowel plus the resonant λ plus iota *ι̯, the semivowel *ι̯ assimilated to the adjacent resonant forming geminate λλ. In this way, στέλλω 'I put up' and κέλλω 'I put a ship to shore' can be traced back to *στέλι̯ω and *κέλι̯ω. The comparison of ἄλλο 'something else' to Lat. *aliud* enables to reconstruct the preform *ἄλι̯οδ in which the assimilation took place before the loss of the final consonant: *ἄλι̯οδ > (36.4) *ἄλλοδ > (x12.2) ἄλλο. **Cf.** Rix §70c; SI §204; LJ §156.

SC 5 Compensatory Lengthening after Loss of ν in the Sequence *λν

In etymological word pairs such as Lesb. βολλᾱ :: Att.-Ion. βουλή 'will' as well as Lesb. στάλλᾱ :: Att.-Ion. στήλη, one finds again that the Aeolic sequence of a short vowel plus a double consonant corresponds to the sequence of a long vowel plus single consonant in Att.-Ion. In these cases, the reconstructed preforms *βολνᾱ́ and *στάλνᾱ exhibit the sequence *λν which assimilated to λλ in Lesbian whereas in Att.-Ion. the *ν was lost with compensatory lengthening of the preceding vowel. In the first example, *βολνᾱ́ became *βǭλᾱ́ before the vowel raising of ǭ > ū and ᾱ > η took place which led to βουλή [būlẹ̄́]. In the second example, *στάλνᾱ became *στᾱ́λᾱ before the vowel raising *ᾱ > η which led to στήλη. This compensatory lengthening is older than the assimilation λν > λλ which is found in *ἀπολνῡμι > (36.1) ἀπόλλῡμι (cf. chap. 21). **Cf.** Rix §77; a different explanation is found in SI §224.2b; LJ §152.

Exercises

E1 Compensatory Lengthening or Assimilation

A φόνος ‘murder’ :: *θένι̯ω > (3.1) ____________ ‘I kill’ **B** aor. ἔκτεινα ‘I killed’ :: prs. *κτένι̯ω > (3.1) ____________ ‘I kill’ **C** ἀμεύομαι ‘I cross’ :: *ἀμύνι̯ω > (3.3) ____________ ‘I repel’ **D** ἡδύς :: f. sg. *ἡδέϝι̯α > (3.1) *____________ > (x21.2) ____________ ‘sweet’ **E** aor. ἤγγειλα ‘I proclaimed’ :: prs. *ἀγγέλι̯ω > (36.4) ____________ ‘I proclaim’ **F** perf. πέπαλμαι ‘I have shaken’ :: prs. *πάλι̯ω > (36.4) ____________ ‘I shake’ **G** ἀγερμός ‘the collecting’ :: *ἀγέρι̯ω > (36.4) ____________ ‘I collect’ **H** σπέρμα ‘seed’ :: prs. *σπέρι̯ω > (3.1) ____________ ‘I sow’ **I** Lat. *sterilis* :: *στέρι̯α > (3.1) ____________ ‘infertile’ **J** aor. ἔβαλον ‘I threw’ :: prs. *βάλι̯ω > (36.4) ____________ ‘I throw’

E2 Iota-Epenthesis

A μέλαν :: f. sg. *μέλανι̯α > (x17) ____________ ‘black’ **B** aor. ἐπέρᾱνα ‘I finished’ :: prs. *περάνι̯ω > (x17) ____________ ‘I finish’ **C** μανίᾱ ‘fury’ :: prs. *μάνι̯ω > (x17) ____________ ‘I am furious’ **D** μαχή ‘fight’ :: *μάχαρι̯α > (x17) ____________ ‘butcher’s knife’ **E** χάρις ‘happiness’ :: *χάρι̯ω > (x17) ____________ ‘I am happy’ **F** Lat. *cum* :: *κομι̯ός > (24.4) *____________ > (x17) ____________ ‘together’ **G** fut. κρανῶ ‘I will finish’ :: prs. *κράνι̯ω > (x17) ____________ ‘I finish’ **H** aor. ἔκλαυσα ‘I closed’ :: prs. *κλάϝι̯ω > (x17) *____________ > (x21.3) ____________ ‘I close’ **I** Hom. δαΐς ‘torch’ :: *δάϝι̯ω > (x17) *____________ > (x21.3) ____________ ‘I ignite’

E3 Compensatory Lengthening after Loss of *v

A Att. εἴλλω :: *ϝέλνω > (5) *____________ > (x21.1) Ion. ____________ ‘I urge’ **B** Lesb. ὀφέλλω :: *ὀφέλνω > (5) Att.-Ion. ____________ ‘I must’ **C** ἀολλίζω ‘I gather’ :: *ἀϝελνής > (5) *____________ > (x21.2) Hom. ____________ [____________] > (9.1) Att. ____________ ‘gathered’

3.1:	*eRi̯ > ẹ̄R	**5:**	*Vln > V̄l	**36.4:**	*i̯ > l / l_	**x21.1:**	*u̯ > Ø / #_(V,R)
3.2:	*iRi̯ > īR	**9.1:**	a + ẹ̄ > ā	**x13.1:**	*s > h / #_V	**x21.2:**	*u̯ > Ø / V_V
3.3:	*yRi̯ > ȳR	**24.4:**	m > n / _(t,d,i̯,s)	**x17:**	*(a,o)Ri̯ > (a,o)i̯R	**x21.3:**	*u̯ > Ø / C_

Vowel Contraction I

SC 7 Contraction of Alike Vowels

Two short or long alike vowels contracted to the respective long vowel: *κάϝαλον > (x21.2) *κάαλον > (7.1) κᾶλον 'firewood'. The contraction of ε and ε resulted in ει [ẹ̄], which can be seen in the 2. sg. imp. *ποίε-ε [pói̯e-e] > ποίει [pói̯ẹ̄] 'do!' which is derived from ποιεῖν. The contraction of o and o resulted in [ọ̄] which was later raised to ου [ū]. The uncontracted Hom. form νόος [nóos] 'mind' corresponds to the contracted Att. form νοῦς. The development was: Hom. νόος > (7.3) *νọ̄ς > (15) νοῦς [nūs]. **Cf.** Rix §59; SI §86; LJ §245–247, 292–297.

SC 8 Contraction of Similar Vowels

Similar vowels are ε/ει [e]/[ẹ̄] and η [ę̄] on the one hand as well as o/ου [o]/[ọ̄] and ω [ǭ] on the other. The contraction of ε/ει [e]/[ẹ̄] and η [ę̄] always resulted in open-mid η [ę̄] regardless of the order of the vowels. This applies to the contracted verbs of the type φιλέ-ω 'I love' in the following forms: 2. sg. subj. *φιλέ-ῃς [pʰiléę̄i̯s] > (8.1) φιλῇς [pʰilę̄̃i̯s]; 3. sg. subj. *φιλέ-ῃ [pʰiléę̄i̯] > (8.1) φιλῇ [pʰilę̄̃i̯]; 2. pl. subj. *φιλέ-ητε [pʰiléę̄te] > (8.1) φιλῆτε [pʰilę̄̃te]; εἰμί 'bin' :: *ἦεν > (8.2) ἦν 'war'. The contraction of o/ου [o]/[ọ̄] and ω [ǭ] always resulted in open-mid [ǭ]. The contracted verbs of the type δουλόω 'I subject' are affected in: 1. sg. *δουλό-ω > (8.3) δουλῶ, ptc. prs. *δουλό-ων > (8.3) δουλῶν 'subjecting'; Hom. λαγωός :: *λαγωός > (8.4) Att. λαγώς 'rabbit'.

SC 9 Contraction of A-Sounds and E-Sounds

In a contraction of an A-sound (α, ᾱ) with an E-sound (ε, ει, η), the first sound prevailed. Examples for αε and αει are: 2. sg. imp. *τίμα-ε > (9.1) τίμᾱ 'honor!', inf. *τῑμά-ειν [tīmáẹ̄n] > (9.1) τῑμᾶν 'to honor', 2. pl. *τῑμά-ετε > (9.1) τῑμᾶτε 'you honor'. Examples for εα are: nom. pl. *ὄρεα > (9.2) ὄρη 'mountains', *γένεα > (9.2) γένη 'families'.

SC 10.1/10.2 Contraction of O-Sounds and A-Sounds

A contraction of an O-sound (o, [ọ̄], ω) plus an A-sound (α, ᾱ) in random order always resulted in open-mid ω [ǭ]. The contracted verbs of the type τῑμά-ω 'I honor' are affected in: 1. pl. *τῑμά-ομεν > (10.1) τῑμῶμεν 'we honor', 1. sg. opt. *τῑμα-οίην > (10.1) τῑμῴην 'I shall honor', ptc. prs. *τῑμάων > (10.1) τῑμῶν 'honoring'. The 3. pl. τῑμῶσι 'they honor' orginated out of *τῑμά-οντι > (x22.1) *τῑμά-ονσι > (2.1) *τῑμά-ọ̄σι > (10.1) τῑμῶσι whereby the contraction might as well have happened at the stage αο. An example for οα is supplied by the acc. sg. of αἰδώς 'shame', which is attested without contraction in Hom. αἰδό-α and with contraction in Att. αἰδῶ.

SC 10.3–10. Contraction of O-Sounds with E-Sounds

If both vowels were close-mid (o, ου, ε, ει), the result of the contraction was close-mid [ọ̄]. Examples for εο are supplied by the contracted verbs of the type φιλέω in: 1. pl. *φιλέ-ομεν > (10.3) *φιλọ̄́μεν > (15) φιλοῦμεν 'we love'; 3. pl. *φιλέ-ọ̄σιν > (10.3) *φιλέ-ọ̄σιν > (15) φιλοῦσιν 'they love'. Examples for οε are supplied by the contracted verbs of the type δούλοω 'I subject' in: inf. prs. *δούλο-ειν > δουλοῦν 'to subject'; 1. sg. ipf. *ἐδούλο-ον > (10.4+15) *ἐδούλουν 'I subjected'; 2. sg. imp. *δούλο-ε > (10.4+15) δούλου 'subject!'.

If one of the contracting vowels was open-mid (ω, η), the contraction resulted in open-mid ω [ǭ]. Examples are supplied by the contracted verbs of the type *φιλέ-ω in: 1. sg. *φιλέ-ω > (10.5) φιλῶ 'I love'; 1. pl. subj. *φιλέ-ωμεν > (10.5) φιλῶμεν 'we love'; ptc. prs. *φιλέ-ων > (10.5) φιλῶν 'loving'.

Exercises

The contraction syllable bears the circumflex if the first of the contracted vowels was accentuated, and it bears the acute if the second of the contracted vowels was accentuated.

E1 Contraction of Alike Vowels

A 3. pl. perf. Hom. βεβάᾱσι :: *βεβά-ᾱσι > (7.1) ___________ 'they have gone' **B** ποιεῖν 'to do' :: 2. pl. *ποιέ-ετε > (7.2) ___________ 'you do' **C** κέρας 'horn' :: pl. *κέρασα > (x15.1) *___________ > (7.1) ___________ 'horns' **D** ὄφις 'snake' :: *ὀφι-ίδιον > (7.4) ___________ 'little snake' **E** λαγώς 'rabbit' :: gen. pl. *λαγώ-ων > (7.7) ___________ 'of the rabbits'

E2 Contraction of Unlike Vowels

A1 θηρᾶν 'to chase' :: 1. pl. *θηρά-ομεν > (10.1) ___________ 'we chase' **A2** 3. sg. ipf. *ἐθήρα-ον > (10.1) ___________ 'he chased' **A3** 3. sg. imp. *θηρα-έτω > (9.1) ___________ 'he shall chase!' **A4** ptc. prs. m. *θηρά-ων > (10.1) ___________ 'chasing' **A5** ptc. prs. f. *θηρά-ọ̄σα > (10.1) ___________ **A6** 2. pl. imp. *θηρά-ετε > (9.1) ___________ 'chase!' **B** σῦκον 'fig' :: pl. *συκέ-ᾱ > (9.2) ___________ 'figs' **C** inf. *ῥῑγώειν > (10.2) ___________ 'to freeze' :: 2. pl. subj. *ῥῑγώητε > (10.2) ___________ **D** Hom. φάος :: *φάος > (10.1) ___________ 'light' **E** ὁρᾶν 'to see' :: 3. pl. *ὁρά-ọ̄σι > (10.1) ___________ **F** ἐστί 'he is' :: 3. sg. ipf. *ἦ-εν > (8.2) ___________ 'he was'

E3 Contraction after Loss of Intervocalic Consonants

A πόλις 'city' :: pl. *πόλεi̯ες > (x16.1) *___________ > (7.1) ___________ 'cities' **B** Hom. σάος > (10.1) Att. ___________ :: nt. pl. *σάϝα > (x21.2) *___________ > (7.1) ___________ 'unhurt' **C** γένος 'kin' :: pl. *γένεσα > (x15.1) *___________ > (9.2) ___________ **D** κλέος 'fame' :: *κλεϝεσνός > (2.2) *___________ > (x21.2) *___________ > (7.2) ___________ [___________] 'famous'

2.2:	*VsR > V̄R	**9.1:**	a + e/ẹ̄ > ā	**10.2:**	o/ọ̄/ǭ + a/e/ẹ̄ > ǭ	**x21.2:**	*u̯ > Ø / V_V
7:	$V_1 + V_1 > \bar{V}_1$	**9.2:**	e + a > ę̄	**x15.1:**	*s > Ø / V_V		
8.2:	ę̄ + e/ẹ̄ > ę̄	**10.1:**	a/ę̄/e + o/ọ̄/ǭ > ǭ	**x16.1:**	*i̯ > Ø / V_V		

14 Vowel Contraction II

SC 23 Resolve of Hiatus through Diphthongization

Att. οἶς [ō̃i̯s] 'sheep' goes back to *ὄϝις [óu̯is] which can be seen by comparing it to Lat. *ovis* and Skr. *ávi-*. After the loss of *ϝ, the vowels ο and ι were in the hiatus position attested in the disyllabic Homeric form ὄϊς [óis]. This hiatus was resolved in Att. οἶς [ō̃i̯s] when ι became the semivowel i̯, which formed an *i*-diphthong with the preceding vowel: **óu̯is* > (x21.2) **óis* > (23.1) οἶς [ō̃i̯s]. The emergence of a *u*-diphthong can be likewise seen in the development of γραῦς 'old woman' which is related to γέρων 'old man'. For Att. γραῦς, one finds the disyllabic Hom. γρηΰς [grę̄ús] with Ionic η for ᾱ and the vowels η and υ in the hiatus position. Starting from a preform *γρᾱΰς [grāús], the long vowel was shortened before a vowel and the resulting hiatus was resolved by transforming υ into its corresponding semivowel *u̯* which led to the formation of the diphthong [au̯] : *γρᾱΰς [grāús] > (1.1) *γραΰς [graús] > (23.2) γραῦς [grãu̯s]. **Cf.** Rix §59d; LJ §267.

Emergence of Long Diphthongs through Contraction

The inf. *τῑμά-εν [tīmáę̄n] > (9.1) τῑμᾶν [tīmā̃n] 'to honor' orginated through the contraction of the verbal stem τῑμά- with the infinitive ending -ειν [ę̄n] and does not have a iota subscript in contrast to the 2. sg. *τῑμά-εις [tīmáei̯s] > (9.1) τῑμᾷς [tīmā̃i̯s] and the 3. sg. *τῑμά-ει [tīmáei̯] > (9.1) τῑμᾷ [tīmā̃i̯] in which cases the endings -εις and -ει stand for an old diphthong [ei̯] which contracted with -α to ᾱͅ [āi̯] according to SC 9.1. In this way, new long diphthongs were formed in Attic after inherited PIE long diphthongs had been shortened in the medial position such as in *Ζηύς > (1.3) Ζεύς (cf. chap. 10). Uncontracted forms are often found in Homer such as ἀείδω [aéi̯dǭ] 'I sing' and ἀοιδή [aoi̯dę̄́] 'song' which correspond to Att. ᾄδω [ā́i̯dǭ] and ᾠδή [ǭi̯dę̄́]. The vowels contracted according to the normal contraction rules and merged to a long vowel which formed a long diphthong together with the semivowel following. **Cf.** Rix §58–59; LJ §197, 235.

Spurious Diphthongs

If the spelling ει does not go back to a former diphthong but displays the result of vowel contraction or compensatory lengthening, one speaks of a spurious diphthong. To decide whether ει stands for a former diphthong [ei̯] or the long vowel [ę̄], one must examine related forms. If a former diphthong [ei̯] contracted with another vowel, the result always shows traces of the semivowel [i̯] whereas the contraction of [ę̄] never resulted in a form which shows traces of the semivowel [i̯]. The inf. τῑμᾶν [tīmā̃n] mentioned in the above paragraph is the result of the contraction of a spurious diphthong whereas the 3. sg. prs. τῑμᾷ [tīmā̃i̯] is the result of the contraction of a real diphthong because the iota subscript is an indication of [i̯]. Another indication of a real diphthong is the retention of ι in other tense forms such as perf. λέλοιπα [léloi̯pa] 'I have left' from λείπω [léi̯pǭ] 'I leave' whereas the ι of φθείρω [pʰtʰę̄́rǭ] 'I destroy' does not appear in the perf. ἔφθαρκα [épʰtʰarka] 'I have destroyed'. **Cf.** SI §76.

Crasis

The Greek term κρᾶσις 'mixture' designates the contraction of a final vowel or diphthong with the initial vowel of the word following. This sound change is indicated by a spiritus lenis written inside the word which is called coronis such as in ἐναντίον > (10.3) τοὐναντίον 'on the contrary'. In other cases such as ὁ ἀνήρ > ἁνήρ 'the man', there is no individual word ἁνήρ that could be found in the lexicon. The normal contraction rules are valid for these contractions unless the sound of the semantically more dominant word prevailed such as in ὁ ἀνέρ > ἁνήρ. **Cf.** Rix §62.

Exercises

E1 Resolve of Hiatus by Diphthongization

A ὄρος ‘mountain’ :: dat. sg. *ὄρεσι [____________] > (x15.1) Hom. ____________ [____________] > (23.1) Att. ____________ [____________] **B** κέρας ‘horn’ :: dat. sg. *κέρασι [____________] > (x15.1) Hom. ____________ [____________] > (23.1) Att. ____________ [____________] **C** Lat. *puer* :: *πάϝις [____________] > (x21.2) Hom. ____________ [____________] > (23.1) Att. ____________ [____________] ‘child’

E2 Emergence of Long Diphthongs through Contraction

A λύω ‘I release’ :: 2. sg. pass. *λύεσαι [____________] > (x15.1) *____________ [____________] > (9.2) ____________ [____________] ‘you are released’ **B1** ζῆν ‘to live’ :: 2. sg. *ζήεις [zdę̄́ei̯s] > (8.2) ____________ [____________] **B2** 3. sg. *ζήει [zdę̄́ei̯] > (8.2) ____________ [____________] **B3** 2. sg. subj. *ζήηις [____________] > (7.6) ____________ [____________] **C1** φιλεῖν ‘to love’ :: 2. sg. subj. *φιλέ-ηις [____________] > (8.1) ____________ [____________] **C2** 3. sg. subj. *φιλέ-ηι [____________] > (8.1) ____________ [____________] **E1** τῑμᾶν ‘to revere’ :: 2. pl. opt. *τῑμάοιτε > (10.1) ____________ [____________] **E2** 3. sg. opt. *τῑμαοίη > (10.1) ____________ [____________]

E3 Crasis

A τὸ ὄπισθεν > (7.3) *____________ > (15) ____________ **B** τὸ ὀπίσω > (7.3) *____________ > (15) ____________ **C** τὰ ἄλλα > (7.1) ____________ **D** ἃ ἐγώ > (9.1) ____________ **E** προ-έλεγον > (10.4) *____________ > (15) ____________ **F** τὸ ἐπέκεινα > (10.4) *____________ > (15) ____________ **G** τὸ ἐλάχιστον > (10.4) *____________ > (15) ____________ **H** τὸ ἔμπαλιν > (10.4) *____________ (15) ____________ **I** τὸ ἐναντίον > (10.4) ____________ **J** τὸ ἔργον > (10.4) *____________ (15) ____________ **K** τὸ ἐντεῦθεν > (10.4) *____________ > (15) ____________

7:	$\breve{\bar{V}}_1 + \breve{\bar{V}}_1 > \bar{V}_1$	**9.1:**	*a + e/ ẹ̄ > ā*	**10.4:**	*o/ ọ̄ + e/ ẹ̄ > ọ̄*	**x15.1:**	**s > Ø / V_V*
8.1:	*e/ ẹ̄ + ę̄ > ę̄*	**9.2:**	*e + a > ę̄*	**15:**	**ọ̄ > ū*	**x21.2:**	**u̯ > Ø / V_V*
8.2:	*ę̄ + e/ ẹ̄ > ę̄*	**10.1:**	*a/ę̄/e + o/ọ̄/ ǭ > ǭ*	**23.1:**	*ĭ̄ > i̯ / V_*		

VOWELS

15 Monophthongization and Raising of Vowels

SC 4.2/7.3/14/15 Sources and further development of [ẹ̄] and [ọ̄]

The spelling ει was originally used for the pre-Att. diphthong *[ei̯] as in δείκνῡμι [dẹ̄́knȳmi] < *[déi̯knūmi] 'I show' in which ει corresponds to <ei> of Old Latin *ex-**deic**-endum* 'for proclaiming'. This can be also seen by comparing Att. τείσει [tẹ̄́sẹ̄] < *[téi̯sei̯] to the syllabic spelling of Cyp. *pe-i-se-i* [pei̯sei̯] because the sequence [pẹ̄sẹ̄] would have been written ˣ*pe-se*. The diphthong [ei̯] monophthongized to [ẹ̄] in preclassical times so that Att. δείκνῡμι [dẹ̄́knȳmi] and τείσει [tẹ̄́sẹ̄] can be traced back to *[déi̯knūmi] and *[téi̯sei̯] only by the comparison with other languages or dialects. The early loanword Lat. *hypotēnūsa* < ὑποτείνουσα already exhibits the monophthongization **ei̯* > (14.2) *ẹ̄* as well as the raising of **ọ̄* > (15) *ū*. After the monophthongization **ei̯* > *ẹ̄* had been completed, the spelling ει could also be used for long close-mid [ẹ̄] which originated out of vowel contraction such as in the 2. pl. *αἰτέ-ε-τε [ai̯téete] > (7.2) αἰτεῖτε [ai̯tẹ̄̂te] 'you ask for' or compensatory lengthening of short ε such as in the aor. *ἔδερσα [édersa] > (2) *ἔδειρα [édẹ̄ra] 'I skinned'. In postclassical times, [ẹ̄] was further raised to [ī] as it can already be seen in occasional spellings of ι for ει in the late 4th century BC as well as in Lat. loanwords such as *pīrātā* for πειρατής or *Aristīdēs* for Ἀριστείδης.

The spelling ου was originally used for the diphthong [ou̯] before it monophthongized to long close-mid [ọ̄] in preclassical times which was again raised to [ū] of the classical language: **spou̯dẹ̄́* > (14.1) **spọ̄dẹ̄́* > (15) σπουδή [spūdẹ̄́] 'hurry'. Long close-mid [ọ̄] also originated out of vowel contractions such as ο + ο e.g. in the 1. pl. *δηλό-ομεν > (7.3) *δηλọ̄̂μεν > (15) δηλοῦμεν [dẹ̄lū̂men] 'we reveal' as well as through the compensatory lengthening of ο such as in the acc. pl. *φίλονς > (4.2) *φίλọ̄ς > (15) φίλους [pʰílūs] 'friends'. **Cf.** Rix §53; SI §57, 61; Allen 1974:66.

SC 12 Palatalization of Proto-Greek *u, *ū > Attic y, ȳ

The comparison of ἐρυθρός 'red' to Skr. *rudhirá-* and Lat. *ruber* as well as the comparison of μῦς 'mouse' to Skr. *mū́ṣ-* and Lat. *mūs* (cf. chap. 37, Z 7/12) shows that Greek υ/ῡ corresponds to *u*, *ū* in other languages. Therefore, it is possible to posit that υ/ῡ had been **u* / **ū* in Proto-Greek. Early Lat. loanwords like *cubus* < κύβος 'cube' and the personal name *Burrus* < Πύρρος show that υ was first spelled <u> whereas in later times the letter <y> was used for spelling υ such as in Lat. *mysticus* for μυστικός 'mystic'. Furthermore, Herodot used the letter υ in Ὑστασπης for Old Persian *Vištaspa-* not for spelling Old Persian /u/ but /u̯i/ just like Lat. *qui* was sometimes spelled κυ. Spellings such as Boeotian ἀσουλίᾱ [asūlíā] für Attic ἀσῡλίᾱ [asȳlíā] 'inviolability' show that the original pronunciation /ū/ was continued in other dialects than Attic. **Cf.** Rix §52,57; SI §38; Allen 1974:62ff; Ruipérez 1956.

The Push-Pull Theorie

The phonemes of a language constitute a coherent system in which changes of individual elements very often affect other elements. The phenomenon that a vacant space in a phoneme system, which has become vacant by sound changes, is filled by the movement of another sound into the vacant position is known as push-pull-theorie. In many cases, it is, however, not clear or investigatable whether the movement of one element pushed another element into another position or the movement of one element pulled another element into a vacant position. Please confer the overview of vowel changes on the page opposite.

Simplified Model of Vowel Changes

1600 BC

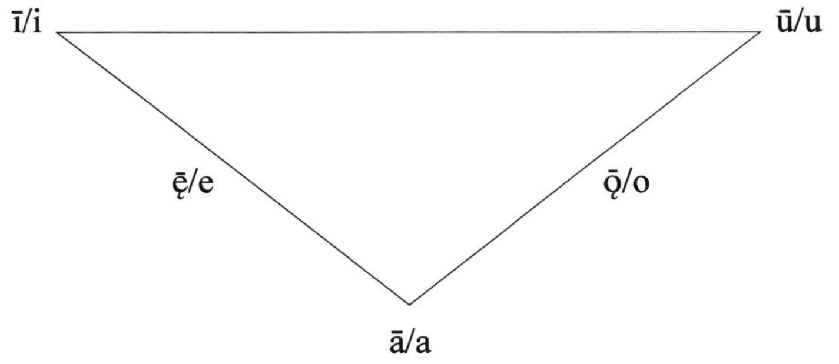

The Proto-Greek vowel system consisted of five short and five long cardinal vowels.

800 BC

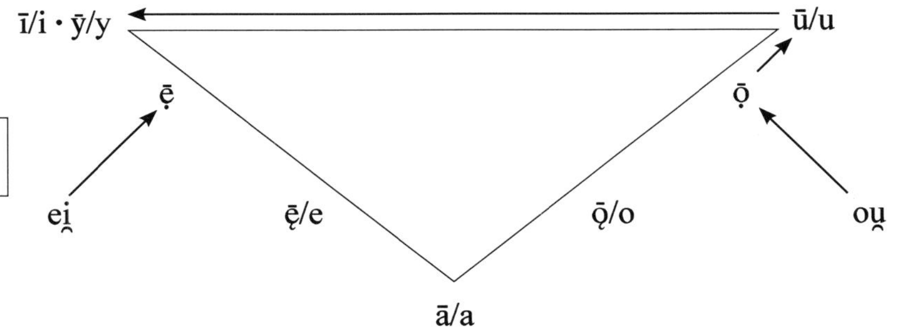

Probably between the 9th and 7th century BC, the new phonemes /ẹ̄/ and /ọ̄/ emerged from different sources (cf. chapter 5). Proto-Greek /ū/ and /u/ were palatalized to /ȳ/ and /y/. The phoneme /ọ̄/ was subsequently raised to /ū/ and filled the gap of the missing cardinal vowel.

500 BC

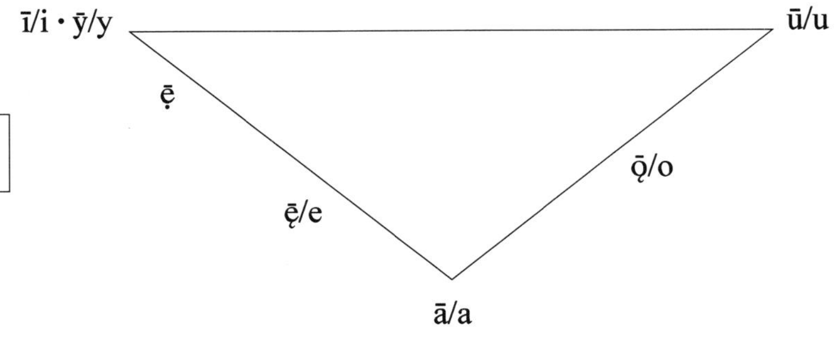

In this way, the Attic vowel system emerged which is described in chapter 5.
Short /e/ was probably realized between /ē̜/ and /ẹ̄/.

16 Qualitative Vowel Changes

SC 11 Cowgill's Law

Words like πρυμνός 'topmost, last', which can be traced back to *προμνός by comparing it to its derivation base πρό 'before', or νύξ 'night', which is related to Lat. *nox*, exhibit υ for expected *o*. This sound change **o* > **u* > υ [y], which was not carried through fully in Greek, is know as Cowgill's law and can be restricted to the position between resonant ρ, λ, ν, μ and labial consonant μ, β, π, φ, *ϝ or one of the Proto-Greek labiovelars *k^w, *g^w, *k^{wh} which developed to Attic π, τ or κ according to the vowel following (cf. chapter 30). This sound change must have happened in Pre-Attic times because it implies the existence of phonemes which were lost in later times. E.g. the labiovelar *k^w caused *o* to become *u* before itself became velar *k* and **u* was fronted to *y*: **nók*^{w}*s* > (11) **núk*^{w}*s* > (x10.1) **núks* > (12.1) νύξ [nyks]. There are, however, numerous counterexamples as well as pairs like πόλος 'pole' and πύλη 'gate' < *πόλη which do not exhibit the respective sound change. In this case πόλος, did not become ˣπύλος although it exhibits exactly the same phonological contexts as πύλη. **Cf.** SI §44.

SC 13 The Att.-Ion. Raising of ᾱ > η and the Att. Reversion after ε, ι, ρ

Doric	Ionic	Attic
σελᾱ́νᾱ	σελήνη	σελήνη
ἁμέρᾱ	ἡμέρη	ἡμέρᾱ

By comparing Dor. σελᾱ́νᾱ 'moon' to Att.-Ion. σελήνη, one finds Dor. ᾱ for Att.-Ion. η. By comparing Dor. ἁμέρᾱ 'day' to Ion. ἡμέρη and Att. ἡμέρᾱ, one does find Dor. ᾱ for Ion. η and initial Att. η, but after ρ, one finds Att. ᾱ for Dor. ᾱ and Ion. η. This sound change is known is the Att.-Ion. raising of ᾱ > η which was carried through fully in Ionic, and in Attic not after ε, ι and ρ. This result is, however, not explained by saying that Att. ᾱ became η in all positions except after ε, ι and ρ, but by saying that in all positions ᾱ became [ǣ], which is an intermediate sound between ᾱ and η, which was transformed back into ᾱ after ε, ι and ρ while [ǣ] further became η in all other positions. This process can be illustrated with the word παρέᾱ 'cheek' which corresponds to Myc. *pa-ra-wo-jo* 'two cheeks' and goes back to *παράϝσᾱ. Due to the loss of *σ, long ᾱ emerged between ρ and ϝ: *παράϝσᾱ > (2.1) *παρᾱ́ϝᾱ. Subsequently, ᾱ became [ǣ] before the loss of *ϝ caused the two vowels to clash: *παρᾱ́ϝᾱ > (13.1) *παρǣϝǣ > (x21.2) *παρǣǣ. The first vowel was shortened to ε before [ǣ] transformed back to ᾱ: *παρǣǣ > (1.1) *παρέǣ > (13.2) παρέᾱ. If ᾱ had been retained after ρ, *παρᾱ́ϝᾱ should have become first ˣπαρᾱ́ϝǣ, then ˣπαρᾱ́ǣ through the loss of *ϝ, and then ˣπαράǣ through vowel shortening, and finally ˣπαράη. In words such as ἡμέρᾱ, ᾱ became [ǣ] in the preform *ᾱ̔μέρᾱ: **hāmérā* > (13.1) **hǣmérǣ* before [ǣ] transformed back to ᾱ after ρ: **hǣmérǣ* > (13.2) **hǣmérā* before [ǣ] became η: **hǣmérā* > (13.3) ἡμέρᾱ [hę̄mérā]. Words such as κόρη 'girl', in which one finds η after ρ, only seem to be exceptions to the above formulated conditions because it can be traced back to *κόρϝᾱ by comparing it to Myc. *ko-wa* [koru̯ā], Arc. κόρϝᾱ, Hom. κούρη and Cret. κώρᾱ. At the time of the change ᾱ > η, the vowel ᾱ did not follow ρ directly but was separated from it through *ϝ. After the sound change ᾱ > η had been completed, η slided into the position after ρ through the loss of *ϝ: *κόρϝᾱ > (13) *κόρϝη > (x21.3) κόρη. Long ᾱ which originated out of compensatory lengthening by SC 2 did undergo the further raising ᾱ > η as it can be seen in the aor. *ἔγαμσε > (2.1) *ἔγᾱμε > (13) ἔγημε 'I married' derived from the prs. γαμέω 'I marry'. The raising ᾱ > η did, however, not affect long ᾱ which originated out of the compensatory lengthening SC 4 as this lengthening took place after the respective sound change had been completed: *πάντι̯α > (x19.2) *πάνσσα > (45.4) *πάνσα > (4.1) πᾶσα 'whole'. **Cf.** Rix §56, 72; SI §55–56; LJ §250.

Exercises

E1 Cowgill's Law

A Lat. *folium* :: *p^{h}óli̯on > (36.4) *__________ > (11) *__________ > (12.1) __________ 'leaf' **B** Lat. *mola* 'millstone' :: **mólā* > (11) *__________ > (12.1) *__________ > (13) __________ 'mill' **C** Skr. *nakhá-* :: gen. sg. **ónok^{wh}os* > (11) *__________ > (x10.3) *__________ > (12.1) __________ 'of the nail' **D** Lat. *formīca* :: **mórmēks* > (11) *__________ > (12.1) __________ 'ant' **E** Lat. *nox* :: **nók^{w}s* > (11) *__________ > (x10.1) *__________ > (12.1) __________ 'night' **F** **smṓnok^{wh}es* > (11) *__________ > (x10.3) *__________ > (12.1) *__________ > (x15.3) Hom. __________ 'solid-hoofed'

E2 The Development *ā > ę̄

A παλΰνω 'to sprinkle' :: *πάλϝᾱ > (13) *__________ > (x21.3) __________ 'flour' **B** Lat. *dūdum* :: *δϝᾱ́ν > (13) *__________ > (x21.3) __________ 'a long time' **C** δαῆναι 'to learn' :: *δάνσος > (2.1) *__________ > (13) __________ 'plan' **D** Skr. *tāvat-* :: *τᾱ́ϝος > (13) *__________ > (x21.2) *__________ > (1.2) __________ 'as long as' **E** Dor. μᾱ́τηϱ :: *μᾱ́τηϱ > (13) Att. __________ 'mother' **F** Lat. *fārī* :: *φᾱμί > (13) __________ 'I speak' **G** aor. Dor. ἐκάθᾱϱα :: *ἐκάθᾱϱα > (13) Att. __________ 'I cleaned' **H** aor. Dor. ἐπέϱᾱνα :: *ἐπέϱᾱνα > (13) Att. aor. __________ 'I finished' **I** Dor. διαφοϱᾱ́ :: *διαφοϱᾱ́ > (13) Ion. __________ 'difference' **J** Dor. σᾶμα :: *σᾶμα > (13) Att. __________ 'sign' **K** Arc. κόϱϝᾱ :: *κόϱϝᾱ > (13) *__________ > (x21.3) __________ 'girl'

E3 Intermediate Steps of the Development *ā > ę̄

A Myc. *pa-ra-wo-jo* 'two cheeks' :: *παϱάϝσᾱ > (2.1) *__________ > (13.1) *__________ > (x21.2) *__________ > (1.1) *__________ > (13.2) __________ 'cheek' **B** dor. ἁμέϱᾱ :: **hāmérā* > (13.1) *__________ > (13.2) *__________ > (13.3) __________ [__________] 'day'

1.1:	*V̄ > V / _V*	**13:**	**ā > ę̄*	**x21.2:**	**u̯ > Ø / V_V*
1.2:	*V̄V̆ > V̆V̄*	**13.1:**	**ā > ǣ*	**x21.3:**	**u̯ > Ø / C_*
2.1:	**VRs > V̄R*	**13.2:**	**ǣ > ā / (e,i,r)_*	**36.4:**	**i̯ > l / l_*
11:	**o > u / B_R, R_B*	**13.3:**	**ǣ > ę̄*	**x10.1:**	**k^w > k / _(u,u̯)_*
12.1:	**u > y*	**x10.3:**	**k^{wh} > k^h / _(u,u̯)_*		

17 Sporadic Vowel Changes

SC 15 Progressive and Regressive Vowel Assimilation

Assimilations can be further subclassified as progressive and regressive assimilations depending on whether sound features are transferred from one element onto a following element, or whether sound features are transferred from one element onto a preceding element. If a vowel assimilates to a preceding vowel, one speaks of progressive assimilation, and if a vowel assimilates to a vowel following, one speaks of regressive assimilation. The difference between Ion. μέγαθος and Att. *μέγαθος > (21.1) μέγεθος 'size', which are both derived from μέγα 'big', can thus be explained by a progressive assimilation of the Attic vowels. Vice versa, a regressive assimilation can be found in the city name Ἐρχομενός > (21.2) Ὀρχομενός which is derived from ἔρχομαι 'I come'. In comparison to the very frequent consonant assimilations, which are discussed in the next chapters, vowel assimilations only appear sporadically. **Cf.** Rix §19; SI §91; LJ §254.

SC 16/18/19 Anaptyxis / Syncope / Hyphaeresis

Anaptyxis is the insertion of an anaptyctic vowel into a group of consonants, as it can be seen in the inscriptional attestations Επιδορομος for Ἐπίδρομος and Τεροπων for Τέρπων. The counterpart to anaptyxis is syncope in which a vowel is elided between two consonants as it can be seen in the difference of Hom. aor. ἤλυθον 'I came' and Att. ἦλθον. Hyphaeresis is the elision of a vowel in a sequence of three vowels as it can be seen in Hom. μυθέαι 'you tell' which can be traced back via *μυθέεαι to *μυθέεσαι. These sound changes occur only sporadically. **Cf.** Rix §66; SI §80; LJ §231, 276.

SC 17 Elision

Elision is the deletion of one of the short vowels α, ε, ι, ο or the diphthong αι before the initial vowel of the next word. Usually, an elision is marked with an apostrophe as in ἀλλὰ ἐγώ > (17) ἀλλ' ἐγώ 'but I' but not if the elision process took place between prefix and verb as in *παρα-έχω > (17) παρέχω 'I give' and *ἀπο-ἔχω > (17) ἀπέχω 'I keep off'. If a tenuis became final by the elision process, it was subsequently aspirated before a spiritus asper as can be seen in ἐπὶ ὁδόν > (17) ἐπ' ὁδόν > (28.1) ἔφοδον which was the base of a newly built nominative ἔφοδος 'access'. Prepositions and conjunctions, which were stressed on their final syllable, lost their accent: ἀλλὰ ἐγώ > (17) ἀλλ' ἐγώ. In all other words e.g. φημὶ ἐγώ > (17) φήμ' ἐγώ 'I say', which were stressed on their final syllable, the accent was replaced by an acute on the preceding syllable. The accent position of words, which were not stressed on their final syllable, did not change: οὔτε σοι οὔτε ἐμοί > (17) οὔτε σοι οὔτ' ἐμοί 'neither to me nor to you'. The final vowels α and ο were never elided in monosyllabic words such as πρό 'vor' or the neuter articles sg. τό, pl. τά. Furthermore, the elision did not take place in the case of a final υ or in the words μέχρι 'as far as', περί 'all around', τί 'what?' and τι 'anything'. **Cf.** LJ §232.

SC 20 Prothetic Vowels

Greek words often exhibit initial vowel which are absent in cognate words from other languages. Examples are ἀνεψιός 'first cousin' compared to Av. *naptiiō* 'descendant' and Lat. *nepōs* 'grandchild' as well as ἀμέλγω 'I milk' compared to Lat. *mulgeō* and Old English *meolcian*. In many cases, these initial vowels go back to PIE laryngeals (cf. chap. 34) but in some cases this phenomenon must be regarded as an internal Greek development. **Cf.** Rix §66; SI § 89–90; LJ §146–149, 213–216; Clackson 1996.

Exercises

E1 Regressive or Progressive Assimilation of the Bold Marked Vowels

A Skr. *jihmá-* :: ***δαχμός*** > (21.2) ___________ 'sloping' **B** λοξός 'sloping' :: λε**κάνη** > (21.2) ___________ 'bowl' **C** ψε**κάς** > (21.2) ___________ 'drop' **D** Skr. *prathimán-* 'extension' :: *πλε**ταμ**ών > (21.2) Hom. ___________ 'even place' **E** **ὀσταφ**ίς > (21.2) ___________ 'raisin' **F** ἥ**μισυς** > (21.2) ___________ 'half' **G** β**υβ**λίον > (21.2) ___________ 'book' **H** Dor. κρᾱ́νᾱ :: *κρ**ᾱ́**ν**ᾱ** > (13) *___________ > (21.2) ___________ 'well' **I** ἐστί 'is' :: 2. sg. imp. *ἔσθ**ι** > (21.2) ___________ 'be!' **J** Arc. ὀδελός :: Att. **ὀ**βελός > (21.1) ___________ 'obol' **K** Lat. *collis* 'hill' :: ***κολα**φών > (21.1) ___________ 'summit' **L** τέμαχος 'piece' :: *τέμ**α**νος > (21.1) ___________ 'piece of land' **M** Ion. χείλιοι :: *χέσλιοι > (2.2) *___________ > (21.2) Att. ___________ 'thousand'

E2 Pretonic and Posttonic Syncope

A οἴομαι > (16.1) ___________ 'I believe' **B** σκόροδον > (16.1) ___________ 'garlic' **C** 2. pl. imp. φέρετε > (16.1) ___________ 'carry!' **D** πέρυσι > (16.1) ___________ 'last year' **E** γέμω 'I am full' :: aor. *γέμετο > (16.1) *___________ > (24.3) hom. ___________ 'he grasped' **F** Φερενίκη > (16.2) ___________ 'bringing victory' **G** 2. sg. imp. *ἐλυθέ > (16.2) ___________ 'come!'

E3 Add the Sound Change Number into the Brackets:

A Ἑρμῆς > (   ) Ἑρεμῆς 'the God Hermes' **B** κλέος 'glory' :: *εὐκλεέος > (   ) εὐκλέος 'glorious' **C** βράγχος > (   ) βαράγχος 'hoarseness' **D** γοάω 'I lament' :: aor. Hom. γόεον > (   ) γόον 'I lamented'

E4 Elision with Possible Aspiration of a Final Tenuis

A ἀπὸ ἐμοῦ > (17) ___________ **B** ἀντὶ ὧν > (17) *___________ > (28.2) ___________ **C** ἀπὸ οὗ > (17) *___________ > (28.1) ___________ **D** ἐπὶ αὐτῷ > (17) ___________ **E** ἐπὶ ἐμοί > (17) ___________

2.2: $*VsR > \bar{V}R$	**16.2:** $V > Ø / C\_C'$	**19:** $Ø > V / C\_C$	**28.1:** $p\#h > p^h$
13: $*\bar{a} > \bar{ę}$	**17:** $V > Ø / C\_\#\#V$	**21.1:** $V_1...V_2 > V_1...V_1$	**28.2:** $t\#h > t^h$
16.1: $V > Ø / 'C\_C$	**18:** $V > Ø / V\_V$	**21.2:** $V_1...V_2 > V_2...V_2$	

18 Assimilation of Consonants I: Voice and Aspiration

Assimilation as the Transition of Phonological Features

Morphological formations continuously create new phonological sequences which are subject to further changes. The root √γραφ- is the base of both the verb γράφ-ω 'I write' as well as the nominal derivation *γράφ-μα > γράμμα 'letter' in which the root final φ assimilated to μ. Likewise, the morphem -θη- was used to form the aor. pass. ἐλείφθην 'was left' from λείπ-ω 'leave' and caused the root final π of the root √λειπ- to become φ before θ. These sound changes, in which sounds become more similar by the harmonization of their features, are known as assimilations. An overview of Attic Greek assimilations can be found in appendix 1.

SC 29/30 Assimilation of Voice

In a sequence of two stops, the manner of articulation of the first stop always assimilated to the manner of articulation of the second stop. The only exception to this rule are combinations of two dental stops which are discussed in the next chapter. Thus, voiceless stops became voiced before voiced stops and voiced stops became voiceless before voiceless stops. As a consequence, β changed to π and γ changed to κ before the suffixes -τος and -τεος, as it can be seen in τρῑ́βω 'I rub' :: *τρῑβτός > (29.2) τρῑπτός 'rubbed' and λέγω 'I speak' :: *λεγτός > (29.10) λεκτός 'spoken'. Voiced stops lost their feature of voice also before the voiceless fricative σ, which played an important role in Attic morphology because it was used for building the aorist morpheme -σα, the future morpheme -σω, the infinitive morpheme -σθαι, the nominative morpheme -ς as well as the dative plural morpheme -σι(ν).

Only few examples can be found for assimilations of voiceless stops to voiced stops as there are only very few suffixes that start with a voiced stop. E.g. the adverb ἐμπλέγδην 'intertwined' can be traced back to *ἐμπλέκδην via SC 30.2 (κ becomes γ before δ) by comparing it to its derivational base ἐμπλέκω 'I intertwine'.

SC 25/26 Assimilation of Aspiration

An aspirated stop lost its feature of aspiration before a non-aspirated stop like in γράφω 'I write' :: *γραφτός > (25.2) γραπτός 'written' and ταράχω 'I confuse' :: perf. *τετάραχται > (25.11) τετάρακται 'has confused'. Conversely, the θ of the aor. pass. morpheme -θη- aspirated a preceding non-aspirated stop as it can be seen in prs. λείπω 'I leave' :: aor. pass. *ἐλείπ-θην > (26.1) ἐλείφθην 'was left' and φυλάττω 'I guard' :: aor. pass. *ἐφυλάκ-θην > (26.3) ἐφυλάχθην 'was guarded'. The loss of the aspiration before *i̯ furthermore explains the alike development of the sequences *κi̯ and χi̯, *τi̯ and *θi̯ as well as *πi̯ and *φi̯ as a prestep of their subsequent palatalization (cf. chapter 29).

Assimilations of Voice and Aspiration

The verb λαμβάνω 'I seize' is the derivational base of 3. sg. aor. pass. ἐλήφθη 'was seized' which can thus be traced back to the preform *ἐλήβ-θη. In a first step, the assimilation of voice occurred: *ἐλήβ-θη > (29.3) *ἐλήπ-θη, and in a second step, the assimilation of aspiration occurred: *ἐλήπ-θη > (26.1) ἐλήφ-θη. Analogically, the verb λέγω 'I speak' is the derivational base of the development of the 3. sg. aor. pass. *ἐλέγθη > (29.11) *ἐλέκθη > (26.3) ἐλέχθη 'was spoken'.

Exercises

E1 Loss of the Feature Voice

A λαμβάνω 'I seize' :: *ληβ-τός > (29.2) ___________ 'seized' **B** νίζω 'I wash' :: *νιβ-τός > (29.2) ___________ 'washed' **C** τρίβω 'I rub' :: perf. *τέτριβ-ται > (29.2) ___________ 'I have rubbed' **D** φλέβιον 'small vein' :: *φλέβ-ς > (29.1) ___________ 'vein' **E** στίγμα 'stitch' :: *στιγ-τός > (29.10) ___________ 'stitched' **F** τρίβω 'I rub' :: fut. *τρίβ-σω > (29.1) ___________ 'I will rub' **G** φλέγω 'I burn' :: *φλόγ-ς > (29.9) ___________ 'flame' **H** λήγω 'I stop' :: fut. *λήγ-σω > (29.9) ___________ 'I will stop' **I** λέγω 'I speak' :: perf. *λέλεγ-ται > (29.10) ___________ 'he has spoken'

E2 Assimilation of Voiceless and Voiced Consonants

A ἑπτά 'seven' :: *ἕπ-δομος > (30.1) ___________ 'seventh' **B** κρύπτω 'I hide' :: *κρύφδην > (25.4) *___________ > (30.1) ___________ 'hidden' **C** ὀκτώ 'eight' :: *ὄκ-δοος > (30.2) ___________ 'eighth' **D** σπέρχω 'I urge' :: *σπέρχδην > (25.13) *___________ > (30.2) ___________ 'urgent'

E3 Loss or Assimilation of Aspiration

A διώκω 'I follow' :: aor. pass. *ἐδιώκ-θην > (26.3) ___________ 'I was followed' **B** ἔχω 'I hold' :: *ἐχ-τός > (25.11) ___________ 'held' **C** πλέκω 'I twine' :: aor. pass. *ἐπλέκ-θην > (26.3) ___________ 'I was twined' **D** βρέχω 'I get wet' :: perf. *βέβρεχ-ται > (25.11) ___________ 'he is wet' **E** τρίβω 'I rub' :: aor. pass. *ἐτρίβ-θην > (29.3) *___________ > (26.1) ___________ 'was rubbed' **F** διορύττω 'I dig out' :: *διῶρυχ-σ > (25.10) ___________ 'complete puncture' **G** τρέφω 'I nourish' :: fut. *θρέφ-σω > (25.1) ___________ 'I will nourish' **H** prs. γράφω 'I write' :: perf. *γέγραφ-ται > (25.2) ___________ 'has written' **I** εὔχομαι 'I pledge' :: fut. *εὔχ-σομαι > (25.10) ___________ 'I will pledge' **J** πέμπω 'I send' :: aor. pass. *ἐπέμπ-θην > (26.1) ___________ 'I was sent' **K** κῆρυξ 'herald' :: perf. pass. *κεκήρυκ-θαι > (19.3) ___________ 'it has been proclaimed'

25.1: $p^h > p\ /\ \_s$	**25.11:** $k^h > k\ /\ \_t$	**29.1:** $b > p\ /\ \_s$	**29.10:** $g > k\ /\ \_t$
25.2: $p^h > p\ /\ \_t$	**25.13:** $k^h > k\ /\ \_d$	**29.2:** $b > p\ /\ \_t$	**30.1:** $p > b\ /\ \_d$
25.4: $p^h > p\ /\ \_d$	**26.1:** $p > p^h\ /\ \_t^h$	**29.3:** $b > p\ /\ \_t^h$	**30.2:** $k > g\ /\ \_d$
25.10: $k^h > k\ /\ \_s$	**26.3:** $k > k^h\ /\ \_t^h$	**29.9:** $g > k\ /\ \_s$	**39.10:** $C^h \ldots C^h > C \ldots C^h$

19 Assimilation of Consonants II: Dental Sequences

Formation and Simplification of Geminate σσ

Geminate σσ, which was always simplified to σ in Attic, originated most often through the assimilation of τ to σ in the sequence *τσ which again had different sources. In the dat. pl. of the *t*-stems like in *πένητ-σιν > (33) *πένησ-σιν > (45.1) πένησιν of πένης 'poor', τ and σ directly met; in the dat. pl. *ἐλπίδ-σιν > (29.4) *ἐλπίτ-σιν > (33) *ἐλπίσ-σιν > (45.1) ἐλπίσιν, which is derived from ἐλπίς 'hope', *τσ originated through the assimilation of voice of δ before σ, and in the dat. pl. *κόρυθ-σιν > (25.6) *κόρυτ-σιν > (33) *κόρυσ-σιν > (45.1) κόρυσιν, which is derived from κόρυς, κόρυθος 'helmet', *τσ originated through the deaspiration of θ before σ. In all three cases, *τσ first became *σσ and was afterwards simplified to σ. Further sources of Attic σ were *τι̯, *θι̯ and *τϝ like in *τότι̯ον > (x19.2) *τόσσον > (45.1) τόσον 'that much', *μέθι̯ος > (25.9) *μέτι̯ος > (x19.2) *μέσσος > (45.1) μέσος 'middle' and *τϝάκος > (x21.5) σάκος 'shield'. Occasionally, morphological derivations like in Hom. ἔσ-σομαι 'you will be', which corresponds to Attic ἔσομαι, led to the formation of σσ. In the Homeric dialect, geminate σσ was mostly preserved after a short vowel if it was not simplified due to metrical reasons in variant forms like ποσσίν/ποσίν, ἔσσομαι/ἔσομαι or μέσσος/μέσος. Already Homeric is the simplification of σσ after a long vowel like in the dat. pl. τάπησιν which is derived from τάπης, τάπητος 'carpet' and goes via *τάπησ-σιν back to *τάπητ-σιν. All Greek dialects furthermore exhibit the simplification of σσ before and after a consonant as well as in the initial and final position. Homeric ἔσκον 'was' < *ἔσ-σκον, which is derived from the root √ἐσ- 'to be', is an example of the simplification before a consonant. The preform *διδόντι̯α, which is the f. prs. ptc. of δίδωμι 'I give', developed via *διδόνσσα > (45.4) *διδόνσα > (2.1) *διδọ́σα to the attested form διδοῦσα 'giving' and is an example of the simplification of σσ after a consonant. The simplification of σσ in the final position can be seen in the development of the preform *φῠ́-ντ-ς which is the prs. ptc. m. of φύω 'I become' and developed to φῡ́ς 'being': *φῠ́-ντ-ς > (33) *φῠ́-νσ-ς > (45.3) *φῠ́-νς > (4.2) φῡ́ς. An example of the simplification in the initial position is furnished by σῆμα 'sign' which goes back to *θι̯ᾱμα: *θι̯ᾱμα > (25.9) *τι̯ᾱμα > (x19.2) *σσῆμα > (45.2) σῆμα. **Cf.** Rix §87b; LJ §92–101.

Combinations of Two Dental Stops

The first sound of the sequences *ττ, *δτ, *θτ, *θθ, *δθ, *τθ always became σ. By comparing it to ἀνύτω 'I complete', the PPP ἀνυστός 'completed' can be traced back to *ἀνυτ-τός; the 2. sg. οἶσθα 'you know' can be traced back to *οἶδ-θα by comparing it to οἶδα 'I know'; 3. sg. perf. πέπεισται 'is persuaded' goes back to *πέπειθ-ται as can be seen in its derivational base πείθω 'I persuade'. In a first step, voiced δ was devoiced to τ before τ or θ (*δτ > *ττ and *δθ > *τθ), θ lost its aspiration before τ (*θτ > *ττ), and τ was aspirated to θ before θ (*τθ > *θθ), whereby all the sequences resulted in *ττ or *θθ. Afterwards, the sound σ [s] was inserted into the sequences which led to *τστ and *θσθ. Since all Greek sequences of the structure C_1sC_1 were simplified to sC_1, the newly formed sequences *τστ and *θσθ finally became στ and σθ (cf. chapter 25). This sound law had already stopped to be active when the Attic sequence ττ developed anew out of *κι̯ and *τι̯ and remained intact. **Cf.** chapt. 29; Rix §106; SI §212; LJ §58.

Dental Stop before Velar Stop

In analogy to the proportion prs. παιδεύω 'I educate' :: perf. πεπαίδευκα 'I have educated', the regularly formed κ-perfect of σπεύδω 'I hurry' is expected to be *ἔσπευδ-κα which should develop to ˣἔσπευτκα via the assimilation of voice *d* > *t* / _*k*. Attic ἔσπευκα 'I have hurried' shows, however, that a dental stop was completely lost before a guttural stop. This was one possibility of avoiding the sequence *τκ which was phonotactically not possible in Attic and therefore also subject to a metathesis to κτ (cf. chapter 22.

Exercises

E1 Simplification of Geminate σσ

A χάρις 'favor' :: dat. pl. *χάριτσιν > (33) *___________ > (45.1) ___________ **B** δατέομαι 'I distribute' :: fut. *δάτσομαι > (33) *___________ > (45.1) ___________ 'I will distribute' **C** πείθω 'I persuade' :: fut. *πείθσω > (25.6) *___________ > (33) *___________ > (45.1) ___________ 'I will persuade' **D** ἐρείδω 'I support' :: fut. *ἐρείδ-σω > (29.4) *___________ > (33) *___________ > (45.1) ___________ 'I will support' **E** μυδάω 'I rot' :: *μύδσος > (29.4) *___________ > (33) *___________ > (45.1) ___________ 'disgust' **F** σπεύδω 'I hurry' :: aor. *ἔσπευδσα > (29.4) *___________ > (33) *___________ > (45.1) ___________ 'I hurried' **G** λύω 'I loosen' :: ptc. aor. f. *λύσαντι̯α > (x19.2) *___________ > (45.4) *___________ > (4.1) ___________ 'loosened' **H** prs. σπένδω 'I pour' :: fut. *σπένδσω > (29.4) *___________ > (33) *___________ > (45.4) *___________ > (4.1) ___________ 'I will pour' **I** τίθημι 'I set' :: ptc. prs. f. *τιθέντι̯α > (x19.2) *___________ > (45.4) *___________ > (4.1) ___________ 'setting'

E2 Complex Development of Dental Sequences

A1 πείθω 'I persuade' :: *ἐπείθ-θην > (46.2) *___________ > (43.2) ___________ 'was persuaded' **A2** *πιθτός > (25.7) *___________ > (46.1) *___________ > (43.1) ___________ 'faithful' **B** σκευάζω 'I equip' :: *ἐσκεύαδ-ται > (29.5) *___________ > (46.1) *___________ > (43.1) ___________ 'he has equipped' **C** ψεύδω 'I lie' :: *ἔψευδ-ται > (29.5) *___________ > (46.1) *___________ > (43.1) ___________ 'he has lied'

E3 Loss of Dental Stop Before Velar Stop

A νομίζω 'I consider' :: perf. *νενόμιδκα > (29.7) *___________ > (44) ___________ 'I have considered' **B** πείθω 'I persuade' :: perf. *πέπειθ-κα > (25.8) *___________ > (44) ___________ 'I have persuaded' **C** σκευάζω 'I equip' :: perf. *ἐσκεύαδ-κα > (29.7) *___________ > (44) ___________ 'I have equipped'

4.1:	$*VnsV > \bar{V}sV$	**29.4:**	$d > t$ / _s	**43.1:**	$t > \emptyset$ / _st	**45.4:**	$ss > s$ / C_
25.6:	$t^h > t$ / _s	**29.5:**	$d > t$ / _t	**43.2:**	$t^h > \emptyset$ / _st^h	**46.1:**	$\emptyset > s$ / t_t
25.7:	$t^h > t$ / _t	**29.7**	$d > t$ / _k	**44:**	$t > \emptyset$ / _k	**46.2:**	$\emptyset > s$ / t^h_t^h
25.8:	$t^h > t$ / _k	**33:**	$t > s$ / _s	**45.1:**	$ss > s$ / V_V	**x19.2:**	$*t\underset{^\frown}{i} > ss$

20 Assimilation of Consonants III: Stop Before Nasal Consonant

SC 32 Labial and Velar Stop Before Nasal Consonant

Before a nasal following, the labial stops β, π, φ transformed into the labial nasal μ and the guttural stops γ, κ, χ transformed into the guttural nasal [ŋ], which was written γ. During this process, the aspirated stops φ and χ were deaspirated and became π and κ, before they were, just like original π and κ, voiced to β and γ and finally completely assimilated to the nasal following, which led to μ and γ [ŋ]: Examples for β, π, φ before μ are: τρίβω 'I rub' :: perf. *τέτρῑβμαι > (32.2) τέτρῑμμαι 'I have rubbed'; λείπω 'I leave' :: perf. *λέλειπμαι > (31.1) *λέλειβμαι > (32.2) λέλειμμαι 'I have left' as well as γράφω 'I write' :: *γράφμα > (25.3) *γράπμα > (31.1) *γράβμα > (32.2) γράμμα 'letter'. The change of the guttural stops γ, κ, χ, which all transformed into the guttural nasal [ŋ], happened in a similar process but was not revealed in the spelling because [g] and [ŋ] were both spelled with the letter γ. Examples for γ and κ are: ἅγιος [hágios] 'holy' :: *ἅγνος [hágnos] > (32.4) ἅγνος [háŋnos] 'holy' as well as κηρύττω 'I proclaim' :: perf. *κεκήρυκ-μαι > (31.2) *κεκήρυγμαι [kekḗrygmai̯] > (32.4) κεκήρυγμαι [kekḗryŋmai̯] 'I have proclaimed'. The morphology of roots such as √φθεγγ- [pʰtʰeŋg] 'to sound', which end in γγ [ŋg], clearly point to the reconstructed pronunciation [ŋm] for γμ. Derived from the verb φθέγγομαι [pʰtʰéŋgomai̯] 'I sound', one finds an expected 3. sg. perf. ἔφθεγκται [épʰtʰeŋktai̯] as well as an unexpected 1. sg. perf. ἔφθεγμαι [épʰtʰeŋmai̯] with γμ instead of γγμ because the regular derivation of √φθεγγ- should be ˣἔφθεγγμαι [épʰtʰeŋgmai̯]. The actually attested form ἔφθεγμαι can be explained by the sound change *g* > *ŋ* / _*m* followed by the simplification of the newly formed geminate nasal *ŋŋ* > *ŋ*: *ἔφθεγγμαι [épʰtʰeŋgmai̯] > (32.5) ἔφθεγγμαι [épʰtʰeŋŋmai̯] > (45.6) ἔφθεγμαι [épʰtʰeŋmai̯]. However, one cannot completely rule out the possibility that the letters γμ and γν werde pronounced [ŋm] and [ŋn] as well as [gm] and [gn]. **Cf.** Rix §105; SI §219, 220; Allen 1974:34.

SC 34 Dental Stop Before Nasal Consonant

Analogous to the above described development of labial and guttural stops to homorganic nasals before a nasal consonant, this development could also be expected for dental stops as it happened e.g. in Lat. *penna* < **petnā* 'feather' and *annus* < **atnos* 'year'. Words like ἀριθμός 'figure' and πότμος 'fate', however, exhibit the retention of the dental consonants θ and τ before a nasal following. The inscriptional form μεσομνη, which corresponds to Hom. μεσό-δμη 'crossbeam', is an example for the expected development μεσό-δμη > (32.3) *μεσόνμη in addition to a subsequent metathesis *μεσόνμη > (42.5) μεσομνη because dental consonants – in this case, dental ν- were avoided as the first element of a sequence (cf. chap. 22).
In single words and certain perfect formations, the development of a dental stop to the fricative σ is met with. Examples are Hom. ὀδμή 'smell' and Hom. ἴδμεν 'we know' which correspond to Att. ὀσμή and Att. ἴσμεν. Further examples are *πεπειθμένος > (34.2) πεπεισμένος 'persuaded' from πείθω 'I persuade' and Dor. κέκαδμαι > (34.1) Att. κέκασμαι 'I have surpassed' from καίνυμαι 'I surpass'. These cases are, however, not explained phonologically but analogically having their starting point in forms like the 2. pl. *ϝίδ-τε > ἴστε 'you know' and *πέπειθται > πέπεισται 'is persuaded' where within the same paradigm the sequence στ developed regularly through the combination of dental stop plus dental stop. Subsequently, κέκαδμαι was reshaped to κέκασμαι in analogy to the 3. sg. κέκασται. After this analogical sound change had been formed to a fixed pattern, it was uncoupled from intraparadigmatic relations and even applied onto completely indepent words like ὀδμή. **Cf.** Rix §105; SI §221.

Exercises

E1 Labial Stop before Nasal Consonant

A σέβομαι ‘I revere’ :: *σεβνός > (32.1) __________ ‘revered’ **B** ἔρεβος ‘darkness’ :: *ἐρεβνός > (32.1) __________ ‘dark’ **C** φυλάττω ‘I guard’ :: perf. *πεφύλακ-μαι > (31.2) *__________ > (32.5) __________ [__________] ‘I have guarded’ **D** τρίβω ‘I rub’ :: *τρῖβμα > (32.2) __________ ‘master’ **E** στέφανος ‘garland’ :: *στέφμα > (25.3) *__________ > (31.1) *__________ > (32.2) __________ ‘band’ **E** ἅπτω ‘I touch’ :: *ἅπμα > (31.1) *__________ > (32.2) __________ ‘knot’

E2 Velar Stop before Nasal Consonant

A σφίγγω [__________] ‘I string’ :: perf. *ἔσφιγγμαι [ésp^{h}iŋgmai̯] > (32.5) *__________ [__________] > (45.6) __________ [__________] ‘I have stringed’ **B** ἐλέγχω [__________] ‘I curse’ :: perf. *ἐλήλεγχμαι [elḗleŋk^{h}mai̯] > (25.12) *__________ [__________] > (31.2) *__________ [__________] > (32.5) *__________ [__________] > (45.6) __________ [__________] ‘I have cursed’ **C** φθόγγος [__________] :: *φθέγγμα [p^{h}t^{h}éŋgma] > (32.5) *__________ [__________] > (45.6) __________ [__________] ‘sound’ **D** πλέκω ‘I twine’ :: ptc. perf. midd. *πεπλεκμένος > (31.2) *__________ > (32.5) __________ [__________] ‘twine’

E3 Dental Stop before Nasal Consonant

A σκευάζω ‘I equip’ :: perf. *ἐσκεύαδ-μαι > (34.1) __________ ‘I have equipped’ **B** πείθω ‘I persuade’ :: *πέπειθμαι > (34.2) __________ ‘I am persuaded’ **C** δατέομαι ‘I distribute’ :: *δατ-μός > (34.3) __________ ‘piece’ **E** φράζω ‘I speak’ :: Hes. πεφραδμένος > (34.1) Att. __________ ‘proclaiming’ **F** κόρυς, κόρυθος ‘helmet’ :: Hom. κεκορυθμένος > (34.2) Att. __________ ‘having a helmet’ **G** καίνυμαι ‘to surpass’ :: Pind. κεκαδμένος > (34.1) Att. __________ ‘surpassed’

25.3:	$p^h > p / \_N$	**31.2:**	$k > g / \_N$	**32.5:**	$g > ŋ / \_m$	**34.3:**	$t > s / \_m$
25.12:	$k^h > k / \_N$	**32.1:**	$b > m / \_n$	**34.1:**	$d > s / \_m$	**45.6:**	$ŋŋ > ŋ$
31.1:	$p > b / \_N$	**32.2:**	$b > m / \_m$	**34.2:**	$t^h > s / \_m$		

21 Assimilationen of Consonants IV: Resonants

Differences of Primary and Secondary Developments

The following tables shows that alike sequences might develop differently. While the primary development was either the insertion of an epenthetic vowel or the deletion of one of the consonants, the secondary development was the assimilation of the consonants.

Sequence	Primary Development	Secondary Development
**nr*	> (47.5) *ndr*	> (35.1) *rr*
**VrsV*	> (2.1) *V̄rV*	> (35.3) *VrrV*
**VsnV*	> (2.2) *V̄nV*	> (37.1) *VnnV*
**Vri̯V*	> (3) *V̄rV*	> (35.4) *VrrV*
**VlnV*	> (5) *V̄lV*	> (36.2) *VllV*

SC 35–37 Assimilation of the Sequences *λι̯, *ρι̯, *ρσ, *σν

The Att. assimilation *ϱσ > (35.3) ϱϱ which is seen by comparing Hom. ταϱσός 'torrefyer' and κόϱση 'temple' to Att. ταϱϱός and κόϱϱη is more recent than the development of *ϱσ in *ἔφθεϱσα [épʰtʰersa] > (2.1) ἔφθειϱα [épʰtʰḗra] in which σ was lost with compensatory lengthening. Likewise, the Att. assimilation *σν > (37.11) νν seen in *ζώσνῡμι > (37.1) ζώννῡμι 'I gird' and *σβέσνῡμι > (37.1) σβέννῡμι 'I extinguish' is more recent than the development of *σν in *σελάσνᾱ > (2.2) Att.-Ion. σελήνη 'moon' in which σ was lost with compensatory lengthening (cf. chapter 11). In the case of *ζώσνῡμι > (37.1) ζώννῡμι, the root √ζωσ- stayed phonologically intact in analogy to forms like ζωστήϱ 'girdle' and survived the phase of the primary development. Similar to the development of *λι̯ > λλ in *ἄλι̯ος > (36.4) ἄλλος 'someone else' (cf. chapter 12), one finds the Att. development *ϱι̯ > (35.4) ϱϱ if *ϱι̯ originated through synizesis which is the development of a vowel to its corresponding semivowel. In this way, the side form βοϱϱᾶς 'north wind' of βοϱέᾱς can be explained through the steps: βοϱέᾱς > (21.2) *βοϱι̯ᾱς > (35.4) βοϱϱᾶς. This assimilation is more recent than the development of *ϱι̯ in *φθέϱι̯ω [pʰtʰéri̯ō] > (3) φθέιϱω [pʰtʰḗrō] in which case *ι̯ was lost with compensatory lengthening.

SC 35–37 Assimilation of the Sequences νρ, νλ, λν, *δλ

For συνϱέω 'I flow together', there also exists an assimilated form συϱϱέω which exhibits the sound change *nr* > *rr* which was more recent than the development **nr* > *ndr* which shows the insertion of an epenthetic consonant like in the gen. sg. *ἀνϱός > (37.5) ἀνδϱός 'of the man' (cf. chapter 32). A similar tendency of assimilation exhibit the sequences νλ, λν and *δλ which all became λλ: συνλέγω > (36.1) συλλέγω 'I gather'; ἀπολνῡμι > (36.2) ἀπόλλῡμι 'I destroy'; **sedlā* > ἕλλᾱ 'seat' which is related to Lat. *sella*. The assimilation *λν > λλ in *ἀπολνῡμι > (36.2) ἀπόλλῡμι is more recent than the development *στάλνᾱ > (5) *στᾱ́λᾱ > (13)Att.-Ion. στήλη in which *ν was lost after λ with compensatory lengthening.

SC 35.2 The Sequence *ϝρ

In the medial position, the sequence *ϝϱ developed to ϱϱ as it can be seen in *ἄ-ϝϱηκτος > (35.2) ἄϱϱηκτος 'tearproof' which is derived from ῥήγνῡμι 'I break'. In the initial position, the semivowel *ϝ vanished like in *ϝϱάτϱᾱ > Att. ῥήτϱᾱ, which is related to Ion. ῥήτϱη. **Cf.** Rix §71.

Exercises

E1 Assimilation of *νρ, ρσ and *σν

A ῥάπτω 'I sew' :: *συνράπτω > (35.1) ___________ 'I sew together' **B** παλίν 'again' + ῥοᾱ́ 'flowing' :: *παλίν-ροια > (35.1) ___________ 'flowing back and forth' **C** German *Arsch* 'ass' :: *ὄρσος > (35.3) ___________ 'buttocks' **D** δέρω 'I skin' :: *δέρσις > (35.3) ___________ 'fur' **E** ἐραστός :: *ἐρασνός > (37.1) ___________ 'lovely' **F** ἀργεστής 'illuminating' ::*ἀργεσνός > (37.1) ___________ 'radiant' **G** ἔρεβος 'evening' :: *ἐρεβεσνός > (37.1) ___________ 'in the evening' **H** Aeol. κλεεννός :: *κλεϝεσνός > (37.1) *___________ > (x21.2) *___________ [___________] > (7.2) *___________ [___________] > (simplification of the double consonant) Att.-Ion. ___________ [___________] 'famous'

E2 Development of Medial *ϝρ

A ῥήτρᾱ 'statute' :: *ἄϝρητος > (35.2) ___________ 'unspeakable' **B** ῥάπτω 'I sew' :: *πολύϝραφος > (35.2) ___________ 'strongly sewed' **C** Myc. *wi-ri-za* = ῥίζα 'root' :: *πολύ-ϝριζος > (35.2) ___________ 'having many roots' **D** Att.-Ion. ῥίπτω 'I throw' :: *ἀναϝρίπτω > (35.2) ___________ 'I throw upwards'

E3 Assimilation of Nasal Consonants

A μένω 'I stay' :: ἐνμένω > (24.1) ___________ 'I stay within' **B** πάλιν 'again' :: παλιν-μήκης > (24.11) ___________ 'twice as long' **C** φαίνω 'I seem' :: *πέφανκα > (24.2) ___________ 'I seemed' **D** κλείω 'I close' :: *ἐνκλείω > (24.2) ___________ 'I enclose' **E** πάλιν 'again' :: παλίν-κοτος > (24.2) ___________ 'recidivist' **F** παροξῡ́νω 'I excite' :: *παρώξυνμαι > (24.1) ___________ 'I have excited'

LWP 24.1:	*n > m / _m*	**LWP 35.1:**	**n > r / _r*	**LWP 35.3:**	**s > r / _r*
LWP 24.3:	*n > ŋ / _(k,g)*	**LWP 35.2:**	**u̯ > r / _r*	**LWP 37.1:**	**s > n / _n*

22 Dissimilation / Dissimilatory Deletion / Haplology / Metathesis

SC 39/40 Regressive and Progressive Dissimilation

The opposite of assimilations, in which sounds become more alike, are dissimilations, in which similar sounds become less alike. This sound change mostly affected non-adjacent sequences of two Greek resonants ϱ, λ and ν which combination was mostly avoided by changing one of the respective resonants into another one. If in a sequence of two similar sounds the second sound is changed, one speaks of progressive dissimilation, if the first sound is changed, one speaks of regressive dissimilation. An example for the progressive dissimilation λ...λ > (40.2) λ...ϱ is the word κεφαλαλγία 'headache' which is also attested as κεφαλαϱγία. An example for the regressive dissimilation ϱ...ϱ > ν...ϱ is the word *δέϱ-δϱ-εον > (39.2) δένδϱεον 'tree' which is a reduplicated formation from the root √δεϱ-, which is also the base of δόϱυ 'wood' and δϱῦς 'oak'. The pattern of *i*-intensive formations like μαι-μάω 'I am very eager', παι-φάσσω 'I rush' probably orginated through the dissimilation of the reduplicated syllable of roots containing resonants. **Cf.** LJ §150; Tichy 1983:296.

SC 41 Dissimilatory Deletion of Sounds and Haplology

If a sequence oft two similar sounds was not resolved through dissimilation but through the complete loss of one of the sounds, one speaks of dissimilatory deletion. This sound change can be seen in *ἔκπλαγλος > (41.1) Hom. ἔκπαγλος 'frigthening' which is derived from ἐκ-πλαγ-ῆναι 'to frighten'. More examples are *δϱύφϱακτον > (41.3) δϱύφακτον 'wooden shed', which is related to φϱάττω < (x19.4) *φϱάκι̯ω 'I fence', as well as φᾱτϱίᾱ > (41.2) φϱᾱτϱίᾱ 'kin'.
Sometimes, morphological formations create two similar or alike syllables which are again often simplified by the speakers, which process is known as haplology. The measure ἡμιμέδιμνον 'half' is also attested as ἡμέδιμνον whereby the syllabic sequence μιμε was simplified to με. The word ἀμφι-φοϱεύς 'large jar' is also attested as ἀμφοϱεύς whereby the syllabic sequence φιφο was simplified to φο. **Cf.** LJ §150.

SC 42 Metathesis

The comparison of the aor. ἔτεκον 'I brought forth' to its respective prs. τίκτω 'I bring forth' shows that the root √τεκ-, which can be deduced from the aor. ἔ-τεκ-ον, is the base of the reduplicated present form τίκτω but not in the expected form τί-τκ-ω* but with a metathesis of the consonants. This is due to the phonological structure of Greek which did not permit consonants sequences with a dental sound as their first element. This Greek internal analysis can be corroborated by material from other IE languages. Cognate forms of χθών [k^ht^hǭn] 'earth' are Hitt. *tekan* and Toch. A *tkaṃ*, both languages exhibit the dental stop *t* before the velar stop *k*. The phonotactic rule that a dental stop cannot be the first element of a sequence also explains the metathesis of **dz* > *zd* which can be assumed as an intermediate step in the development of **gi̯* > *zd* and **di̯* > *zd*. **Cf.** chapt. 28; Rix §106b; LJ §577.

Exercises

E1 Dissimilation and Dissimilatory Deletion

A θηράω 'I hunt' :: θηρητήρ > (39.1) ___________ 'hunter' **B** ναῦς 'ship' :: *ναύ-κρασρος > (2.2) *___________ > (39.1) *___________ > (13) ___________ 'captain' **C** Ion. τέρας :: Hom. Aeol. *πέρωρ > (39.1) ___________ 'monster' **D** παλύνω 'I sprinkle' :: *παλ-πάλη > (39.5) ___________ 'flour' **E** δέλτος 'writing tablet' :: *δάλ-δαλον > (39.5) ___________ 'artwork' **F** νάρναξ > (39.7) ___________ 'container' **G** πνέω 'I breathe' :: *πον-πνύω > (39.8) ___________ 'I gasp' **H** Skr. *grás-ati* 'eats' :: *γρασ-τήρ > (41.2) ___________ 'stomach' **I** κλίβανος > (39.6) ___________ 'oven' **J** νίτρον > (39.9) ___________ 'natron' **K** Lat. *Cerberus* :: Κέρβερος > (40.1) ___________ 'hellhound' **L** ἄλγος 'pain' :: *ἀλγαλέος > (39.3) ___________ 'difficult'

E2 Loss of One Syllable through Haplology

A κελαινός 'black' + νέφος 'cloud' :: *κελαι**νονε**φής > ___________ 'of black clouds' **B** Lat. *pōtus* 'drinking' :: *πο**τοτής** > ___________ 'drink' **C** ποινή 'fine' :: *ἀ**πόποι**να > *___________ > (Vendryes' law, cf. chap. 8) ___________ 'ransom' **D** τετρα- 'four' + δραχμή 'drachma' :: *τέ**τρα-δρα**χμον > ___________ 'four drachmas' **E** κάλαμος 'shaft' + μίνθη 'mint' :: *καλα**μο-μίν**θη > ___________ 'peppermint' **F** ἀρήν 'sheep' + νάκη 'fur' :: *ἀρ**νο-να**κίς > ___________ 'sheepskin' **G** ὄπισθεν 'behind' + θέναρ 'hand' :: *ὀπισ**θο-θέ**ναρ > ___________ 'back of the hand'

E3 Metathesis

A Lat. *quippe* :: *k^w*ídpe* > (29.8) *___________ > (x23.1) *___________ > (42.3) ___________ 'why then?' **B1** PIE **tken-* 'to injure' :: 1. pl. aor. *ἔτκαμεν > (42.1) Hom. ___________ 'we slayed' **B2** 3. sg. aor. pass. *ἔτκατο > (42.1) Hom. ___________ 'he was slayed' **C** PIE **tk̂ei̯-* 'to settle' :: *τκίζω > (42.1) ___________ 'I found' **D** Skr. *ṛ́kṣa-* :: *ἄρτκος > (42.1) ___________ 'bear'

2.2:	**VsR* > *V̄R*	**39.3:**	*l…l* > *r…l*	**39.8:**	*n…n* > *i̯…n*	**42.1:**	**tk* > *kt*
13:	**ā* > *ę̄*	**39.5:**	*l…l* > *i̯…l*	**39.9:**	*n…r* > *l…r*	**42.3:**	**tp* > *pt*
29.8:	*d* > *t* / _*p*	**39.6:**	*l…n* > *r…n*	**40.1:**	*r…r* > *r…l*	**x23.1:**	*k^w > *t* / _(*i,e*)
39.1:	*r…r* > *l…r*	**39.7:**	*n…n* > *l…n*	**41.2:**	*r…r* > Ø*…r*		

23 Grassmann's Law

SC 39.10 Loss of Aspiration Through Dissimilation

The perfect tense form κεκέλευκα 'I have commanded' which is derived from κελεύω 'I command', exhibits the perfect tense morpheme -κ- besides the ending -α and the regular reduplication of the Greek perfect stem. The verb φεύγω 'I flee' does, however, not have a perfect *φέφευγα but πέφευγα'I have fled' in which initial φ was changed to its corresponding tenuis π. This sound change is known as Grassmann's law and can generally be stated as: If two syllables of a word start with an aspirate consonant, the first aspirate is changed to the corresponding tenuis. This rule is especially necessary to explain forms derived from roots like √θρεφ-, √θαφ-, √θαχ-, √θρεχ-, √θρυφ-, √θριχ- which have two aspirate consonants. In this way, the present *θρέφω > (39.10) τρέφω 'I nourish' originated by Grassmann's law of the first aspirate. The future *θρέφσω > (25.1) θρέψω 'I will nourish' does, however, not exhibits this sound change because in the preform *θρέφσω the second aspirate φ lost its aspiration before σ and became π before Grassmann's law could take effect.

This sound change also effected the glottal fricative *h* which developed out of *i̯, *ϝ or *σ and was written with spiritus asper. This explains the variation between ἔχω [ékʰǭ] 'I have' and its fut. ἕξω [héksǭ] 'I will have'. The present *ἕχω goes back to *σέχω [sékʰǭ] and its fut. ἕξω goes back to *σέχσω in which χ was deaspirated before σ before Grassmann's law took effect. The 3. sg. aor. ἔσχον 'I got' as well as the inf. aor. σχεῖν 'to have' exhibit the zero-grade -σχ- of the root √σεχ- whose initial σ was retained before a consonant. The coexistence of ἔχω, ἕξω and σχεῖν clearly shows how morphologically related words may develop phonological differences through sound change. **Cf.** Rix §107; LJ §45.

Analogy Prevented Rampant Sound Changes

An exception to the above formulated rule can be seen in the 2. sg. imp. aor. pass. *παιδεύ-θη-θι > παιδεύ-θη-τι 'be educated!' because in this case it was not the second but the first aspirate which was changed into a tenuis. This was due to analogy to other forms of the passive aorist which all had the suffix -θη-. The regular form παιδεύ-τη-θι* would have been phonologically to different in comparison to other aorist forms. In this case, it was more important to retain the form of the tense morpheme rather than to change the form according to regular sound laws.

Further exceptions to Grassmann's law are the 3. sg. aor. ἐφάνθη 'it became clear' and the 2. sg. imp. aor. φάθι 'speak!' in which cases the sound change was prevented in analogy to φαίνω 'I show' and φημί 'I say' because the regular forms ἐπάνθη* and πάθι* would have lost their phonological relation to their base forms φαίνω and φημί.

Grassmann's law in Greek and Sanskrit

Grassmann's law was found by Hermann Grassmann, a German polymath, who was renowned as a linguist and mathematician but also as a physicist and a general scholar. Aside from Greek, Grassmann's law also affected Sanskrit although it does not date back to PIE times but occurred independently in Greek and Sanskrit. This can be shown by tracing the reduplicated present τίθημι 'I put' from the root √θη-, which corresponds to Skr. *dhā-*, back to its preform PIE **dʰídʰēmi*. If Grassmann's had been active in PIE times already, **dʰídʰēmi* would have become ˣ*dí-dʰēmi*, which should have resulted in ˣδίθημι.

Exercises

E1 Loss of Aspiration

A1 θάπτω 'I bury' :: nom. sg. *θάφος > (39.10) ____________ 'grave' **A2** aor. pass. *ἐθάφην > (39.10) ____________ 'I was buried' **B** θάττων 'faster' :: *θαχύς > (39.10) ____________ 'fast' **C** ἅπτω 'I touch' :: prs. *ἁφάσσω [____________] > (39.10) Ion. ____________ [____________] 'I feel' **D** aor. ἔθρεξα 'I ran' :: prs. *θρέχω > (39.10) ____________ 'I run' **E** θρύπτω 'I grind' :: *θρυφή > (39.10) ____________ 'debauchery' **F1** θρίξ 'hair' :: nom. pl. *θρίχες > (39.10) ____________ 'hairs' **F2** gen. sg. *θριχός > (39.10) ____________ 'of the hair' **H** nom. sg. *φάϝος > (x21.2) ____________ 'light' :: prs. *φιφαύσκω > (39.10) ____________ 'I let appear' **I** θύω 'I sacrifice' :: aor. pass. *ἐθύθην > (39.10) ____________ 'I was sacrificed' **J** τίθημι 'I set' :: aor. pass. *ἐθέθην > (39.10) ____________ 'was set' **K** θεσμός :: *θεθμός > (39.10) Dor. ____________ 'statute' **L** χείρ 'hand' + ἔχω 'I hold' :: *ἐχε-χειρίᾱ > (39.10) ____________ 'caesefire'

E2 Reconstruct the Preforms:

A φιλέω 'I love' :: perf. *____________ > (39.10) πεφίληκα 'I have loved' **B** χράομαι 'I need' :: perf. *____________ > (39.10) κέχρημαι 'I needed' **C** φύω 'I become' :: perf. *____________ > (39.10) πέφῡκα 'I have become' **D** Lat. *fīdō* 'I have confidence' :: *____________ > (39.10) πείθω 'I persuade' **E** *____________ > (39.10) κιχάνω 'I achieve' **F** χέω 'I pour' :: perf. *____________ > (39.10) κέχυμαι 'I have poured'

E3 Which of the Following Forms is an Analogical Formation?

τρέφω 'I nourish' :: 3. sg. ind. perf. midd. τεθράφθαι 'having nourished'

τρέπω 'I turn' :: 3. sg. ind. perf. midd. τετράφθαι 'having turned'

Answer:

E4 Why is it Difficult to Trace φάτνη 'Manger' back to *φάθνη?

Answer:

24 Loss and Re-Emergence of the Fricative σ

LWP x13.1 Buccalization of Initial *s

The PIE fricative **s* remained only before and after a stop consonant and in the final position: **$h_1$es-ti* > ἐστί 'is'; **deḱsiterós* > δεξιτερός 'right'; **u̯oi̯ḱos* > οἶκος 'house'. In all other positions, *s became *h* which remained in the initial position if it did not vanish through Grassmann's law (cf. chapter 22) or psilosis. This development **s* > (x13.1) *h* can be seen by comparing *σέξ > ἕξ [héks] 'six', *σεπτά > ἑπτά [heptá] 'seven' and *σέρπω > ἕρπω [hérpǭ] 'I crawl' to their cognate forms Lat. *sex*, *septem*, *serpō* and Skr. *ṣaṭ*, *sapta*, *sarpāmi*. **Cf.** Rix §86.

LWP x13.2/x14.2 = x15.1 Buccalization and Loss of Intervocalic *s

The comparison of νόστος 'return' and νέομαι 'I come', which are both derived from the root √νεσ-, enables to trace νέομαι back to *νέσομαι whose *σ vanished between vowels. This loss of intervocalic *σ occurred via the intermediate step *h* which was still preserved in e.g. Myc. *pa-we-a_2* /pʰarweha/ 'clothes' in which the syllabogram a_2 stands for /ha/. The corresponding Attic form φάρη developed via: *φάρϝεhα > (x14.1) *φάρϝεα > (x21.3) *φάρεα > (9.2) φάρη 'clothes'. This sound change explains the endings of the 2. sg. ind. midd. παιδεύ-ῃ 'you educate for yourself' and the 2. sg. imp. midd. παιδεύ-ου 'educate for yourself!' in which intervocalic *σ vanished before the vowel hiatus was resolved by contraction: *παιδεύεσαι > (x15.1) *παιδεύεαι > (9.2) παιδεύῃ as well as *παιδεύεσο > (x15.1) *παιδεύεο > (10.3) *παιδεύǭ > (15) παιδεύου. The sound changes **s* > (x13.1) *h* and *h* > (x14.1) Ø are expressed by **s* > (x15.1) Ø in a single step. **Cf.** Rix §87.

LWP x14.2 Transposition of the Glottal Fricative *h*

The buccalization of intervocalic *σ produced at first the glottal fricative *h* which was transposed to the initial position in some words. The words for 'dawn' Att. ἕως, Hom. ἠώς and Dor. ἀϝός can be traced back to PIE **$h_2$éu̯sōs* by comparing it to Lat. *aurōra* und Skr. *uṣā́s-*. The laryngeal in the preform **$h_2$éu̯sōs* colored **e* to *a* before vanishing in the initial position before vowel which resulted in **āu̯sōs*. Next, intervocalic **s* became *h* which was transposed to the initial position: **āu̯sōs* > (x13.2) **āu̯hōs* > (x14.2) **hāu̯ōs*. Finally, intervocalic **u̯* vanished before **ā* was raised to η and the long vowel was shortened before a vowel: **hāu̯ōs* > (x21.2) **hāōs* > (13) **hēōs* > (1.1) att. ἕως [héǭs].

LWP x21.5/6 Re-Emergence of σ from *τϝ

The loss of initial PIE **s* was partially compensated through the formation of new initial σ out of the sequence *τϝ. The Cretan form τϝε 'you' of the enclitic personal pronoun enables to trace Att. σε back to *τϝε as well. By the comparison with Lat. *tuus* 'your', the possessive pronoun 2. sg. σός 'your' can be traced back to *τϝός. Theoretically, the development has to be modeled as **tu̯* > **ss* with subsequent degemination **ss* > *s* but this detail is disregarded in this book.

In the medial position, the sequence *τϝ was continued by Att. ττ / Ion. σσ, the same result as for *τι̯ and *κι̯ (cf. chapt. 29). By the comparison with Skr. *catvā́ras* 'four', Att. τέτταρες and Ion. τέσσαρες can be traced back to **k^wétu̯r̥es*, whereby the labiovelar **k^w* became τ, syllabic **r̥* became αρ and **tu̯* became ττ/σσ: **k^wétu̯r̥es* > (x23.1) **tétu̯r̥es* > (x25.1) *τέτϝαρες > (x21.6) Att. τέτταρες / Ion. τέσσαρες. This sound change also explains the phonological difference of the synonymous verbs *τϝάω > (x21.5) σάω and *δια-τϝάω > (x21.6) διαττάω 'I sieve'. **Cf.** Rix §104.

Exercises

E1 Development of *σ in the Initial and Medial Position

A Lat. *sāl* :: *σάλς > (x13.1) ____________ 'salt' **B** Lat. *sulcus* 'plow' :: *σέλκω > (x13.1) ____________ 'I drag' **C** Lat. *sēmi* :: *σημι- > (x13.1) ____________ 'half' **D** γένος 'kin' :: gen. sg. *γένεσος > (x15.1) *____________ > (10.3) *____________ > (15) ____________ **E** Skr. *trásāmi* :: *τρέσω > (x15.1) ____________ 'I tremble' **F** μένω 'I stay' :: fut. *μενέσω > (x15.1) *____________ > (10.1) ____________ 'I will stay'

E2 Transposition of the Glottal Fricative *h*

A Lat. *ūrō* 'I burn' :: *εὔσω > (x13.2) *____________ > (x14.2) ____________ 'I singe' **B** ὁράω 'I see' :: *προ-ὁρά́ [prohorá́] > (x14.2) *____________ [____________] > (7.3) *____________ > (15) ____________ [____________] 'guard' **C** ὁδός 'way' :: *πρό-ὁδος [próhodos] > (x14.2) *____________ [____________] > (7.3) *____________ > (15) ____________ [____________] 'vanished' **D** Skr. *iṣirá-* 'agile' :: *ἰσερός > (x13.2) *____________ > (x14.2) ____________ 'strong'

E3 Re-Emergence of Initial σ from *τϝ

A1 Skr. *tavás-* 'strong, brave' :: *τϝάϝος > (x21.2) *____________ > (x21.5) ____________ 'healthy' **A2** *τϝῶκος > (x21.5) ____________ 'strong' **B** Skr. *tveṣá-* 'vehement' :: *τϝείσω > (x15.1) *____________ > (x21.5) ____________ 'I shake' **C1** Lith. *tveriù* 'to grasp' :: *τϝωρός > (x21.5) ____________ 'heap' **C2** *τϝορός > (x21.5) ____________ 'urn' **C3** *τϝεροι̯ά > (3) *____________ > (x21.5) Att. ____________ > (13) Ion. ____________ 'rope' **D** aor. ἔσαξα 'I crammed' :: prs. *τϝάκι̯ω > (x21.5) *____________ > (x19.4) Att. ____________ 'I cram' **E** Skr. *tváṣṭar-* 'name of a creator deity' :: *tu̯r̥ks > (x25.1) *____________ > (x21.5) ____________ 'meat'

3:	*VRi̯ > V̄R*	**15:**	*ǭ > ū*	**x14.2:**	*#V…h > #hV…*	**x21.2:**	*u̯ > Ø / V_V*
7.3:	*o + o > ǭ*	**x13.2:**	*s > h / V_V*	**x15.1:**	*s > Ø / V_V*	**x21.5:**	*tu̯ > s / #_*
10.1:	*e + ǭ > ǭ*	**x13.5:**	*s > h / C_C*	**x16.1:**	*i̯ > Ø / V_V*	**x25.1:**	*r̥ > ar*
10.3:	*e + o > ǭ*	**x14.1:**	*h > Ø / V_V*	**x19.4:**	*ki̯ > att. tt*		

25 Consonant Sequences Containing the Fricative σ

SC x13.3/x14.3/x15.3 Initial *σ plus Resonant

The development of initial *s > h, which was described in the preceding chapter, also happened before resonant in the sequences *sr-, *sl-, *sm-, *sn-, *$su̯$-, *$si̯$- which resulted in *hr-, *hl-, *hm-, *hn-, *$hu̯$-, *$hi̯$-. Subsequently, these initial resonants were allophonically realized as voiceless aspirate resonants [r^h], [l^h], [m^h], [n^h], [$u̯^h$], [$i̯^h$] which was expressed by inscriptional spellings such as ϱh, λh, ϝh. Examples are: Dor. ϱhoϝαισι, which belongs with Att. ῥοή 'stream' to the root √σϱεϝ-, and Pamph. ϝhέ and Att. ἑ 'self' which go back to *σϝε. The aspiration of the voiceless aspirate resonants was preserved in Att. ῥ [r^h] and analogically transferred onto every initial ϱ even if it had not developed out of *sr- because the initial sequence *hr- was frequent. The resonants [l^h], [m^h], [n^h] lost their aspiration and became [l], [m], [n], and [$u̯^h$], [$i̯^h$] developed to h as it can be seen in *σϝεκυϱός > ἑκυϱός 'father in law' (~Lat. *socer*, Skr. *śváśura-*), and *$si̯um\bar{e}n$ > ὑμήν 'small ribbon' (~Skr. *syūman-* 'strap'). The development of *s > h > Ø is expressed by SC x15.3 in a single step. **Cf.** Rix §86; LJ §112–115, 127–129.

SC x13.5/x14.2/x14.3/x15.2 Medial *σ plus Resonant

As it was stated in chapter 11, *σ caused the gemination of a resonant following in Att. compounds. This can be seen in pairs like ῥέω 'I flow' :: ἐπι-ϱϱέει 'he flows hither' from the root √σϱεϝ-, λήγω 'I stop' :: ἄ-λληκτον 'incessantly' from the root √σληγ- and μοῖϱα 'part' :: ἄ-μμοϱος 'without share of' from the root √σμεϱ-. Some cases like ὁϱμή 'onrush, assault', which is related to ὄϱνῡμι 'I excite', are furthermore examples for the transposition of the glottal fricative h (cf. the preceding chapter) which happened after *σ had become h between consonants: *ὀϱσμά > (x13.5) *ὀϱhμά > (x14.2) *ὁϱμά > (13) ὁϱμή. Another example is ἀϱαϱίσκω 'I join' :: *ἄϱσμα > (x13.5) *ἄϱhμα > (x14.2) ἅϱμα 'chariot'. Both examples exhibit the development *σ > h next to a resonant. This observation makes it probable that in the obove mentioned examples *ἐπι-σϱέει > (x15.2) ἐπι-ϱϱέει, *ἄσληκτον > (x15.2) ἄλληκτον and *ἄσμοϱος > (x15.2) ἄμμοϱος, the fricative *σ first became *h and then assimilated to the adjacent resonant. Rule x15.2 sums up this process *s > *h > R / _R in a simgle step. **Cf.** Rix §88.

SC 38 Aspiration of κ or π by *σ following

The comparison of Myc. *ai-ka-sa-ma* [ai̯ksmā] to Hom. αἰχμή [ai̯kʰmḗ] 'lance' shows that Myc. retains s after k whereas it was lost in the Homeric form where [kh] is found instead of [ks] because after the development s > h the sequence [kh] was interpreted as monophonemic /k^h/. In this way, πλέκω 'I twine' and πλοχμός 'locks, braids of hair' can be connected as the former goes back to *$pl\acute{e}\hat{k}$-$\bar{o}$ and the latter goes back to *$plo\hat{k}$-$sm\acute{o}s$. **Cf.** Rix §87; LJ §132.

SC 32 Simplification of Consonant Sequences Containing σ

If σ was surrounded by two alike consonants, the first consonant was lost such as in *δίκσκος > (43.3) δίσκος 'discus' which is derived from δικεῖν 'to throw'. If, however, σ was surrounded by unlike consonants, σ was lost and the clashing consonants were often subject to further modifications. The 2. pl. perf. midd. πεφύλαχθε 'you have guarded for yourself' < *πε-φύλακ-σθε which is derived from φυλάττω < (x19.4) *φυλάκι̯ω 'I guard' is an example for the loss of σ between consonants whereby *πε-φύλακ-σθε became *πεφύλακθε before κθ assimilated to χθ. If the consonant before σ was ν, ν was lost such as in *σύν-στημα > (43.7) σύστημα 'collocation'. **Cf.** Rix §87; LJ §133–134.

Exercises

E1 *σ plus Resonant in the Initial and Medial Position

A OHG *snuor* ‘string’ :: prs. *σνήι̯ω > (x16.1) *___________ > (x15.3) *___________ > (1.1) ___________ ‘I spin’ **B** prs. *σνέι̯ω > (x16.1) *___________ > (x15.3) ___________ ‘I swim’ :: ipf. *ἔσνεον > (x15.2) ___________ ‘I swam’ **C** prs. *σρέϝω > (x13.3) *___________ > (x21.2) ___________ ‘I flow’ :: ipf. *ἔσρεϝον > (x15.2) *___________ > (x21.2) ___________ ‘I flowed’ **D** prs. *σλήγγω > (x15.3) ___________ ‘I stop’ :: aor. *ἔσληγγσα > (x15.2) ___________ ‘I stopped’ **E** Lith. *smagus* ‘heavy’ :: *σμόγος > (x15.3) ___________ ‘effort’ **F** Skr. *smárati* ‘he thinks of’ :: *σμέριμνα > (x15.3) ___________ ‘sorrow’ **G** Latv. *smaida* ‘smile’ :: *φιλο-σμειδής > (x15.2) ___________ ‘loving to laugh’ **H** Lat. *frīgus* ‘coldness’ :: prs. *σρῑγέω > (x13.3) ___________ ‘I shudder’ **I** λαμβάνω ‘I grasp’ :: ipf. *ἔσλαβον > (x15.2) ___________ ‘I grasped’ **J** *σμικρός > (x15.2) ___________ ‘small’ **L** Av. *snāvarə* :: *σνηῦρον > (x15.2) *___________ > (1.3) ___________ ‘tendon’

E2 Aspiration of κ by *σ

A Lat. *texō* ‘I weave’ :: *τέκσνᾱ > (x13.5) *___________ > (27.2) *___________ > (13) ___________ ‘art’ **B** λευκός ‘shining’ :: *λύκσνος > (x13.5) *___________ > (27.2) ___________ ‘lamp’ **C** Lat. *arānea* :: *ἀράκσνᾱ > (x13.5) *___________ > (27.2) *___________ > (13) ___________ ‘spider’ **D** ἀκίς ‘pointed object’ :: *ἄκσνᾱ > (x13.5) *___________ > (27.2) *___________ > (13) ___________ ‘chaff’

E3 Loss or Preservation of σ in Consonant Sequences

A aor. ἔλακον ‘I cried’ :: prs. *λάκ-σκω > (43.3) ___________ ‘I cry’ **B** βλαβή ‘damage’ :: perf. inf. midd. *βεβλάπσθαι > (43.6) *___________ > (26.1) ___________ ‘having damaged’ **C** τρίβω ‘I rub’ :: perf. inf. midd. *τετρίβσθαι > (29.1) *___________ > (43.6) *___________ > (26.1) ___________ ‘I have rubbed’ **D** Skr. *pā́rṣṇi-* :: *πᾱ́ρσνᾱ > (43.6) *___________ > (13) *___________ > (1.3) *___________ > (x20) ___________ ‘heel’ **E** Lat. *cēnseō* ‘I estimate’ :: *κόνσμος > (43.7) ___________ ‘jewellery’ **F** πάλιν ‘again’ :: *παλίνσκιος > (43.7) ___________ ‘thick-shaded’ **G** Skr. *dámpati-* :: *δεμσπότης > (24.3) *___________ > (43.7) ___________ ‘master, lord’

1.1: *V̄ > V̆ / _V̄*	**27.2:** *kh > kʰ*	**43.7:** *n > Ø / _sC*	**x15.2:** **s > R / _R_*	**x20:** *p > pt / #_V*
1.3: *V̄ > V̆ / _RC*	**29.1:** *b > s / _p*	**x13.3:** **s > h / #_R*	**x15.3:** **s > Ø / #_R*	**x21.2:** **u̯ > Ø / V_V*
13: **ā > ē̜*	**43.6:** *s > Ø / C_1_C_2*	**x13.5:** **s > h / C_C*	**x16.1:** **i̯ > Ø / V_V*	

26 The Semivowel *ϝ

SC x21.1/x21.4 Loss and Debuccalization of Initial *ϝ

The semivowel *ϝ = [u̯], also known as digamma, remained in Att. words only as the second element of diphthongs such as in ἔπνευσα [épneu̯sa] 'I breathed' whereas it was lost in all other positions. The comparison of the initial positions of Att.-Ion. οἶκος 'house', ἔτος 'year', ἄστυ 'city' to Dor. ϝοῖκος, ϝέτος, ϝάστος shows that the semivowel *ϝ remained in Dor. whereas it was lost in Att.-Ion. In ἑκών [hekǭn] 'voluntary' < *ϝεκών [u̯ekǭn], which is related to Skr. *váśas-* 'desire', the semivowel *ϝ contrarily developed to aspirate *h* which process is known as debuccalization. No adequate explanation has been found for this double representation of *ϝ -its complete loss in *ϝοῖκος > (x21.1) οἶκος and its aspiration to *h* in *ϝέκων > (x21.4) ἑκών- except that the development *ϝ > *h* mostly happened in words such as *ϝέσπερος > (x21.4) ἕσπερος 'evening', in which the fricative σ appears somewhere in the word. A counterexample to this observation is, however: *ϝάστυ > (x21.1) ἄστυ. In some cases, it is, however, not possible to determine whether initial *h* is the continuant of *ϝ or was caused by the transposition of *h* which goes back to *σ (cf. chapter 24). By the comparison with Skr. *vásman-* 'garment', it is possible to trace εἷμα [hę̄ma] 'garment' back to *ϝέσμα whereby initial *h* might either go back to *ϝ directly or it might as well be aspirate *h*, which has been transposed from the medial to the initial position. A similar example is the development of *ϝέρσμα > ἕρμα [hérma] 'hill' which is related to Skr. *várṣman-* 'elevation'. **Cf.** Rix §71; SI §182, 187–188; LJ §179–183.

SC x21.2 Loss of Intervocalic *ϝ

In Att.-Ion., the semivowel *ϝ was also lost between vowels, as revealed by the comparison of Dor. κλέϝος with Att. κλέος 'fame'. This sound change affected presents like *πλέϝω > (x21.2) πλέω 'I sail' whose aor. ἔπλευσα [épleu̯sa] 'I sailed' still exhibits the respective sound as the second element of the diphthong [eu̯]. After the loss of intervocalic *ϝ, vowels were in the hiatus position which was preserved in many Hom. words.

The nom. pl. ἡδεῖς [hę̄dę̄s] from ἡδύς [hę̄dýs] 'sweet' goes back to *ἡδέϝες [hę̄déu̯es] > (x21.2) *ἡδέες > (7.2) ἡδεῖς in contrast to the gen. sg. *ἡδέϝος > (x21.2) ἡδέος which did not contract to ˣἡδους because the loss intervocalic *ϝ happened after the productive phase of the contraction of unlike vowels. Therefore, the nom. pl. ἄστη 'cities' from ἄστυ can be identified as an analogical formation to *s*-stems like nom. sg. γένος :: nom. pl. γένη because in the Homeric preform ἄστεα the vowels should not have been contracted. **Cf.** Rix §72; SI §182; LJ §186–187.

SC x21.3 Loss of *ϝ after Consonant

After a consonant, *ϝ was lost without a trace in Attic and with compensatory lengthening of the preceding vowel in Ionic. Lat. *laevus* 'left' and Lat. *scaevus* 'left' correspond to λαιός 'left' and σκαιός 'left hand', which are the same forms in Attic and Ionic because after a diphthong no compensatory lengthening took place in Ionic. Dialect forms like ξένϝος, κόρϝα, καλϝός show the retention of the semivowel *ϝ, which was completely lost in Att. ξένος 'foreigner', κόρη 'girl' and καλός 'beautiful' and with compensatory lengthening in Ion. ξεῖνος, κούρη, κᾱλός. The word κόρη < *κόρϝᾱ gives an important clue for the chronology of sound changes because it has η after ρ although η should have been reversed to ᾱ after ρ (cf. chapter 16) which means that the development ᾱ > η and the Attic reversion η > ᾱ must have been completed before the loss of *ϝ because at that time ᾱ was not in the position after ρ but still after *ϝ: *κόρϝᾱ > (13) *κόρϝη > (x21.3) *κόρη **Cf.** Rix §72; SI §190.

Exercises

E1 Loss and Debuccalization of Initial *ϝ

A Skr. *vidmá* :: 1. pl. *ϝίδμεν > (x21.1) ____________ 'we know' **B** Lat. *vīnum* :: *ϝοῖνος > (x21.1) ____________ 'wine' **C** Lat. *vīs* :: *ϝίς > (x21.1) ____________ 'force' **C** Lat. *Vesta* 'goddess of the hearth :: *ϝεστίᾱ > (x21.4) ____________ 'hearth' **D** Lat. *lāna* :: *ϝλᾶνος > (13) *____________ > (x21.1) ____________ 'wool' **E** German *Werk* :: *ϝέργον > (x21.1) ____________ 'work' **F** Skr. *vácas-* 'word' :: **u̯ék^{w}os* > (x24.2) *____________ > (x21.1) ____________ 'speech'

E2 Loss of Intervocalic *ϝ

A Myc. *di-wo* :: gen. sg. *Διϝός > (x21.2) ____________ 'of Zeus' **B** aor. ἔπνευσα 'I breathed' :: *πνέϝω > (x21.2) ____________ 'I breath' **C** Skr. *kravíṣ-* 'raw meat' :: *κρέϝας > (x21.2) ____________ 'meat' **D** Skr. *avidam* 'I found' :: aor. *ἔϝιδον [____________] > (x21.2) *____________ [____________] > (23.1) *[____________] > (14.2) ____________ [____________] 'I saw' **E** ἀπο-λαύω 'I benefit' :: *λᾱϝίς > (13) *____________ > (x21.2) Hom. ____________ 'prey' **F** ἀήρ 'wind' :: *ἄϝελι̯α > (36.4) *____________ > (x21.2) ____________ 'storm' **J** Lat. *ventus* 'wind' :: *ἄϝητι > (x22.1) *____________ > (x21.2) ____________ 'it blows'

E3 *ϝ after Consonant in Ionic and Attic

A Myc. *wo-wo* :: *ϝόρϝος > (x21.4) *____________ > (x21.3) Att. ____________ / Ion. ____________ 'border' **B** Dor. μῶνος :: *μόνϝος > (x21.3) Att. ____________ / Ion. ____________ 'alone' **C** *μάνϝος > (x21.3) Att. ____________ / Ion. ____________ 'thin' **D** Skr. *sárva-* :: *σόλϝος > (x13.1) *____________ > (x21.3) Att. ____________ / Ion. ____________ 'whole' **E** Myc. *ke-se-nu-wo* :: *ξένϝος > (x21.3) Att. ____________ / Ion. ____________ 'foreigner' **F** Skr. *dvíṣ* :: *δϝίς > (x21.3) ____________ 'twice' **G** *δέρϝᾱ > (13) *____________ > (x21.3) ____________ / Ion. ____________ 'neck' **H** Arc. ὀλοϝά :: *ὀλϝαί > (x21.3) Att. ____________ / Ion. ____________ 'barley-corns' **I** Skr. *dagh-* 'to reach' :: *φθάνϝω > (x21.3) Att. ____________ / Ion. ____________ 'I come'

13:	**ā > ę̄*	**36.4:**	**i̯ > l / l_*	**x21.2:**	**u̯ > Ø / V_V*	**x22.1:**	**ti > si*
14.2	**ei̯ > ẹ̄*	**x13.1:**	**s > h / #_V*	**x21.3:**	**u̯ > Ø / C_*	**x24.2:**	**k^{w} > p / _(o,a)*
23.1:	*ĭ > i̯ / V_*	**x21.1:**	**u̯ > Ø / #_(V,R)*	**x21.4:**	**u̯ > h / #_V*		

27 The Semivowel *i̯

SC x16.1 Loss of Intervocalic *i̯

Intervocalic *i̯ was lost between vowels before the remaining vowel hiatus was resolved by contraction of the vowels. By the comparison with Ved. *tráyaḥ*, Greek τρεῖς [trẹ̄s] 'three' can be traced back to *τρέi̯ες whereby intervocalic *i̯ was lost before ε and ε contracted to ει [ẹ̄]: *τρέi̯ες > (x16.1) *τρέες > (7.2) τρεῖς. Based on Myc. evidence in spellings like *qe-te-ha* / *qe-te-jo* / *qe-te-a*, in which the spellings *h*, *j* and zero alternate, and Cretan forms like τρέες 'three' which lack vowel contraction of alike vowels, one can assume that similar to the development of intervocalic *σ also intervocalic *i̯ became *h* before it vanished completely. This intermediate step *h* which seems to have been preserved in Mycenaean and retarded the contraction in Cretan τρέες [tréʰes] is, however, not further considered in the sound change exercises of this book. **Cf.** Rix §69; SI§ 192; LJ §170.

Re-Emergence and Anew Loss of Intervocalic i̯

Intervocalic i̯ could re-emerge out of the sequence *ϝi̯ such as in the present *κλάϝi̯ω > (x17) *κλάi̯ϝω > (x21.3) κλαίω 'I close'. It then vanished again with compensatory lengthening which can be seen in the variant form κλαίω > (6.1) κλᾴω. This process is also seen in the difference of *αἰϝεσί > Hom. αἰεί and Att. ᾀεί which is also attested as ἀεί with the shortening of the initial vowel: *αἰϝεσί > (x15.1) *αἰϝεί > (x21.3) Hom. αἰεί > (6.1) Old-Att. ᾀεί > (1.1) Att. ἀεί. The loss of i̯ is also attested in the variant form ὑός of υἱός 'son'. **Cf.** Rix §73; SI §205–6; LJ §265.

SC x16.2/3 Correspondences of Initial i̯ in Other Languages

Meaning	Greek	Sanskrit	Latin	Reconstruction	Sound Change
Liver	ἧπαρ [hẹ̄par]	*yákr̥t* [i̯ákr̥t]	*iecur* [i̯ekur]	**Hi̯ē/ekʷr̥t*	x16.2
Joke	ζυγόν [zdygón]	*yugám* [i̯ugám]	*iugum* [i̯ugum]	**i̯ugom*	x16.3

The above table shows that Latin and Sanskrit initial i̯ corresponds to Greek *h* or ζ. This double representation is usually explained through the assumption of an initial laryngeal in those words which exhibit initial Greek *h* because Sanskrit equivalents sometimes show the lengthening of a final vowel in compounds whose second element is one of the respective words, and this lengthening can be explained by an initial laryngeal. Therefore, by the comparison with Old Latin *ioubēre* [i̯ou̯bēre] 'to command' and Skr. *yúdhyati* [i̯údʰi̯ati] 'he fights', one can trace ὑσμίνη [hysmínẹ̄] 'fight' in a first step back to **i̯udʰ-smīnā*. Due to the long *ā* of the first element of the Sanskrit compound *amitrā-yúdh-* 'fighting enemies', the respective PIE root can be reconstructed as **Hi̯eu̯dʰ-* with an initial laryngeal, which enables to trace the preform **i̯udʰ-smīnā* further back to **Hi̯udʰ-smīnā*. This argumentation implies that initial ζ must go back to *i̯. The evidence of words which support this argumentation is, however, scarce and partially contraditory. E.g. the comparison of ζυγόν :: Skr. *yugá-* :: Lat. *iugum* hints to PIE **i̯ugóm* without initial laryngeal but the 3. sg. ipf. Ved. *āyunak* 'he harnessed' with its lengthened augment speaks for an initial laryngeal and must therefore be explained through analogy to other regular forms. Exercises for SC x16.3 can be found in the next chapter. **Cf.** SI §191; LJ §167; an opposite view is found in Rix §68, §80e.

Exercises

E1 Loss of Intervocalic *i̯

A1 πειθώ 'persuasion' :: dat. sg. *πειθόι̯ι [____________] > (x16.1) *____________ [____________] > (23.1) ____________ [____________] **A2** gen. sg. *πειθόι̯ος > (x16.1) *____________ > (7.3) *____________ > (15) ____________ **B** πόλις 'city' :: gen. sg. *πόληι̯ος > (x16.1) *____________ > (1.2) ____________ 'of the city' **C** σταῖς 'bread dough' :: *στᾱ́ι̯αρ > (x16.1) *____________ > (13) *____________ > (1.1) ____________ 'hard fat' **D** Skr. *dyati* 'he binds' :: *δέι̯ω > (x16.1) ____________ 'I bind' **E** Skr. *dīdā́ye* 'it shines' :: *δέι̯αται > (x16.1) ____________ 'he seems **F** Lat. *plēnus* :: *πλήι̯ος > (x16.1) *____________ > (1.1) ____________ 'full' **G** fut. νήσω 'I will spin' :: prs. *νήι̯ω > (x16.1) *____________ > (1.1) ____________ 'I spin' **H** Hitt. *ariyezzi* 'he investigates' :: *ἐρέι̯ω > (x16.1) ____________ 'I ask'

E2 Change of **Hi̯* to *h* in the Initial Position

A1 Av. *yārə* :: **Hi̯ǭ̃rā* > (x16.2) ____________ 'time' **A2** **Hi̯ǭ̃ros* > (x16.2) ____________ 'year' **B** **Hi̯óp*^{h}*ra* > (x16.2) *____________ > (39.10) Hom. ____________ 'as long as' **C** Skr. *yájāmi* :: **Hi̯ági̯ō* > (x16.2) *____________ > (x18.1) ____________ 'I worship' **D** Skr. *yad* :: nt. sg. **Hi̯ód* > (x16.2) *____________ > (x12.2) ____________ 'which'

E3 Loss of *i̯ after α with Compensatory Lengthening

A Lat. *lēvir* :: *δαι̯ϝήρ > (x21.3) *____________ > (6.1) Hom. ____________ 'brother-in-law' **B** ἔλαιον 'oil' :: *ἐλαί̯ϝᾱ > (x21.3) Old Att. ____________ > (6.1) Att. ____________ 'olive tree' **C** κλαίειν > (6.1) ____________ 'to cry' **D** Ἀθᾱναίᾱ > (13) ____________ > (6.1) ____________ > (7.1) ____________ 'Athena' **E** Lat. *avis* 'bird' :: *ἀϝι̯ετός > (x17) *____________ > (21.2) Hom. ____________ 'eagle'

1.1:	*V̄ > V / _V*	**7.3:**	*o/ǭ + o/ǭ > ǭ*	**31.10:**	C^h…C^h > C…C^h	**x18.1:**	**gi̯ > zd*
1.2:	*V̄V̆ > V̆V̄*	**10.1:**	*e + ǭ > ǭ*	**x12.2:**	**VC(C)# > V#*	**x21.3:**	**u̯ > Ø / C_*
4.1:	**VnsV > V̄sV*	**13:**	**ā > ę̄*	**x16.1:**	**i̯ > Ø / V_V*		
6:	*ai̯ > ā / _V*	**15:**	**ǭ > ū*	**x16.2:**	**Hi̯ > h / #_V*		
7.1:	*ă + ă > ā*	**23.1:**	*ĭ > i̯ / V_*	**x17:**	**(a,o)Ri̯ > (a,o)i̯R*		

28 Palatalization of Voiced Sounds

SC x18 Palatalization of *di̯, *gi̯ and *gʷi̯

The verb ἁρπάζω [harpázdǭ] 'to rob' < *ἁρπάγι̯ω is related to ἁρπαγή 'robbery' and an example for the sound change *gi̯ > (x18.1) ζ. A similar sound change *di̯ > (x18.2) ζ can be seen the verb ἐλπίζω [elpízdǭ] 'I hope' < *ἐλπίδι̯ω, which is related to ἐλπίς, ἐλπίδος 'hope'. The sequence *gi̯ could also originate out of *gʷi̯ because *i̯ was lost after the labial coarticulation of the labiovelar *gʷ. In this way, νίζω 'I wash' can be connected to ἄ-νιπτος 'unwashed' by tracing νίζω back to *νίγι̯ω which itself goes back to **nígʷ-i̯ō*. The labiovelar *gʷ lost its labial coarticulation before *i̯ and the resulting sequence *gi̯ developed further to ζ: **nígʷi̯ō* > (x11.2) *νίγι̯ω > (x18.1) νίζω. The zero-grade PPP **n̥-nigʷ-tós*, which is also built from the respective root **nei̯gʷ-* and furnished with the negation particle **n̥-*, developed to ἄνιπτος because syllabic *n̥ became α, and the labiovelar *gʷ became β before a consonant which itself became π before τ: **ń̥-nigʷ-tos* > (x26.1) **ánigʷtos* > (x24.3) *ἄνιβτος > (29.2) ἄνιπτος. **Cf.** Rix §102; SI §200; LJ §103.

Phonetic Value and Origin of the Sound Cluster [zd] Denoted by ζ

This book identifies the phonetic value of Greek ζ as [zd] for the following reasons: One argument for the pronunciation [zd] is the present πλάζω 'I hit' in which ν vanished before ζ just like ν vanished before σ in *σύνστημα > (43.7) σύστημα. The root of πλάζω is √πλαγγ- [plaŋg] because its aorist ἔπλαγξα [éplaŋksa] and its future πλάγξω [pláŋksǭ] can be traced back to *ἔ-πλαγγ-σα [éplaŋgsa] and *πλάγγ-σω [pláŋgsǭ] by assimilation of voice. In the present πλάζω [plázdǭ], there is, however, no nasal because the sequence *gi̯ became [zd] in the preform *πλάγγι̯ω [pláŋgi̯ǭ] before ν was lost before [zd]: *πλάγγι̯ω [pláŋgi̯ǭ] > (x18.1) *πλάνζω [plánzdǭ] > (43.8) πλάζω [plázdǭ].
Another argument for the pronuciation [zd] is the verb ἔρδω [érdǭ] 'I do' < *ϝέργι̯ω which is related to ἔργον 'work' < *ϝέργον. In the preform *ϝέργι̯ω [u̯érgi̯ǭ], the sequence *gi̯ developed to ζ [zd]: *ϝέργι̯ω [u̯érgi̯ǭ] > *ϝέρζω [u̯érzdǭ]. According to SC 43.6, a fricative /s/ was lost between dissimilar consonants so that in a first step *ϝέρζω [u̯érzdǭ] became *ϝέρδω [u̯érdǭ] and subsequently ἔρδω [érdǭ] by the loss of the initial digamma (SC x21.1). If ζ had been pronounced [dz], [u̯érgi̯ǭ] should have led via [u̯érdzǭ] to Att. ˣἔρζω. Nevertheless, it is phonologically very probable that the palatalization of *gi̯, *di̯ and initial *i̯ initially generated an affricate [dz] due to the typological frequency of this sound change. In Attic sequences, dental stops could, however, not be the first element of a sequence so that [dz] became [zd] by metathesis. **Cf.** chapt. 22; LJ §104–105.

ζ Originated out of the Combination */sd/

The combination of the sounds σ and δ also resulted in ζ, which is another argument for interpreting ζ phonetically as [zd] because [z] is the voiced variant of /s/ before /d/. The attachment of the directive particle δε 'to, into the direction of', which is seen in οὐρανόν-δε 'to the sky' and οἴκα-δε '(to) home', to the acc. pl. Ἀθήνας led to Ἀθήναζε 'to Athens' as well as to the formation of the word θύρᾱζε 'out of' built from the acc. pl. θύρᾱς of θύρᾱ 'gate'. The phoneme combination */sd/ was probably pronounced [zd] in PIE times already so that the reduplicated verb PIE **si-sd-ō* 'I sit down', which is derived from the root **sed-* 'to sit', was phonetically realized as [sizdō]. This can be seen in its continuants Lat. *sīdō* and Skr. *sīdati* in which voiced [z] was lost before a voiced stop with compensatory lengthening, as in ἵζω [hízdǭ] 'I set' in which initial **s* became *h* and the phoneme combination */sd/ is continued by ζ. **Cf.** SI §201; LJ §104b.

Exercises

E1 ζ from the Sound Cluster *γι̯

A ἁγνός 'holy' :: *ἅγι̯ω > (x18.1) ___________ 'I worship' **B** σταγών 'drop' :: *στάγι̯ω > (x18.1) ___________ 'I drop' **C** μέγα 'big' :: *μέγι̯ων > (x18.1) Ion. ___________ 'bigger' **D** στέναγμα 'roaring, raging' :: *στενάγι̯ω > (x18.1) ___________ 'I moan' **E** βίος 'life' :: **g^wi̯ēn* > (x11.2) *___________ > (x18.1) ___________ 'to live'

E2 ζ from the Sound Cluster *δι̯

A Lat. *scindō* 'I split' :: *σχίδι̯α > (x18.2) ___________ 'piece of wood' **B** Skr. *dyā́us* 'sky' :: *Δι̯ηύς > (1.3) *___________ > (x18.2) ___________ 'Zeus' **C** πέδον 'ground' :: *πεδι̯ός > (x18.2) ___________ 'on foot' **D** κομιδή 'I transport' :: *κομίδι̯ω > (x18.2) ___________ 'to transport' **E** κλύδων 'wash of waves' :: *κλύδι̯ω > (x18.2) ___________ 'I rinse' **F** Hom. ὀδμή 'smell' :: *ὄδι̯ω > (x18.2) ___________ 'I smell' **G** νόμος 'custom' :: *νομίδι̯ω > (x18.2) ___________ 'I have in use'

E3 ζ from Initial *ι̯

A Lat. *iūs* 'broth' :: *ι̯ῦσμᾱ > (x16.3) *___________ > (2.2) *___________ > (13) ___________ 'leaven' **B** ζωστός 'girded' :: *ι̯ώσνᾱ > (x16.3) *___________ > (2.2) *___________ > (13) ___________ 'belt' **C1** Skr. *yásyati* 'it becomes hot' :: *ι̯εστός > (x16.3) ___________ 'boiling hot' **C2** *ι̯έσω > (x16.3) *___________ > (x15.1) ___________ 'I boil' **D** Skr. *yáva-* 'cereal' :: *ι̯εϝι̯αί > (x16.3) *___________ > (3) *___________ > (x21.2) ___________ [___________] 'spelt'

E4 ζ from the Sound Cluster */sd/

A German *Ast* :: **ó-sd-os* > ___________ 'twig'

B *χαμᾱ́ 'earth' :: acc. pl. *χαμᾱ́σ-δε > ___________ 'to the ground'

1.3: *V̄ > V̆ / _RC*	**x11.2:** *g^w > *g / _i̯*	**x18.1:** *gi̯ > zd*
2.2: **VsR > V̄R*	**x15.1:** **s > Ø / V_V*	**x18.2:** **di̯ > zd*
3: **VRi̯ > V̄R*	**x16.3:** **i̯ > zd / #_V*	**x21.2:** **u̯ > Ø / V_V*
13: **ā > ę̄*		

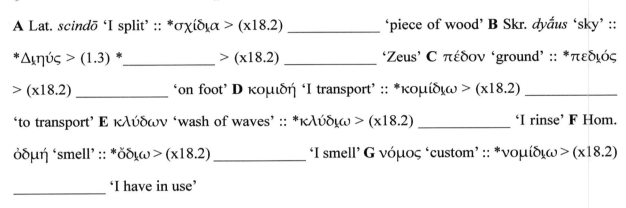

29 Palatalization of Voiceless Sounds

SC x19.2/3/4 Palatalization of *ti̯ and *ki̯

Att. ττ regularly corresponds to Ion. σσ in φυλάττω :: φυλάσσω 'I protect', γλῶττα :: γλῶσσα 'tongue', πέττω :: πέσσω 'I cook', ἐλᾱ́ττων :: ἐλάσσων 'smaller', μέλιττα :: μέλισσα 'bee', κορύττω :: κορύσσω 'I equip'. The etymologies of these words show that ττ/σσ go back to the following sequences: *κι̯ (*φυλάκι̯ω > φυλάττω), *χι̯ (*γλῶχι̯α > γλῶττα), *k^wi̯ (*$pék^w$i̯ō > πέττω), *k^{wh}i̯ (*$elénk^{wh}$i̯ōn > ἐλᾱ́ττων), *τι̯ (*μέλιτι̯α > μέλιττα) and *θι̯ (*κορύθι̯ω > κορύττω). Due to de-aspiration and de-labialization, the sequences *k^wi̯, *k^{wh}i̯, *χι̯, *κι̯ merged in *κι̯, and the sequences *θι̯, *τι̯ merged in *τι̯ before *κι̯ and *τι̯ further developed to ττ/σσ.
In the following words, however, the sequences *τι̯ and *θι̯ are uniformly continued by σ in Ion. as well as in Att: *τότι̯ος > Att.-Ion. τόσος 'so great', *μέθι̯ος > Att.-Ion. μέσος 'amidst', *πάντι̯α > Att.-Ion. πᾶσα 'whole' and *$ti̯eg^w omai̯$ > Ion.-Att. σέβομαι 'I revere'. This difference is due to the fact that the development of *τι̯ and *θι̯ to Att.-Ion. σ happened earlier than the development of *κι̯ to Att. ττ/ Ion. σσ but was delayed in some morphological contexts so that it coincided with the later development of *κι̯ > ττ/σσ. In a first step, the palatal semivowel *ι̯ caused the palatalization and affrication of *τι̯ to *τσ^ɩ which originated out of *τι̯. The sequence *τσ^ɩ de-palatalized and assimilated to *σσ via the intermediate steps *τσ^ɩ > *στ^ɩ > *σσ^ɩ > *σσ before it merged with original *σσ which was simplified to σ (cf. chapter 19 and appendix 1). In this way, *μέθι̯ος > (25.9) *μέτι̯ος > (x19.2) *μέσσος > (45.1) μέσος as well as *τότι̯ος > (x19.2) *τόσσος > (45.1) τόσος and *$ti̯ég^w omai̯$ > (x19.5) > *$ség^w omai̯$ > (x24.4) σέβομαι originated. This development took place only in morphologically opaque words but not in words like *ἐρέτ-ι̯ω > Att. ἐρέττω / Ion. ἐρέσσω 'I row' because its connection to its derivation base ἐρέτης 'rower' was still clear and the speakers could clearly analyze ἐρέττω as *ἐρέτ-ι̯ω. Therefore, the phonological development of *τι̯ halted at the stage *τσι̯ in morphologically transparent words until *κι̯, which originated out of the sequences *ki̯, *k^hi̯, *k^wi̯, *k^{wh}i̯, reached the stage *τσ^ɩ and merged with *τσ^ɩ which originated out of *τι̯. This chronological sequence is the reason why *τι̯ has partly uniform and partly varying results in Ion. And Att. whereas *κι̯ is always represented by ττ/σς. **Cf.** Rix §102–103; SI §195–199; LJ §93–101.

SC x22.1 South Greek Palatalization τι > σι

The development τι > σι took place in all Greek *ti*-stems, *i̯ă*-stems and *ios*-adjectives which were dervived from *t*-stems. Examples are: Skr. *gati-* 'action of going' :: *βατίς > (x22.1) βασίς 'step'; ἄμβροτος 'immortal' :: *ἀμβροτίᾱ > (x22.1) ἀμβροσίᾱ 'ambrosia'; πλοῦτος 'wealth' :: *πλούτιος > (x22.1) πλούσιος 'rich'. In contrast to Northern Greek, this sound change happened in Southern Greek also in the endings of the third person sg. and pl. Examples are: Dor. ἔχοντι :: Att.-Ion. ἔχουσι 'they have' and Myc. *e-ko-si* /ek^{h}onsi/ respectively. **Cf.** Rix §101; SI §148; LJ §51.

SC x19.1 Palatalization of Labial Sounds

All Greek dialects have πτ as the continuant of *πι̯ and *φι̯. By the comparison with χαλεπός 'difficult', the verb χαλέπτω 'I oppress' can therefore be traced back to *χαλέπι̯ω. Likewise, βάπτω 'I immerse' can be traced back to *βάφι̯ω by comparing it to βαφή 'immersion'. First, φ lost its aspiration before *ι̯ before the resulting sequence *πι̯ developed further just like original *πι̯. No examples can be found for the development of *βι̯ although one often finds the verb βλάπτω 'I damage' being traced back to *βλάβι̯ω by comparing it to βλάβη 'damage'. In this case, however, βλάπτω goes back to *βλάπι̯ω which can be inferred from Cret. ἀβλοπης 'without damage', and βλάβη originated from *βλάπη through assimilation. **Cf.** Rix §102; SI §202; LJ §68.

Exercises

E1 ππ from the Sequences *πι̯ and *φι̯

A κλοπή 'theft' :: *κλέπι̯ω > (x19.1) ___________ 'I steal' **B** κόπος 'striking' :: *κόπι̯ω > (x19.1) ___________ 'I hit' **C** τύπος 'hit' :: *τύπι̯ω > (x19.1) ___________ 'I hit' **D** τάφος 'funeral' :: *θάφι̯ω > (25.5) *___________ > (x19.1) ___________ 'I bury'

E2 The Development τι > σι

A δοτός 'given' :: *δότις > (x22.1) ___________ 'gift' **B** Skr. *sthití-* :: *στατίς > (x22.1) ___________ 'setting' **C** Skr. *páti-* :: *πότις > (x22.1) ___________ 'husband' **D** ἐσ-τί 'is' :: *τίθη-τι > (x22.1) ___________ 'he puts' **E** ἐργάτης 'worker' :: *ἐργατίᾱ > (x22.1) ___________ 'work' **F** Ved. *-dhiti-* :: *θέτις > (x22.1) ___________ 'setting' **G** ἄμβροτος 'immortal' :: *ἀμβρότιος > (x22.1) ___________ 'divine' **H** Dor. ϝίκατι :: Att. *εἴκοτι > (x22.1) ___________ 'twenty' **I** Dor. διᾱκάτιοι :: Att. *διᾱκότιοι > (x22.1) ___________ 'two hundred'

E3 Attic and Ionic Forms

A φρακτός 'fenced' :: *φράκι̯ω > (x19.4) Att. ___________ / Ion. ___________ 'I fence' **B** ἐρέτης 'rower' :: *ἐρέτι̯ω > (x19.3) Att. ___________ / Ion. ___________ 'I row' **C** τάξις 'order' :: *τάκι̯ω > (x19.4) Att. ___________ / Ion. ___________ 'I arrange' **D** λῖτός :: *λιτι̯ός > (x19.3) Ion. ___________ 'smooth' **E** Lat. *pix* :: *πίκι̯α > (x19.4) Att. ___________ / Ion. ___________ 'pitch' **F** νακτός 'solid' :: *νάκι̯ω > (x19.4) Ion. ___________ 'I stamp' **G** aor. ἔμαξα 'I kneaded' :: prs. *μάκι̯ω > (x19.4) Att. ___________ / Ion. ___________ 'I knead' **H** λευκός 'shining' :: *λεύκι̯ω > (x19.4) Ion. ___________ 'I watch' **I** λιτή 'imploration' :: *λίτι̯ομαι > (x19.3) Ion. ___________ 'I implore' **J** ταραχή 'confusion' :: *ταράχι̯ω > (25.14) *___________ > (x19.4) Att. ___________ / Ion. ___________ 'I confuse' **K** βήξ, βηχός 'cough' :: *βήχι̯ω > (25.14) *___________ > (x19.4) Att. ___________ / Ion. ___________ 'I cough' **L** κοροπλάθος 'producer of figurines' :: *πλάθι̯ω > (25.9) *___________ > (x19.3) Att. ___________ / Ion. ___________ 'I produce'

25.5: $p^h > p$ / _*i̯*	**x19.1:** **pi̯ > pt*	**x22.1:** **ti > si*
25.9: $t^h > t$ / _*i̯*	**x19.3:** **ti̯* > att. *tt* / ion. *ss*	
25.14: $k^h > k$ / _*i̯*	**x19.4:** **ki̯* > att. *tt* / ion. *ss*	

CONSONANTS

Development of PIE Labiovelars

The PIE labiovelars *k^{w}, *g^{w}, *g^{wh} were velar stops articulated with the additional feature of lip rounding, which is indicated by superscript ^{w}. Depending on the vowel following, the labiovelars developed to dental, labial or velar stops in Attic. This can be seen in the different behavior of *k^{w} in the following derivations of the root *k^{w}elh1- 'to make a turn': *k^{w}élh1os > (x3.1)*k^{w}élos > (x23.1) τέλος 'terminal point', *k^{w}l̥h$_{1}$im > (x8.1)*k^{w}álim > (x24.2) πάλιν 'backwards' and Akk. *k^{w}é-k^{w}lh$_{1}$om > (x3.1) *k^{w}é-k^{w}lom > (12.3) *k^{w}ó-k^{w}lom > (11) *k^{w}ú-k^{w}lom > (x10.1) *kúklom > (12.1) κύκλον 'circle'. In these cases, the labiovelar *k^{w} developed to τ before ε, to π before α and to κ next to υ. The context-sensitive development of *g^{wh} is illustrated in chapter 31 more thoroughly. **Cf.** Rix §97–99; SI §161–164; LJ §30–41.

SC x17 Dentalization of Labiovelars

The labiovelars *k^{w}, *g^{w}, *g^{wh} became the dental stops τ, δ, θ before the front vowel ε. Therefore, Att. τε [te] 'and' < *k^{w}e directly corresponds to Lat. *que* [ku̯e]. In Att. δελφῦς < *g^{w}elb^{h}us 'womb', which is related to the synonymous Skr. *gárbha-*, the media aspirate *b^{h} was devoiced to φ before *g^{w} became δ before ε: *g^{w}elb^{h}us > (x9.1) *g^{w}elp^{h}us > (x23.2) δελφῦς. An example for the development of *g^{wh} before a front vowel is furnished by the comparison of Lat. *formus* 'warm' and Skr. *gharmá-* 'embers' to θερμός 'warm' < *g^{wh}ermós whereby *g^{wh} was devoiced *k^{wh} before it sound became θ before ε. The labiovelar *k^{w} became τ before ι, too, as it can be seen in the comparison of Lat. *quis* [ku̯is] and Hitt. *kwis* [ku̯is] to τίς [tís] 'who?', which are go back to *k^{w}ís.

SC x18 Labialization of Labiovelars

Before *a*, *o* or a consonant, the labiovelars *k^{w}, *g^{w}, *g^{wh} became the labial stops π, β, φ; *g^{w} and *g^{wh} became β and φ also before ι. In this way, the root √ὀπ- of ὄψις [ópsis] 'seeing' can be connected to Lat. *oculus* 'eye' and Skr. *ákṣan-* 'eye' and traced back to *ok^{w}-, which can be reconstructed as *h$_{3}$ek^{w}- using laryngeals (cf. chapter 34). The comparison of Skr. *rájas-* 'airspace' to ἔρεβος 'dark' enables the reconstruction of the preform *éreg^{w}os, in which*g^{w} became β before *o*. The comparison of Skr. *ahí-* 'snake' to the synonymous ὄφις enables the reconstruction of the preform *óg^{wh}is, in which *g^{wh} was devoiced to *k^{wh} before it became φ before ι: *óg^{wh}is > (x9.4) *ók^{wh}is > (x24.6) ὄφις [óp^{h}is].

SC x9/x10 Loss of Labial Coarticulation next to *u̯/u and before *i̯

The second element of the composite forms αἰ-πόλος 'goatherd' and βου-κόλος 'cowherd', which are derived from αἶξ 'goat' and βοῦς 'cow', both go back to *k^{w}olos, whereby in the first case *k^{w} became π before *o*, and in the second case it became κ due to the dissimilatory effect of the preceding υ. This loss of the labial coarticulation also happened before *i̯ as it can be seen by the comparison of *pek^{w}tos > (x24.1) πεπτός 'cooked' to *pek^{w}i̯ō > (x11.1) *πέκι̯ω > (x19.4) Att. πέττω 'I cook'. A Ionic example is the derivation of *ók^{w}i̯e > Hom. Ion. ὄσσε 'two eyes' in which *k^{w}i̯ first became*ki̯ before it developed to σσ: *ók^{w}i̯e > (x11.1) *óki̯e > (x19.4) ὄσσε.
As Hom. βίοτος 'life' can be traced back to *g^{w}iotos by comparing it to Lat. *vīvus* und Skr. *jīvá-* 'alive', also ζωός 'alive' can be traced to a formation *g^{w}i̯ō(u̯)ós of the same root, in which *g^{w}i̯ became *gi̯ and subsequently ζ: *g^{w}i̯ōós > (x11.2) *gi̯ōós > (x18.1) ζωός. **Cf.** LJ §31–32.

Exercises

E1 Context-Sensitive Development of Labiovelars

A Lat. *vorāre* 'to devour' :: **gʷorā́* > (x24.4) ____________ 'food' **B** Skr. *carati* 'he walks' :: **kʷélos* > (x23.1) ____________ 'end' **C** Lat. *quid* :: **kʷíd* > (x12.2) *____________ > (x23.1) ____________ 'what?' **D** Skr. *páñca* :: **pénkʷe* > (x23.1) ____________ 'five' **E** Lat. *oculus* 'eye' :: **ókʷsetai̯* > (x24.1) fut. ____________ 'he will see' **F** Lat. *sequor* :: **sékʷomai̯* > (x13.1) *____________ > (x24.2) ____________ 'I follow' **G** Lith. *káina* 'price' :: **kʷoi̯nā́* > (x24.2) *____________ > (13) ____________ 'penitence' **H** Myc. *qe-ja-me-no* :: **kʷínu̯ō* > (x23.1) *____________ > (x21.3) ____________ 'I pay' **I** πέντε 'five' :: **pénkʷtos* > (x24.1) ____________ 'the fifth' **J** Skr. *jyā́-* 'bowstring' :: **gʷiós* > (x24.4) ____________ 'bow' **K** Skr. *paktí-* 'cooked meal' :: **pékʷtos* > (x24.1) ____________ 'cooked'

E2 Loss of Labial Coarticulation next to Velar Vowels

A Lat. *lupus* :: **lúkʷos* > (x10.1) ____________ 'wolf' **B** Lat. *nox* :: **nókʷts* > (11) *____________ > (x10.1) *____________ > (33) *____________ > (45.3) ____________ 'night' **C** βίος 'life' :: **sugʷīu̯ḗs* > (x10.2) *____________ > (x13.1) *____________ > (x21.2) *____________ > (1.1) ____________ 'healthy'

E3 Loss of Labial Coarticulation with Subsequent Palatalization

A ὄμμα 'eye' :: **ókʷi̯omai̯* > (x11.1) *____________ > (x19.4) Ion. ____________ 'I anticipate' **B** acc. **u̯ókʷa* > (x24.2) *____________ > (x21.1) Hom. ____________ 'voice' :: nom. **u̯ókʷi̯a* > (x11.1) *____________ > (x19.4) *____________ > (x21.1) Hom. Ion. ____________ 'rumor' **C** Skr. *pácati* :: **pékʷi̯ō* > (x11.1) *____________ > (x19.4) Att. ____________ 'I cook' **E** χέρ-νιψ 'water for washing the hands' :: **nígʷ-i̯ō* > (x11.2) *____________ > (x18.1) ____________ 'I wash'

11: **o > u / R_B*	**x10.2:** **gʷ > g / _(u,u̯)_*	**x18.1:** **gi̯ > zd*	**x23.1:** **kʷ > t / _(i,e)*
13: **ā > ę̄*	**x11.1:** **kʷ > *k / _*i̯*	**x19.4:** **ki̯* > att. *tt*	**x24.1:** **kʷ > p / _C*
33: *t > s / _s*	**x11.2:** **gʷ > *g / _*i̯*	**x21.1:** **u̯ > Ø / #_V*	**x24.2:** **kʷ > p / _(a,o)*
45.3: *ss > s / _#*	**x12.2:** *C > Ø / V_#*	**x21.2:** **u̯ > Ø / V_V*	**x24.4:** **gʷ > b / _(a,o,i)*
x10.1: **kʷ > k / _(u,u̯)_*	**x13.1:** **s > h / #_V*	**x21.3:** **u̯ > Ø / C_*	

Development of PIE Mediae Aspiratae

SC x9 Standard Development of the PIE Mediae Aspiratae in Greek

The PIE mediae aspiratae *b^h, *d^h, *g^h, *$\hat{g}^h$, *g^{wh} were devoiced and became the tenuis aspiratae p^h, t^h, k^h, *k^{wh} in Proto-Greek times already (cf. chapt. 38, L41–46). In Sanskrit, however, the PIE mediae aspiratae *b^h, *d^h, *g^h usually remained which led to regular correspondences exemplified by Gr. φ and Skr. *bh* in φέρω 'I carry' :: Skr. *bhárati* 'he carries', φράτηρ :: Skr. *bhrā́tā* 'brother', νέφος :: Skr. *nábhas-* 'fog', as well as Gr. θ and Skr. *dh* in θρασύς :: Skr. *dhṛṣú-* 'bold', ἔθηκα :: Skr. *ádhāt* 'he put', αἶθος 'heat' :: *édha-* 'fire wood', and furthermore Gr. χ and Skr. *gh* in ὀμίχλη :: Skr. *meghá-* 'cloud'. The correspondence χ :: Skr. *h* such as in χειμών 'winter' :: Skr. *himá-* 'cold' and ἄγχω 'I throttle' :: Skr. *áṃhas-* 'fear' is found in those cases in which Gr. χ and Skr. *h* continue PIE *$\hat{g}^h$ or in the case of the secondary development of Skr. *gh* > *h*. The tenuis aspiratae φ θ χ could could lose their feature of aspiration due to Grassmann's law (SC 39.10) and become the tenuis π τ κ. **Cf.** Rix §94; SI §143, 147, 158, 163; LJ §22.

SC x9.4 The PIE Voiced Aspirated Labiovelar *g^{wh}

The PIE voiced aspirated labiovelar *g^{wh} was devoiced to Proto-Greek *k^{wh} before the labiovelars split into the Attic threefold results: velar stop next to υ and before *i̯, dental stop before ε, labial stop before ο, α, ι or a consonant (cf. chapter 30). This development explains the phonological difference of *k^{wh}én-i̯ō > θείνω 'I kill' and its reduplicated aor. Hom. *é-k^we-k^{wh}n-e > ἔπεφνε 'he killed' because *k^{wh} became θ before ε in θείνω, and it became φ before ν in ἔπεφνε, which should have been ἔτεφνε* according to the regular development of *k^w > τ but it was analogically remodeled.

Another example for the representation of *k^{wh} is the development of *elak^{wh}rós > ἐλαφρός 'fast, little', *elak^{wh}ús > ἐλαχύς 'small' and its comparative form *elénk^{wh}i̯ōn > Att. ἐλάττων, Ion. ἐλάσσων 'smaller'. By the comparison with Skr. *raghú-* 'fast' and Av. *rənjiiō* 'faster', the root *elak^{wh}- can be identified as the zero-grade of *h_1l̥ŋg^{wh}- of the PIE root *$h_1$leng^{wh}- whose initial laryngeal *h_1 became *e* and syllabic *n̥ became *a*: *h_1l̥ŋg^{wh}- > *el̥ŋg^{wh}-> *elŋ̥g^{wh}- > *elag^{wh}-. Subsequently, the devoicing of *g^{wh} > *k^{wh} resulted in the root forms *elag^{wh}- > *elak^{wh}- and *eleng^{wh}- > *elenk^{wh}-. Before a consonant, *k^{wh} became φ as it can be seen in *elak^{wh}rós > (x24.5) ἐλαφρός. Before labial *u*, the labiovelar *k^{wh} lost its labial coarticulation due to dissimilation whereby *k^{wh} became χ as it can be seen in *elak^{wh}ús > (x10.3) ἐλαχύς. The explanation of the related Att. comparative ἐλάττων is, however, somewhat more difficult because the presumable preform *elak^{wh}i̯ōn could in fact explain Ion. ἐλάσσων via the intermediate steps *elak^{h}i̯ōn > (25.14) *elaki̯ōn > ἐλάσσων but not the vowel length of Att. ἐλάττων. As it is described in chapter 29, the sequence *k^{wh}i̯ developed via *k^hi̯ to *ki̯ before it resulted in Att. ττ and Ion. σσ respectively. The development*ki̯ > Att. ττ / Ion. σσ proceeded via the intermediate steps *τσ^ʲ und *στ^ʲ, which are in some cases actually attested as <T> e.g. in the Ionic inscription ελαΤων for ἐλάσσων. The intermediate step *στ^ʲ is necessary for explaning the vowel length in Att. ἐλάττων as in this case the starting point of derivation is not *elak^{wh}- with the zero-grade of the root but *elenk^{wh}- with the *e*-grade of the root. The bold printed root vowel *e of *elenk^{wh}- was reshaped to *a* in analogy to the vowels of ἐλ**α**φρός and ἐλ**α**χύς so that *elénk^{wh}i̯ōn became *elánk^{wh}i̯ōn before the further development *elánk^{wh}i̯ōn > (x11.3) *elánk^{h}i̯ōn > (25.14) *elánki̯ōn. After *ki̯ had reached the intermediate step *στ^ʲ on its way to ττ during the palatalization process, ν was lost with compensatory lengthening which led to *ἐλᾱ́στων which further developed to the attested form ἐλᾱ́ττων. **Cf.** Rix §97–99, 103.

Exercises

E1 Standard Development

A Skr. dhūmá- 'smoke' :: *d^{h}ūmós > (x9.2) __________ 'courage' **B** Skr. prá dhanvati 'he dies' :: *d^{h}nātós > (x9.2) *__________ > (13) θνητός 'dead' **C** Skr. dádhāmi :: *d^{h}í-d^{h}ē-mi > (x9.2) *__________ > (39.10) __________ 'I put' **D** Lat. ānser :: gen. sg. *ĝ^{h}ansós > (x1.3) *__________ > (x9.3) *__________ > (2.1) *__________ > (13) __________ 'of the goose' **E** θύρᾱ 'door' :: *d^{h}u̯r̥-i̯ó-s > (x9.2) *__________ > (x25.1) *__________ > (x17) *__________ > (x21.3) __________ 'door hinge' **F** Skr. bhā́ti 'he speaks' :: *b^{h}āmí > (x9.1) *__________ > (13) __________ 'I speak' **G** Skr. bahú- 'arm' :: *b^{h}n̥ĝ^{h}ús > (x1.3) *__________ > (x9.1 + x9.3) *__________ > (x26.1) *__________ > (39.10) __________ 'thick' **H** Goth. bindan 'to bind' :: *b^{h}énd^h-sma > (x9.1+x9.2) *__________ > (39.10) *__________ > (25.6) *__________ > (33) *__________ > (45.4) *__________ > (4.1) __________ 'rope'

E2 Context-Sensitive Development of *g^{wh}

A Skr. gharmá- 'burning heat' :: *g^{wh}ermós > (x9.4) *__________ > (x23.3) __________ 'warm' **B** θείνω 'I kill' :: *g^{wh}ónos > (x9.4) *__________ > (x24.6) __________ 'murder' **C** Skr. áhi- :: *óg^{wh}is > (x9.4) *__________ > (x24.6) __________ 'snake' **D** Lat. nix :: acc. Hes. *níg^{wh}m̥ > (x9.4) *__________ > (x26.3) *__________ > (x24.6) __________ 'snow' **E** Goth. bidjan 'to ask for' :: *g^{wh}od^{h}éi̯ō > (x9.2+x9.4) *__________ > (x16.1) *__________ > (39.10) *__________ > (x24.2) Hom. __________ 'I desire' **F** Hom. ποθέω 'I desire' :: *k^{wh}ét^{h}i̯est^{h}ai̯ > (25.9) *__________ > (x23.3) *__________ > (x19.3) Ion. __________ 'to implore' **G** Lat. voveō 'I promise' :: *éu̯g^{wh}omai̯ > (x9.4) *__________ > (x10.3) __________ 'I pray'

2.1: *VRs > V̄R	**39.10:** C^h…C^h > C…C^h	**x9.4:** *g^{wh} > *k^{wh}	**x23.3:** *k^{wh} > t^h / _e
4.1: *VnsN > V̄sV	**45.4:** ss > s / C_	**x10.3:** *k^{wh} > k^h / _(u,u̯)_	**x24.2:** *k^w > p / _(a,o)
13: *ā > ę̄	**x1.3:** *ĝ^h > *g^h	**x16.1:** *i̯ > Ø / V_V	**x24.6:** *k^{wh} > p^h / _(a,o,i)
25.6: t^h > t / _s	**x9.1:** *b^h > p^h	**x17:** *(a,o)Ri̯ > (a,o)i̯R	**x25.1:** *r̥ > ar
25.9: t^h > t / _i̯	**x9.2:** *d^h > t^h	**x19.3:** *ti̯ > ion. ss	**x26.1:** *n̥ > a
33: t > s / _s	**x9.3:** *g^h > k^h	**x21.3:** *u̯ > Ø / C_	**x26.3:** *m̥ > a

Epenthetic and Final Consonants

SC 47.1/3/6 The Initial Development of Nasal before Resonant

By comparison with μέλι, μέλιτος 'honey', the verb βλίττω 'to harvest honey' can be traced back to *μλίττω and further to *μλίτι̯ω due to the fact that initial μ became β before λ, and ττ is the Att. result of *τι̯ according to SC x19.3. The development of nasal to homorganic stop also happened before ϱ and enables to trace βϱοτός 'mortal' back to *μϱοτός which is confirmed by Lat. *mortuus* and Ved. *mr̥tá-* 'dead'. One finds the gloss δϱώψ· ἄνθϱωπος attested at Hesychius, who was an ancient lexicographer, which could be an example for the development of ν to δ before initial ϱ if δϱώψ is to be considered as a composite form which goes back to *νϱώψ. The first element νϱο- could then be interpreted as being derived from ἀνήϱ, and the second element –οψ would be similar to the second element of Αἰθίοψ 'Ethiopian'. The word δϱώψ could therefore be translated as 'male' for literal 'someone who has a male appearance'. **Cf.** Rix §78; SI §224; LJ §153.

SC 47.2/4/5 Epenthetic Consonants in the Medial Position

Similar to the development in the initial position, one finds the insertion of consonants between a nasal and a resonant in the medial position, which explains the development of gen. sg. *ἀνϱός > (47.5) gen. ἀνδϱός 'of the man' from ἀνήϱ 'man'. The etymological correspondences Skr. *nára-* 'man' and Lat. *Nerō, -ōnis* literally 'the virile one' expectably do not exhibit the inserted stop at the respective place. The place of articulation of the inserted stop depended on the preceding nasal so that one finds δ inserted between ν and ϱ in ἀνδϱός, and β inserted between μ and ϱ in *γαμϱός > (47.2) γαμβϱός 'brother in law' which is related to γάμος 'marriage'. **Cf.** Rix §78; SI §224; LJ §153.

SC x12.1 Final **m* became –ν in Proto-Greek already

The comparison of the endings of the acc. sg. Lat. *amīcu-m* and Skr. *deva-m* to φίλο-ν shows that PIE final*-*m* was preserved in Lat. and Skr. and became -ν in Greek. This sound change must have taken place in Proto-Greek times because all Greek dialects exhibit this sound change. **Cf.** Rix §77; SI §236; LJ §142.

SC x12.2 Loss of Final Consonants Except for ν, ϱ, σ

Alle Greek words end either in a vowel, a diphthong or in one of the three consonants ν, ϱ, σ because all other final consonants were lost. An example for this process is furnished by the disyllabic Hom. πάϊς [páis] 'child' which corresponds to monosyllabic Att. παῖς [pāi̯s]. From the gen. παιδ-ός, one can see that πάϊς must go back *πάϊδς [páids] which changed via assimilation and simplification of the double consonant to the attested form: *πάϊδ-ς > (29.4) *πάϊτ-ς > (33) *πάϊσ-ς > (45.3) πάϊς. For the vocative one would thus expect the the bare stem *πάιδ; the attested forms Hom. πάϊ [pái] and Att. παῖ [pāi̯] do, however, exhibits the loss of final δ. Further examples showing the loss of final consonants are Lat. *is-tud* 'this' in comparison zu *τόδ > (x12.2) τό 'this' and Skr. *járant-* 'old' in comparison to the voc. *γέϱοντ > (x12.3) γέϱον 'old man!'. Without correspondences in cognate languages, it would in many cases not be possible to detect that Greek also had had one or several consonants at the respective place. **Cf.** Rix §100; SI §236; LJ §29.

Exercises

E1 Epenthetic Consonants in the Initial and Medial Position

A1 μορμύρω :: *μρέμω > (47.1) ___________ ‘I roar’ **A2** *μρόμος > (47.1) ___________ ‘roaring’ **A3** *μρομτή > (24.4) *___________ > (47.1) ___________ ‘thunder’ **B** aor. ἔμολον ‘I came’ :: prs. *μλώσκω > (47.3) ___________ ‘I come’ **C** μέλδομαι ‘I melt’ :: *μλαδύς > (47.3) ___________ ‘smooth’ **D** μαλακός ‘smooth’ :: *μλάξ > (47.3) ___________ ‘limp’ **E** Skr. *marcáyati* :: *μλάπτω > (47.3) ___________ ‘I harm’ **F** βλώσκω ‘I come’ :: perf. *μέ-μλω-κα > (47.4) ___________ ‘I have come’ **G** ἀμαλός ‘smooth’ :: *ἀμλύς > (47.4) ___________ ‘weak’ **H** Av. *mərəzu-* :: *mr̥ǵ^{h}ús > (x1.3) *___________ > (x9.3) *___________ > (x25.2) *___________ > (47.1) ___________ ‘short’ **I** Russ. *morozgá* ‘drizzling rain’ :: *μρέχω > (47.1) ___________ ‘I make wet’ **J** Skr. *mūrtá-* ‘coagulated’ :: *μρότος > (47.1) ___________ ‘coagulated blood’ **K** Skr. *amŕ̥ta-* :: *ἄμροτος > (47.2) ___________ ‘immortal’

E2 Loss of Final Consonants except for ν, ρ, σ

A gen. ἑκόντος :: nom. nt. *ἑκόντ > (x12.3) ___________ ‘voluntary’ **B** gen. γυναικός :: voc. *γύναικ > (x12.2) ___________ ‘woman!’ **C** gen. μέλιτος :: nom. *μέλιτ > (x12.2) ___________ ‘honey’ **D** gen. γάλακτος :: nom. *γάλακτ > (x12.2) ___________ ‘milk’ **E** gen. Hom. ἄνακτος :: voc. *ἄνακτ > (x12.2) ___________ ‘master!’ **F** κρῖθή :: nom.-acc. *κρῖθ > (x12.2) Hom. ___________ ‘barley’ **G** Hom. πόρσω :: *πόρσωδ > (x12.2) *___________ > (35.3) ___________ ‘forward’ **H** δέρκομαι ‘I see’ :: *ὑπόδρακ > (x12.2) ___________ ‘glowering’ **I** Skr. *yákr̥t* :: *Hi̯ēk^{w}r̥t > (x16.2) *___________ > (x24.1) *___________ > (x25.1) *___________ > (x12.3) ___________ ‘liver’ **J** Skr. *abharant* :: 3. pl. ipf. *ἔφεροντ > (x12.3) ___________ ‘they carried’ **K** Skr. *abharat* :: 3. sg. ipf. *ἔφερετ > (x12.2) ___________ ‘he carried’

24.3: *m > n / _(t,d,i̯,s)*	**47.3:** *m > b / #_l*	**x12.2:** $*VC_1(C_2)\# > V\#$	**x24.1:** *k^w > p / _C
35.3: *s > r / r_*	**47.4:** *Ø > b / m_l*	**x12.3:** $*VC_1(C_2)\# > C_1V\#$	**x25.1:** *r̥ > ar
47.1: *m > b / #_r*	**x1.3:** *ǵ^h > *g^h	**x16.2:** *Hi̯ > h / #_	**x25.2:** *r̥ > ra
47.2: *Ø > b / m_r*	**x9.3:** *g^h > k^h		

33 Development of PIE Syllabic Resonants *m̥, *n̥, *r̥, *l̥

SC x19 Development of PIE *r̥ and *l̥

The PPP *dr̥-tó-s* > (x25.1) δαρτός 'skinned', which is derived from δέρω 'I skin', exhibits the zero-grade *dr̥-* of the root *der-*, in which the PIE resonant *r* became syllabic *r̥* between two consonants and resulted in Att. αρ. A similar example is seen in the relation of στέλλω 'I send' and its PPP *stl̥-tó-s* > (x25.3) σταλτός 'sent', in which syllabic *l̥ resulted in Att. αλ. In addition to the development *r̥ > αρ and *l̥ > αλ, the development *r̥ > ρα and *l̥ > λα is also met with in *t^hr̥sús* > θρασύς 'bold' and in *ml̥dús* > βλαδύς 'weak', which is related to Skr. *mr̥dú-* and Lat. *mollis*. No clear rules for this divergent distribution have been found yet. Other Greek dialects have furthermore examples of a development *r̥ > ορ / ρο seen in the comparison of Att. καρδίᾱ 'heart' with Pamph. κορζια, as well as Att. θρασύς in comparison with Lesb. θορσέως. In the case of βροτός 'mortal', which is related to Lat. *mortuus* and Skr. *mr̥tá-* 'dead', a word from another dialect has appearently become Attic because PIE *mr̥tós* should have given Att. βρατός*. In cases like τρέφω 'I nourish' :: τρεπτός 'nourished' or στρέφω 'I turn' :: στρεπτός 'turned', whose PPPs should be τραπτός* and στραπτός* according to regular sound laws, the vowel of their derivation base was analogically transferred onto the PPP. **Cf.** chapt. 37, L19–22; Rix §75–76; SI §93–100.

SC x20.1 Development of PIE *n̥

The PPP *tn̥-tó-s* > (x26.1) τατός 'stretched', which is derived from τείνω 'I stretch' < *tén-i̯ō*, exhibits the zero-grade *tn̥-* of the root *ten-*, in which the PIE nasal *n* became syllabic *n̥ between consonants and resulted in Att. α. This relation is also seen in λανθάνω [lant^hánǭ] 'I hide' and its aor. ἔλαθον [élat^hon] 'I hid' < *é-ln̥t^hon*, as well as in μανθάνω [mant^hánǭ] 'I learn' and its aor. ἔμαθον [émat^hon] 'I learned' < *é-mn̥t^hon*. Further examples for the development of PIE *n̥ are furnished by privative alpha formations which express absence, lack or the opposite of their derivation base: ἄ-μοιρος 'having no part', ἀ-νομία 'lawlessness', ἄ-νιπτος 'unwashed' and ἄν-ιππος 'without horse', ἀν-ύποπτος 'unsuspicous', in which initial *n̥ is continued by α before consonants and by αν before vowels.

SC x20.3 Development of PIE *m̥

The acc. sg. of the vocalic declensions (δόξα-ν, λόγο-ν, πόλι-ν) is formed with the case ending -ν, whereas the ending of the consonantic declension is -α (ἀγῶν-α, ἄρχοντ-α). Also the 1. ps. sg. exhibits the two functionally identical personal endings -ν and α- which can be seen in ipf. ἐπαίδευο-ν 'I educated' and in aor. ἐπαίδευσ-α 'I educated'. The difference of the two variant forms goes back to two phonologically identical but functionally different PIE morphemes */m/ of which one was used for the acc. sg. and the other one as the personal ending of the 1. sg. After a vowel, */m/ remained a consonant and became -ν in the final position: *lógom* > (x12.1) λόγον. After a consonant, */m/ became its syllabic allophone *[m̥] which became α in the final position: *e-pái̯deu̯s-m̥* > (x26.3) ἐπαίδευσ-α. The same development is found between consonants: *k̂m̥tóm* > ἑκατόν. Before a vowel, *m̥ was continued as αμ: *g^wm̥-i̯ō* > (x26.4) *g^wami̯ō* > (24.3) *g^wani̯ō* > (x24.4) *bani̯ō* > (x17) βαίνω 'I go'.

> **INFO** If a long vowel is found in the PPP of verbs like βάλλω 'I throw' :: βλητός 'thrown' or τέμνω 'I cut' :: PPP τμητός 'cut', this is an indication for a former laryngeal in the PIE root. (cf. chap. 35).

Exercises

E1 Development of *r̥ and *l̥

A σπείρω 'I sow' :: **spr̥tós* > (x25.1) ___________ 'sowed' **B** Skr. *pr̥thú-* :: **pl̥tús* > (x25.4) ___________ 'flat' **C** Lat. *saliō* :: **sl̥i̯omai̯* > (x25.3) *___________ > (36.4) *___________ > (x13.1) ___________ 'I jump' **D** τρέπω 'I turn' :: perf. **té-tr̥p-mai̯* > (x25.2) *___________ > (31.1) *___________ > (32.2) ___________ 'I have turned' **E** Lat. *porrum* :: **pŕ̥son* > (x25.2) ___________ 'leek' **F** Boiotian πέτταρες :: **k*^{w}*étu̯r̥es* > (x25.1) *___________ > (x21.6) *___________ > (x23.1) Att. ___________ 'four' **G** βέλος 'missile' :: **bl̥i̯ō* > (x25.3) *___________ > (36.4) ___________ 'I throw'

E2 Development of *n̥ and *m̥

A Lat. *inguen* 'abdomen' :: **n̥g*^{w}*ḗn* > (x26.1) *___________ > (x23.2) ___________ 'gland' **B** δδόμος 'house' :: **dḿ̥pedom* > (x26.3) *___________ > (x12.1) ___________ 'ground' **C** λανχάνω 'I draw lots' :: **lń̥k*^{h}*os* > (x26.1) ___________ 'alloted portion' **D** Hom. βένθος :: **bń̥t*^{h}*os* > (x26.1) ___________ 'depth' **E** πένθος 'grief' :: **pń̥t*^{h}*os* > (x26.1) ___________ 'suffering' **F** βαίνω 'I go' :: **g*^{w}*m̥tós* > (x26.3) *___________ > (x24.4) ___________ 'gone' **G** βατός 'gone' :: **g*^{w}*m̥-i̯ō* > (x26.4) *___________ > (24.3) *___________ > (x24.4) *___________ > (x17) ___________ 'I go' **H** Skr. *sanitúr* 'without' :: **sń̥ter* > (x13.1) *___________ > (loss of aspiration) *___________ > (x26.1) ___________ 'far from' **I** νόστος 'return' :: **ń̥smenos* > (x26.1) ___________ 'saved' **J** χανδόν 'with open mouth' :: **k*^{h}*ń̥u̯os* > (x26.1) *___________ > (x21.2) ___________ 'airspace' **K** Skr. *dáṃśati* 'he bites' :: **é-dn̥kon* > (x26.1) ___________ 'bit' **L** Lat. *densus* :: **dn̥sús* > (x26.1) ___________ 'thick' **M** Skr. *ánudra-* :: **ń̥-udro-s* > (x26.2) ___________ 'without water'

24.3:	*m > n / _(t,d,i̯,s)*	**x13.1:**	**s > h / #_V*	**x23.2:**	**g*^{w} *> d / _e*	**x25.4:**	**l̥ > la*
31.1:	*p > b / _N*	**x17:**	**(a,o)Ri̯ > (a,o)i̯R*	**x24.4:**	**g*^{w} *> b / _(a,o,i)*	**x26.1:**	**n̥ > a*
32.2:	*b > m / _m*	**x21.2:**	**u̯ > Ø / V_V*	**x25.1:**	**r̥ > ar*	**x26.2:**	**n̥ > an / _V*
36.4:	**i̯ > l / l_*	**x21.6:**	**tu̯* > att. *tt / V_V*	**x25.2:**	**r̥ > ra*	**x26.3:**	**m̥ > a*
x12.1:	*m > n / _#*	**x23.1:**	**k*^{w} *> t / _(i,e)*	**x25.3:**	**l̥ > al*	**x26.4:**	**m̥ > am / _V*

34 Development of PIE Laryngeals I

SC x5/x6 Laryngeals Become Vowels

The PIE laryngeals *h_1, *h_2, *h_3 (cf. chap. 38, L69–75) become vowels in the initial position before a consonant, in the final position after a consonant and in the medial position between consonants. Laryngeal *h_1 became ε, laryngeal *h_2 became α and laryngeal *h_3 became *o*. In the following contexts, a word boundary is represented by the hash sign #. **Cf.** Rix §79–85.

	Initial Position			**Between Consonants**			**Final Position**	
PIE	*#h_1C-*	*#h_2C-*	*#h_3C-*	*-Ch_1C-*	*-Ch_2C-*	*-Ch_3C-*	*-Ch_1#*	*-Ch_2#*
Vowel	*#εC-*	*#αC-*	*#oC-*	*-CεC-*	*-CαC-*	*-CoC-*	*-Cε#*	*-Cα#*

Laryngeal *h_1: 1. Initial position: Att. ἐγείρω 'I wake up' goes back to **$h_1$gér-i̯ō* and is related to Skr. *járati* 'he awakes'. **2. Medial position:** Att. βέλεμνα 'missiles' < **gʷélemna* < **gʷél$h_1$mnh_2* is derived from βάλλω 'I throw' and furnishes an examples for interconsonantal *h_1 als well as for final *h_2. **3. Final position:** Hom. Ion. ὄσσε 'two eyes' goes back to **ókʷi̯h_1*: **ókʷi̯h_1* > (x6.4) **ókʷi̯e* > (x11.1) *ὄκι̯ε > (x19.4) ὄσσε.
Laryngeal *h_2: 1. Initial position: By the comparison with Lat. *Nerō* and Skr. *nára-*, Att. ἀνήρ can be traced back to **h_2nēr*. **2. Medial position:** Att. στατός can be traced back to **st$h_2$tós* by comparing it to Lat. *status* and Skr. *sthitá-*. **3. Final position:** Att. τρία 'three' goes back to **tríh$_2$* and is related to Skr. *trī́*.
Laryngeal *h_3: 1. Initial position: Att. ὀρέγω 'I stretch out' < **$h_3$régō* is related to Lat. *regō*. **2. Medial position:** Att. δοτός 'given' goes back to **d$h_3$tós* and is related to Lat. *datus* and Skr. *datá-*. **For the final position,** there are no examples.

SC x2/x3 Vowel-Coloring and Loss of Laryngeals

In the position before the vowel **e*, laryngeal *h_2 caused the coloring of **e* to α, and laryngeal *h_3 caused the coloring of **e* to o. Laryngeal *h_1 did not change the quality of adjacent vowels, and only **e* was affected by laryngeals. Subsequently, the laryngeals were lost before a vowel without a trace.

PIE	*-h_1e-*	*-h_2e-*	*-h_3e-*
Coloring	*(-h_1e-)*	*-h_2a-*	*-h_3o-*
Loss	ε	α	ο

Laryngeal *h_1: The PIE root **$h_1$es-* 'to be' had the present **$h_1$és-ti* > ἐστί 'is' in which laryngeal *h_1 was lost before **e* without affecting the vowel.
Laryngeal *h_2: The PIE root **h_2eĝ-* 'to drive, to compel' had the present **h_2éĝō* > ἄγω 'I lead' in which laryngeal *h_2 caused **e* to become *a* before the larygeal was lost before this vowel. Before this change, palatal **ĝ* had become velar **g*: **h_2éĝō* > (x1.2) **$h_2$égō* > (x2.1) **$h_2$ágō* > (x3.2) ἄγω.
Laryngeal *h_3: The PIE root **$h_3$ed-* 'to smell', which is also found in Hom. ὀδμή and Lat. *odor* 'smell', had the present **$h_3$éd-i̯ō* > ὄζω 'I smell'. After the initial laryngeal *h_3 had caused **e* to become *o*, the laryngeal was lost before this vowel before **di̯* was palatalized to ζ: **$h_3$éd-i̯ō* > (x2.3) **$h_3$ódi̯ō* > (x3.3) **ódi̯ō* > (x18.2) ὄζω.

Exercises

E1 Laryngeals Become Vowels

A Lat. *līber* :: *$h_1$léu̯d^heros* > (x5.1) *____________ > (x9.2) ____________ 'free' **B** Skr. *urú-* :: *$h_1$urús* > (x5.1) ____________ 'broad' **C** Skr. *úkṣati* :: *$h_2$uks-ō* > (x5.2) ____________ 'I grow' **D** Lat. *migrāre* 'to wander' :: *$h_2$méi̯g^wō* > (x5.2) *____________ > (x24.4) ____________ 'I change' **E** Skr. *óhate* 'he praises' :: *h_1u̯g^{wh}omai̯* > (x5.1) *____________ > (x9.4) *____________ > (x10.3) ____________ 'I pray' **F** Skr. *rákṣati* :: *$h_2$léksō* > (x5.2) ____________ 'I repel' **G** Skr. *patnī́-* :: *pótnih_2* > (x6.5) ____________ 'mistress' **H** Skr. *máhi-* :: *még̑h_2* > (x1.2) *____________ > (x6.4) ____________ 'big' **I** Lat. *pater* :: *ph_2tḗr* > (x6.2) ____________ 'father' **J** Hom. ὄπα 'voice' :: *u̯ók^{w}i̯h_2* > (x6.5) *____________ > (x11.1) *____________ > (x19.4) Ion. *____________ > (x21.1) Ion. ____________ 'rumor' **K** Skr. *hitá-* :: *$d^h$$h_1$tós* > (x6.1) *____________ > (x9.2) ____________ 'set' **L** Lat. *fānum* 'sanctuary' :: *$d^h$$h_1$s-$b^h$$h_2$tos* > (x6.1+x6.2) *____________ > (x9.1+x9.2) ____________ 'said by a deity' **M** Skr. *jánitar-* :: *ĝenh_1tōr* > (x1.2)* ____________ > (x6.1) ____________ 'creator' **N** τέρω 'I drill' :: *tér$h_1$trom* > (x6.1) *____________ > (x12.1) ____________ 'drill'

E2 Coloring and Non-Coloring of Initial Vowels

A Lat. *aevum* :: *$h_2$ei̯u̯esí* > (x2.1) *____________ > (x3.2) *____________ > (x15.1) *____________ > (x21.2) Hom. Ion. ____________ 'eternal' **C** Skr. *édhas-* 'firewood' :: *$h_2$ei̯d^hos* > (x2.1) *____________ > (x3.2) *____________ > (x9.2) ____________ 'embers' **D** Hitt. *ḫanti* :: *$h_2$entí* > (x2.1) *____________ > (x3.2) ____________ 'before' **E** Skr. *ásmi* :: *$h_1$ésmi* > (x3.1) *____________ > (2.2) ____________ 'I am' **F** Lat. *ite* :: 2. pl. imp. *$h_1$íte* > (x3.1) ____________ 'go!' **G** Lat. *uncus* :: *h_2óŋkos* > (x3.3) ____________ 'barb' **H** Lat. *animus* :: *$h_2$én$h_1$mos* > (x2.1) *____________ > (x3.2) *____________ > (x6.1) ____________ 'wind'

x1.2: *ĝ > g	**x6.1:** *h_1 > e / C_C	**x9.4:** *g^{wh} > *k^{wh}	**x21.1:** *u̯ > Ø / #_(V,R)
x2.1: *e > a / *h_2_	**x6.2:** *h_2 > a / C_C	**x10.3:** *k^{wh} > k^h / _(u,u̯)_	**x21.2:** *u̯ > Ø / V_V
x3.1: *h_1 > Ø / _V	**x6.3:** *h_3 > o / C_C	**x11.1:** *k^w > *k / _*i̯	**x24.4:** *g^w > b / _(a,o,i)
x3.2: *h_2 > Ø / _V	**x6.5:** *h_2 > a / C_#	**x12.1:** *m > n / _#	
x5.1: *h_1 > e / #_C	**x9.1:** *b^h > p^h	**x15.1:** *s > Ø / V_V	
x5.2: *h_2 > a / #_C	**x9.2:** *d^h > t^h	**x19.4:** *ki̯ > ion. ss	

35 Development of PIE Laryngeals II

SC x2/x4 Coloring and Loss with Compensatory Lengthening after Vowel

The PIE vowel **e* was changed by laryngeal *h_2 to *a* and by laryngeal *h_3 to *o* before the laryngeals were lost with compensatory lengthening of the vowel if in position after the vowel. Laryngeal *h_1 did not change vowel quality but was also lost with compensatory lengthening. **Cf.** Rix §81–82.

PIE	*-eh$_1$-*	*-eh$_2$-*	*-eh$_3$-*
Change of Vowel Quality	*(-eh$_1$-)*	*-ah$_2$-*	*-oh$_3$-*
Loss with Compensatory Lengthening	η	ᾱ	ω

Laryngeal *h_1: The PIE root **d^{h}eh$_1$-* 'to put' had a reduplicated present tense formation **d^{h}í-d^{h}eh$_1$-mi* 'I put' > τίθημι in which case laryngeal *h_1 was lost with compensatory lengthening before **d^h* was devoiced to θ and the first aspirate lost its aspiration: **d^{h}í-d^{h}eh$_1$-mi* > (x4.1) **d^{h}i-d^{h}ē-mi.* > (x9.2) *θίθημι > (39.10) τίθημι.
Laryngeal *h_2: The PIE root **b^{h}eh$_2$-* 'to speak' had a present tense formation **b^{h}eh$_2$-mi* 'I speak' > Dor. φᾱμί, Att.-Ion. φημί in which case laryngeal *h_2 changed **e* zu **a* before the laryngeal was lost with compensatory lengthening. Subsequently, **b^h* was devoiced to φ and ᾱ was raised to η: **b^{h}eh$_2$mi* > (x2.2) **b^{h}ah$_2$mi* > (x4.2) **b^{h}āmi* > (x9.1) *φᾱμί > (13) φημί.
Laryngeal *h_3: The PIE root **deh$_3$-* 'to give' had a nominal derivation **déh$_3$-rom* 'gift' > δῶρον whose laryngeal *h_3 changed **e* zu **o* before the laryngeal was lost with compensatory lengthening: **déh$_3$rom* > (x2.4) **dóh$_3$rom* > (x4.3) **dōrom* > (x12.1) δῶρον.

SC x7 Syllabic Resonant plus Laryngeal plus Consonant

A combination of syllabic resonant plus laryngeal **R̥H* transformed into resonant plus long vowel *RV̄* or a sequence of a short vowel plus resonant plus short vowel *V̆RV̆*. The reason for this double representation is mostly seen in different accentuation patterns so that unaccentuated **R̥H* changed to *RV̄* and accentuated **Ŕ̥H* changed to *V̆RV̆*. Examples cannot be found for all contexts. **Cf.** Rix §83; SI §109.
Laryngeal *h_1: Unaccentuated **r̥h$_1$* became ρη in **tr̥h$_1$tós* > (x7.1) τρητός 'perforated', which is derived from τείρω 'I perforate'. Unaccentuated **l̥h$_1$* became λη in **g^{w}l̥h$_1$tós* > (x7.5) **g^{w}lētós* > (x24.3) βλητός 'thrown', which is derived from βάλλω 'I throw'.
Laryngeal *h_2: Att. τλητός 'carried' goes back to **tl̥h$_2$-tós* from the root **telh$_2$-* which is also the derivational base of τελαμῶν < **telh$_2$mṓn* 'broad strap for carrying' and Lat. *lātus* 'carried'. Unaccentuated **l̥h$_2$* became λᾱ before ᾱ was raised to η: **tl̥h$_2$-tós* > (x7.6) Dor. τλᾱτός > (13) Att. τλᾱτός. The accentuated sequence **ĺ̥h$_2$* became αλα in **g^{w}ĺ̥h$_2$nos* > βάλανος 'acorn' which is related to Lat. *glāns*: **g^{w}ĺ̥h$_2$nos* > (x7.7) **g^{w}álanos* > (x24.4) βάλανος. A similar case is **d^{h}ń̥h$_2$tos* > θάνατος 'death' in which accentuated **ń̥h$_2$* became ανα before **d^h* was devoiced to θ: **d^{h}ń̥h$_2$tos* > (x7.12) **d^{h}ánatos* > (x9.2) θάνατος. In **d^{h}n̥h$_2$tós* > θνητός 'dead', νη is the representation of the unaccentuated sequence **n̥h$_2$*.

SC x8 Syllabic Resonant plus Laryngeal plus Vowel

Before a vowel, the sequence of syllabic resonant plus laryngeal **R̥HV* transformed into the sequence of vowel plus resonant *VR* which can be exemplified by Att. πάρος 'formerly' < **pr̥h$_3$os* which is related to Skr. *purás*. Another example is the etymology of καλέω 'I call out': **kl̥h$_1$ei̯ō* > (x8.1) **kálei̯ō* > (x16.1) καλέω whereas its PPP κλητός 'called out' goes back to **kl̥h$_1$tós* built from the PIE root **kelh$_1$-*.

Exercises

E1 Unaccented Syllabic Resonant Plus Laryngeal Before Consonant or Vowel

A στόρνῡμι 'I spread out' :: **str̥h_3-tós* > (x7.4) ___________ 'spread out' **B** ἁμαρτάνω 'I miss' :: **n̥-$h_2$mertēs* > (x7.11) *___________ > (13) ___________ 'unfailing' **C** πίμπλημι 'I fill' :: 3. sg. aor. midd. **pl̥h_1-to* > (x7.5) Hom. ___________ 'it became full' **D** Skr. *ā́śīrta-* :: **ń̥-ḱr̥h_2-tos* > (x1.1) *___________ > (x7.2) *___________ > (x26.1) ___________ 'unmixed' **E** Myc. *no-pe-ra-ha* :: **n̥-h_3b^{h}elēs* > (x7.13) *___________ > (x9.1) *___________ > (+privative alpha) ___________ 'useless' **F** Dor. λᾶνος :: **u̯l̥$h_2$nos* > (x7.6) *___________ > (x21.1) *___________ > (13) ___________ 'wool' **G** aor. ἔμολον 'I came' :: **ml̥h_3sḱō* > (x1.1) *___________ > (x7.8) *___________ > (47.4) ___________ 'I come' **H** Dor. ἄδμᾱτος :: **ń̥-dm̥$h_2$tos* > (x7.15) *___________ > (x26.1) *___________ > (13) ___________ 'untamed' **I** δέμω 'I build' :: **neu̯ó-dm̥$h_2$tos* > (x7.15) *___________ > (x21.2) *___________ > (13) *___________ 'newly built' **J** κάμνω 'I become tired' :: **ḱe-ḱm̥h_2-u̯ōs* > (x1.1) *___________ > (x7.15) *___________ > (13) *___________ > (x21.2) Hom. ___________ 'tired' **K** aor. ἔγρετο 'he woke up' :: **n̥$h_1$gretos* > (x7.9) ___________ 'without waking up' **L** κάμνω 'I am tired' :: aor. **ḱḿ̥$h_2$om* > (x1.1) *___________ > (x8.3) *___________ > (x12.1) *___________ > (+ accentuated augment) ___________ 'I became tired'

E2 Accented Syllabic Resonant Plus Laryngeal Before Consonant

A Skr. *adāṃta-* :: **n̥-dḿ̥$h_2$tos* > (x7.16) *___________ > (x26.1) ___________ 'untamed' **B** Skr. *śīrṣán-* :: **ḱŕ̥$h_2$sn̥h_2* > (x1.1) *___________ > (x6.5) *___________ > (x7.3) *___________ > (2.2) *___________ > (13) Hom. ___________ 'head' **C** Lat. *palma* :: **pĺ̥$h_2$meh_2* > (x2.2) *___________ > (x4.2) *___________ > (x7.7) *___________ > (13) ___________ 'palm of the hand'

2.2: *VsR > V̄R	**x6.5:** *h_2 > a / C_#	**x7.7:** *ĺ̥h_2 > ala	**x7.16:** *ḿ̥h_2 > ama
13: *ā > ę̄	**x7.2:** *r̥h_2 > rā	**x7.8:** *l̥h_3 > lǭ	**x8.3:** *m̥h_2 > am / _V
47.3: m > b / #_l	**x7.3:** *ŕ̥h_2 > ara	**x7.9:** *n̥h_1 > nę̄	**x9.1:** *b^h > p^h
x1.1: *ḱ > k	**x7.4:** *r̥h_3 > rǭ	**x7.11:** *n̥h_2 > nā	**x21.1:** *u̯ > Ø / #_(V,R)
x2.2: *e > a / _*h_2	**x7.5:** *l̥h_1 > lę̄	**x7.13:** *n̥h_3 > nǭ	**x21.2:** *u̯ > Ø / V_V
x4.2: *ah_2 > ā	**x7.6:** *l̥h_2 > lā	**x7.15:** *m̥h_2 > mā	**x26.1:** *n̥ > a

36 Analogical Changes

Levelling of Intraparadigmatic Differences

If sound laws altered a language unrestrictedly, some morphologically related word forms would lose their phonological relation and would not be perceptible as being related. It is due to analogy, which is the formation of a word based on the model of another word, that morphologically related words do not diverge too strongly phonologically. According to regular sound laws, the inf. ἕπ-εσθαι 'to follow' should be ἕτ-εσθαι* because it relies on the PIE root *sek^w-, the labiovelar of which should have become τ before ε according to SC x17.1. The whole paradigm according to sound laws would be: 1. sg. *$sék^w$omai̯ > ἕπομαι, 2. sg. *$sék^w$esai̯ > ἕτεσαι*, 3. sg. *$sék^w$etai̯ > ἕτεται*, 1. pl. *sek^wómet^{h}a > ἑπόμεθα, 2. pl. *$sék^w$est^{h}ai̯ > ἕτεσθαι*, 3. pl. *sek^wontai̯ > ἕπονται. The divergence π :: τ was resolved in favor of π in order to ensure a coherent phonological shape of the words.

Analogical Preservation of Tense and Mood Signs

The verb παιδεύω has the aor. ἐπαίδευσα and the fut. παιδεύσω although intervocalic σ should have vanished in Proto-Greek times already according to SC x15. It was retained in analogy to the numerous verbs having a consonantic stem such as διώκω [di̯ǭkǭ] 'I follow' which has the aor. ἐδίωξα [edíǭk-sa] and the fut. διώξω [di̯ǭk-sǭ] in which forms σ remained after a consonant. Therefore, the tense morpheme -σ- was reintroduced in ἐπαίδευσα and παιδεύσω because its loss in παιδεύσω would have resulted in παιδεύω which would have been identical to the present tense so that a tense distinction would not have been possible without further means. Another example is the 2. sg. imp. aor. pass. *παιδεύ-θη-θι > παιδεύ-θη-τι 'be educated!', which should have been παιδεύ-τη-θι* due to Grassmann's law (cf. chap. 22). But as the morpheme -θη- was used in all the other forms of the aor. pass., the second aspirate was deaspirated instead of the first.

Reenforcement of Meaning After Loss of Semantic Content

In some cases, a morpheme is added onto an already existing and functionally similar morpheme to clarify its meaning which has been obscured through sound changes. The nom. τίς 'who?' goes back directly to PIE *$k^w$is, which can be seen by comparing it to Lat. *quis* [ku̯is]. The expected acc. *k^wim first became Greek τίν* before it was remodelled to τίνα by the attachment of the acc. sg. morpheme -α of the consonant stems. Furthermore, other paradigmatic forms such as gen. sg. τίνος, dat. sg. τίνι and nom. pl. τίνες were built from the stem τιν- although the final sound -ν had originally been the morpheme of the acc. sg.

A similar process can be seen in the paradigmatic forms of the *s*-aor. ἐπαίδευσα, ἐπαίδευσας, ἐπαίδευσε, ἐπαιδεύσαμεν, ἐπαιδεύσατε, ἐπαιδεύσαν. The ending of the first person sg. *-*m* was attached to the PIE aor. morpheme *-*s*- which phonetically led to the articulation of */m/ as syllabic *[m̥], which resulted in Greek -*a*: **epái̯deu̯s-m̥* > ἐπαίδευσα 'I educated'. The regular development of the preforms of the 2. sg. **epái̯deu̯s-s* and 3. sg. **epái̯deu̯s-t* with the morphemes *-*s* and *-*t* would have both led to ἐπαίδευς*, which would not have guaranteed a clear distinction of tense or person. In this case, the form ἐπαίδευσα, which goes back to **epái̯deu̯sm̥*, was used as the stem onto which the morpheme for the 2. sg. -ς was attached which led to ἐπαίδευσα-ς. The ending -ε of the 3. sg. aor. ἐπαίδευσε was formed in analogy to the regular ending -ε of the 3. sg. perf. πεπαίδευκε 'I have educated'.

Exercises

E1 The *s*-stem ἔπος, ἔπους, ἔπει goes back to the preforms **u̯ék^{w}os*, **u̯ék^{w}esos*, **u̯ék^{w}esi*. Is this the regular result? Where did analogy take place?

Answer:

E2 Why is the difference of the paradigmatic forms prs. θείνω 'I kill' :: aor. ἔπεφνε 'I killed' a peculiarity?

Answer:

E3 Is the nom. pl. ὀστᾶ of ὀστοῦν 'bone' regular if it goes back to *ὀστέα?

Answer:

E4 Seen in relation to ἅπτω 'I touch', why is ἀφάσσω 'I touch' a regular form and ἀφάω 'I touch' not?

Answer:

E5 The numeral διᾱκόσιοι 'two hundred' should be διᾱκασιοι* with α instead of ο, because the second element -κασι- goes back to *κατι which is a variant of ἑκατόν 'hundred'. What is the origin of the analogical formation?

Answer:

E6 The paradigms of the contracted verbs τῑμάω, ποιέω, δουλόω with their future forms τῑμήσω, ποιήσω, δουλώσω were analogically leveled. While ποιέω < *ποιέ-ω and δουλόω < *δουλό-ω are nominal derivations with a short vowel ε/ο, verbs like τῑμάω < *τῑμᾱ-ω are derivations from ᾱ-stems. Where did analogy take place if one assumes that rule SC 1.1 "a vowel before a vowel was shortened" took place in a relatively recent period of time and definitively after the vowel raising ᾱ > η?

Answer:

37 The Reconstruction of PIE Phonemes

Systematic Correspondences in Vocabulary and Grammar

If different languages exhibit systematic correspondences regarding their vocabulary and grammar, and the frequency of these correspondences is so high that it cannot be attributed to mere chance, it is possible to posit a genetic relationship between these languages and reconstruct a common ancestor or proto-language. Lat. *tremō* and Gr. τρέμω, which both mean 'I shiver', enable the reconstruction of a common preform **trémō*, out of which the two language forms originated without any changes. The comparison of Lat. *serpō* and Gr. ἕρπω, which both mean 'I creep', furthermore shows that these two forms are not identical, but that Lat. /s/ corresponds to Gr. /h/. One could thus posit **sérpō* as the preform and derive Gr. ἕρπω by the sound change **s > h / #_V*, or posit **hérpō* as the preform and explain the Lat. form via the sound change **h > s / #_V*. If one additionally takes into account Skr. *sárpā-mi* 'I creep' (*-mi* is the extended ending of the 1. ps. sg.), the first solution is corroborated because two languages have /s/ in the initial position. Nonetheless, **hérpō* could still be the preform of all the forms, in which case Latin and Sanskrit would exhibit a parallel development. But regarding the majority of IE languages, in which /s/ corresponds to Lat. and Skr. /s/, as well as to Gr. /h/, the preform **serpō* with initial */s/ is reconstructed. This accords to the linguistic principle of majority and simplicity. The sound, which is exhibited by most languages and which takes the fewest intermediate steps from the preform to the attested language form, can be most often reconstructed for the preform.

Phonological Correspondences Between Sanskrit, Attic and Latin

The following charts are examples for etymological word correspondences between Sanskrit, Greek and Latin on the left side, the PIE preform and its meaning in the middle and the sound correspondences illustrated by the examples on the right side. One example often furnishes results for more than one sound. The sound, which is being compared in a line, is printed in **bold**. The following description serves as an introduction to the comparative method and does not exhaustively present and explain all the correspondences and irregularities of the given words. Usually, the meanings of the attested forms and the meaning of the preform are the same. Otherwise, they will be mentioned in the commentary. The abbreviation **L** stands for line. The following charts do not give an exhaustive presentation of PIE phonology but serve for giving an overview of the most important sound correspondences.

1. Short Vowels

There were only little changes regarding the development of short vowels from PIE to Attic. PIE *a, *e, *i, *o remain and *u, which was still *u in Proto-Greek, became Att. y. Sometimes, PIE *o changed via *u to Att. y. In Sanskrit, PIE *e and *o merge to Skr. a. Sometimes, PIE *o is represented by Skr. ā. Latin preserves the PIE short vowels except for *o, which became u in many positions.

	Compared Languages			Preform and Meaning		Sound Correspondences			
	Sanskrit	**Attic**	**Latin**	**PIE**	**Meaning**	**Skr.**	**Att.**	**Lat.**	**PIE**
1	*mádati*	μαδαρός	*madeō*	*√*mad-*	'to be wet'	*a*	*a*	*a*	***a***
2	*~ahám*	ἐγώ	*egō*	**eĝóh$_2$*	'I'	*a*	*e*	*e*	***e***
3	*~tíṣṭhati*	ἵστησι	*~sistit*	**sti-steh$_2$-ti*	'he stands, sets'	*i*	*i*	*i*	***i***
4	*sthitá-*	στατός	*status*	**sth$_2$tós*	PPP 'set'	*a*	*o*	*u*	***o***
5	*pā́da-*	πόδα	*(pedem)*	**pód-m̥*	'foot'	*ā*	*o*	-	***o***
6	*~nákta-*	νύξ	*nox*	**nók^{w}t-s*	'night'	*a*	*y*	*o*	***o***
7	*rudhirá-*	ἐρυθρός	*ruber*	**(h$_1$)rud^{h}rós*	'red'	*u*	*y*	*u*	***u***

L1: PIE *a remains in Skr., Att., Lat. *a*. PIE *a is relatively seldom in PIE roots. Skr. *mádati* 'it bubbles', Gr. μαδαρός 'wet', Lat. *madeō* 'I am wet' are different formations derived from the root *mad- 'to be wet'.

L2: PIE *e remains in Att., Lat. *e* and becomes Skr. *a*. Att. ἐγώ and Lat. *egō* go back to *eĝóh$_2$, whereby palatal *ĝ became velar *g before the laryngeal was lost with compensatory lengthening: *eĝóh$_2$ > (x1.2) *egóh$_2$ > (x4) ἐγώ. In Latin, the accent position was changed to the initial syllable. Skr. *ahám* goes back to the apophonical variant *eĝh$_2$óm, whereby the sequence *ĝh$_2$ first became *ĝ^h and then *h*, before *e and *o became *a*: *eĝh$_2$óm > *eĝ^{h}óm > *ehóm > *ahám*.

L3: PIE *i remains in Skr., Att., Lat. *i*. The laryngeal in the preform *stí-steh$_2$-ti changed *e zu *a* before it was lost with compensatory lengthening. The Pre-Greek sequence *stistā was simplified to *sistā: *stí-steh$_2$-ti > (x2.2) *stí-stah$_2$-ti > (x4.2) *στίστᾱτι > (simplification) *σίστᾱτι. Subsequently, initial *σ was buccalized to *h*, and the sequence *τι became σι before *ᾱ was raised to η: *σίστᾱτι > (x13.1) *ἵστᾱτι > (x22.1) *ἵστᾱσι > (13) ἵστησι. Skr. *tíṣṭhati* and Lat. *sistit* go back to the apophonical variant *stí-sth$_2$-e-ti, whereby in Skr., laryngeal *h$_2$ aspirated the adjacent *t* > *th* and changed *e to *a*. The phenomenon that Skr. *s was changed to retroflex *ṣ* after the sounds *r*, *ŭ*, *k*, *ĭ* is known as the *ruki*-rule.

L4: PIE *o remains in Att. *o*, Old Latin *o* and becomes Skr. *a*, Lat. *u*. Therefore, the Gr. ending *-os* regularly corresponds to Old Lat. *-os* > Lat. *-us* as well as Skr. *-as*. Between consonants, the laryngeals *h$_1$, *h$_2$, *h$_3$ became Gr. *e*, *a*, *o*, Lat. *a* and Skr. *i* (cf. L72–75). As in L3, *h$_2$ caused the aspiration of Skr. *t* > *th*.

L5: Sometimes in open syllables, PIE *o became Skr. *ā*, which is known as Brugmann's law. The first *e* of Lat. *pedem* does not go back to PIE *o but was caused by apophony *e :: *o (cf. chap. 9). The syllabic acc.-morpheme *m̥ resulted in Skr., Att. *a*, Lat. *em* (cf. L19). In Skr., an additional *-m* was added for indicating the acc. more strongly.

L6: PIE *o remains Lat., Gr. *o* and Skr. *a*. as it was described in L4. In Gr., PIE *o first became *u and then Att. *y* in the position between the resonant *n* and the labialized consonant *k^w (SC 11). In all three languages, the labial coarticulation of *k^w was lost. Final *ts was simplified to *s* in Gr. and Lat., whereas it was lost completely in Skr.

L7: PIE *u remains Skr., Lat., Proto-Greek *u* and becomes Att. *y*. For *d^h cf. L43–45. It is not clear whether the initial ε in ἐρυθρός goes back to *h$_1$ or is a Greek development. Therefore, it has been put into parentheses in the preform *(h$_1$)rud^{h}rós. For Lat. *-er* < *-ros* cf. L48.

37

2. Long Vowels

It is possible to reconstruct long vowels for PIE which mostly go back to the combination of a short vowel plus laryngeal. The loss of the laryngeal caused a compensatory lengthening of the preceding vowel. Original long vowels are apophonical **ē* and **ō* of the ablaut vowel **e/o*. In Att., PIE **ē*, **ī*, **ō*, **ū* remained whereas **ā*, which was still **ā* in Proto-Greek, became**ę̄* (cf. SC 13, chap. 16) and **ū* became *ȳ*. In Skr., **ē* and **ō* became *ā* analogous to the development of **e* and **o* to *a*. In Lat., the PIE long vowels were preserved.

	Compared Languages			Preform and Meaning		Sound Correspondences			
	Sanskrit	Attic	Latin	PIE	Meaning	Skr.	Att.	Lat.	PIE
8	*sv**ā**dú-*	ἡδύς	*su**ā**vis*	**su̯**eh**$_2$dús*	'sweet'	*ā*	*ę̄*	*ā*	***ā* < **eh$_2$***
9	*~dá-dh**ā**-mi*	τίθημι	*~f**ē**-cī*	**dí-d^h**eh**$_1$-mi*	'to put'	*ā*	*ę̄*	*ē*	***ē* < **h$_1$***
10	*~v**ī**rá-*	ῑ̓ς	*v**ī**s*	**u̯**ī́**s*	'force'	*ī*	*ī*	*ī*	***ī* < **iH***
11	***ā**śú-*	ὠκύς	*~**ō**cior*	**h$_2$**ō**k̂ús*	'fast'	*ā*	*ǭ*	*ō*	***ō***
12	*m**ū́**ṣ-*	μῦς	*m**ū**s*	**m**ū́**s*	'mouse'	*ū*	*ȳ*	*ū*	***ū***

L8: PIE **ā* remains in Skr., Lat. *ā*, Proto-Greek **ā* and results in Att. *ę̄* if it was not reversed to *ā* after ε, ι, ϱ (SC 13.2). In L8, **ā* resulted from **eh$_2$* because PIE **su̯ādús* can be traced further back to **su̯eh$_2$dús*. Initial **su̯* resulted in Att. *h*. In Lat., **su̯ādús* was transferred into the *i*-declension, and **d* was lost before *u̯*: **su̯ādus* > **su̯ādu̯is* > Lat. *suāvis* [su̯āu̯is].
L9: PIE **ē* remains in Att. *ę̄*, Lat. *ē* and results in Skr. *ā*. In L9, **ę̄* resulted from **eh$_1$* because **d^{h}íd^{h}ēmi* can be traced further back to **d^{h}íd^{h}eh$_1$mi* which resulted via *θίθημι in τίθημι 'I put'. Skr. *dádhāmi* 'I put' goes back to **d^{h}éd^{h}ēmi* with the vowel *e in the reduplicated syllable. Loss of aspiration in the initial position through Grassmann's law (cf. chapter 23).
L10: PIE **ī* remains *ī* in all three languages. In this case, **ī* goes back to **iH*. The root noun **u̯iHs* 'strength', which was built from the root **u̯iH-* 'to be strong', resulted in Att. ῑ̓ς and Lat. *vīs*. For Att. *u̯* > Ø cf. L34 and SC x21.1. The nominalized derivation **u̯iH-ró-s* 'strong' resulted in Skr. *vīrá-* and Lat. *vir* 'man'.
L11: PIE **ō* remains in Lat. *ō*, Att. *ǭ* and results in Skr. *ā*. The initial laryngeal **h$_2$* was lost without a trace. In Gr. and Lat., **k̂* became *k* similar to the development of **ĝ* > *g* in L2/54/55. For **k̂* > *ś* in Skr. cf. L52/53. No positive is found for the Lat. comparative *ōcior* 'faster'.
L12: PIE **ū* remains in Skr., Lat. *ū*, Proto-Greek **ū* and results in Att. *ȳ*. Skr. *ṣ* after *ū* according to the *ruki*-rule (cf. L3).

3. Diphthongs

Due to the sound changes **e* > *a* and **o* > *a* mentioned in L4/5, the PIE diphthongs **ei̯*, **oi̯* and **ai̯* merged in Pre-Sanskrit **ai̯* before it monophthongized to Skr. *ē*. Likewise, **eu̯*, **ou̯* and **au̯* merged in **au̯* before it monophthongized to Skr. *ō*. Traditionally, the vowel length of Skr. *ē* and *ō* is not used in the transcription of Skr. words.

	Compared Languages			Preform and Meaning		Sound Correspondences			
	Sanskrit	**Attic**	**Latin**	**PIE**	**Meaning**	**Skr.**	**Att.**	**Lat.**	**PIE**
13	*édhas-*	αἶθος	~*aedēs*	**$h_2$ei̯d^hos*	'burning'	*ē*	*ai̯*	*ae*	***ai̯**
14	*dídeśati*	δείκνῡμι	*dīcō*	√**dei̯k̂-*	'to show'	*ē*	*ẹ̄*	*ī*	***ei̯**
15	*veśá-*	οἶκος	*vīcus*	**u̯oi̯k̂ós*	'dwelling place'	*ē*	*oi̯*	*ī*	***oi̯**
16	~*ójas-*	αὐξάνω	*augēre*	√**$h_2$eu̯g-*	'to augment'	*ō*	*au̯*	*au̯*	***au̯**
17	*óṣati*	εὕω	*ūrō*	**$h_1$éu̯s-ō*	'to burn'	*ō*	*eu̯*	*ū*	***eu̯**
18	*loká-*	(λευκός)	*lūcus*	**lou̯kos*	'clearing'	*ō*	*ū*	*ū*	***ou̯**

L13: PIE **ai̯* remains in Att. *ai̯*, Old Lat. *ai̯* > Lat. *ae* as the prestep of the Vulgar Lat. monophthongization *ae* > *ē*. In Skr., **ai̯* monophthongizes to *ē*. Skr. *édhas-* 'fire wood' and Att. αἶθος 'heat' go back to the PIE *s*-stem **$h_2$éi̯d^hos*. For **h_2e* > *a* cf. L69; for **d^h* > Att. θ, Lat. *d* cf. L44. Transition of the PIE *s*-stem **$h_2$éi̯d^hos* into the *e*-declension in Lat. *aedēs* 'house, temple' < * 'fire-place'.
L14: PIE **ei̯* remains in Old Lat. *ei̯*, Proto-Greek **ei̯* and monophthongizes to Att. *ẹ̄* and Skr. *ē*. In Skr., **ei̯* became **ai̯* through the Sound change **e* > *a* before **ai̯* monophthongized to Skr. *ē*. In Proto-Greek and Pre-Attic, **ei̯* was a real diphthong (Pre-Att. *δείκνῡμι [déi̯knūmi]) and monophthongized to Att. *ẹ̄* (δείκνῡμι [dẹ̄knȳmi]) before it was raised to *ī* after the classical period. In Old Lat. *deicō* [dei̯kō], the diphthong *ei̯* was preserved before it monophthongized via *ẹ̄* to *ī* in Lat. *dīcō*, similar to the Attic development. The meaning changed from *to show* > *to speak*. In Skr. *dídeśati* 'he shows', one finds the reduplicated formation **di-dei̯k̂-e-ti*. For **k̂* > Gr., Lat. *k*, Skr. *ś* cf. L52/53.
L15: PIE **oi̯* remains in Att. *oi̯*, it becomes Skr. *ē* and Lat. *oe* or *ī* such as in*vīcus* 'village'. In Skr., **oi̯* became **ai̯* through the sound change **o* > *a* and monophthongized to *ē* (cf. L4). For the ending Skr. *-as*, Gr. *-os*, Lat. *-us* cf. L4. In Att., initial **u̯* was lost but it remained in other dialects as ϝ (cf. L34). In Lat., **oi̯* became **ei̯* through the influence of the initial **u̯* before it monophthongized via *ẹ̄* to Lat. *ī*, just like original **ei̯*. The Lat. standard development is, however, **oi̯* > *ū* such as in **oi̯nos* > Old Lat. *oinos* > Lat. *ūnus* 'one'.
L16: PIE **au̯* remains in Att., Lat. *au̯* and monophthongizes to Skr. *ō*. In this case, the diphthong **au̯* goes back to **$h_2$eu̯*. In αὐξάνω [au̯ksánọ̄] 'I augment', one finds the assimilation of voice *g* > *k* _*s* according to SC 29.9.
L17: PIE **eu̯* remains in Att. *eu̯*. In Lat., **eu̯* merges with the development of **ou̯*. In Skr., **eu̯* becomes **au̯* through the sound change **e* > *a* before it monophthongizes to *ō*. The initial laryngeal is lost (cf. SC x3.1). In Skr. *ṣ* < **s* due to the *ruki*-rule (cf. L3). In Att., intervocalic *σ is lost via the intermediate step *h* which caused the initial aspiration (cf. chap. 24). In Lat., PIE **eu̯* had become **ou̯* in Proto-Italic times already before it monophthongized via *ọ̄* to *ū*. Between vowels, **s* became *r* via voiced [z] which is known as rhotazism
L18: Skr. *loká-* 'world, open space' and Old Lat. *loucos* 'grove, wood' > Lat. *lūcus* go back to **lou̯kos* 'clearing' built from the root **leu̯k-* 'to shine'. In Att., the root is attested with *e*-vocalism in λευκός 'shining'.

4. Syllabic Resonants

The PIE nasals */n/, */m/ and liquids */r/, */l/ had syllabic allophones *[n̥], *[m̥], *[r̥], *[l̥] if they functioned as the nucleus of a syllable.

	Compared Languages			Preform and Meaning		Sound Correspondences			
	Sanskrit	**Attic**	**Latin**	**PIE**	**Meaning**	**Skr.**	**Att.**	**Lat.**	**PIE**
19	***dáśa***	**δέκα**	***décem***	****dék̂m̥***	'ten'	*a*	*a*	*em*	****m̥***
20	***nā́man-***	**ὄνομα**	***nōmen***	****(h*$_1$*)neh*$_3$*mn̥***	'name'	*a*	*a*	*en*	****n̥***
21	***r̥̄kṣa-***	**ἄρκτος**	***ursus***	****h*$_2$*ŕ̥tk̂os***	'bear'	*r̥*	*ar*	*ur*	****r̥***
22	***pr̥thú-***	**πλατύς**	***(mollis)***	****pl̥th*$_2$*ú-***	'wide'	*r̥*	*la*	*(ol)*	****l̥***

L19: PIE **m̥* results in Lat. *em* and Skr., Att. *a* before a consonant or in the final position (cf. SC x26.3). For **k̂* > Gr., Lat. *k*, Skr. *ś* cf. L52/53.
L20: PIE **n̥* results in Lat. *en* and Skr., Att. *a* before consonant or in the final position (cf. SC x26.1). The initial vowel of ὄνομα originated probably through vowel assimilation from *ενομα (cf. SI §90). Lat. *nōmen* and Skr. *nā́man-* probably continue the lengthened ablaut grade **ō* of the preform **nōmn̥* < **(h*$_1$*)neh*$_3$*mn̥*.
L21: PIE **r̥* remains in Skr. *r̥*, it becomes Att. *ar* or *ra* with unclear distribution (cf. chap. 33) and Lat. *ur* via **or*. In Greek, metathesis of **tk̂* > *kt*. For the development of the so-called "thorn-cluster" **tk̂* > Skr. *kṣ*, Gr. κτ, Lat. *s* cf. L40. The cognate form Het. *ḫartaga*, the meaning of which cannot be definitely asserted to have been 'bear', clearly exhibits an initial laryngeal as well as a sequence of dental stop before velar stop.
L22: PIE **l̥* becomes Skr. *r̥*, Att. *al* or *la* with unclear distribution (cf. chap. 33) and Lat. *ol*. In Skr., laryngeal **h*$_2$ aspirated the precedent stop: **th*$_2$ > *th* (cf. L2/3). In Lat, there is no cognate form of **pl̥th*$_2$*ú-* but PIE **l̥* is continued e.g. in Lat. *mollis* 'soft' < **ml̥du̯is*.

5. Syllabic Resonant plus Laryngeal

The sequence of syllabic resonant plus laryngeal was known as "long sonants" in former times. For a complete list of Att. results cf. SC x7 as well as chap. 35. Due to the threefold Greek vowel coloring caused by the laryngeals, these sequences exhibit many possible developments, out of which the following table gives only a few examples.

	Compared Languages			Preform and Meaning		Sound Correspondences			
	Sanskrit	**Attic**	**Latin**	**PIE**	**Meaning**	**Skr.**	**Att.**	**Lat.**	**PIE**
23	*adānta-*	ἄδμητος	-	**n̥-dm̥h*$_2$*-tós*	'untamed'	*ān*	*mę̄*	*mā*	****m̥h*$_2$**
24	*jātá-*	γνητός	***nātus***	****ĝn̥h*$_1$*tós***	'born'	*ā*	*nę̄*	*nā*	****n̥h*$_1$**
25	*(stīrṇá-)*	στρωτός	*strātus*	****str̥h*$_3$*tós***	'spread out'	*īr*	*rǭ*	*rā*	****r̥h*$_3$**
26	***ū́rṇā-***	(λῆνος)	***lāna***	****h*$_2$*u̯l̥H-neh*$_2$**	'wool'	*ūr*	*lę̄*	*lā*	****l̥H***

L23: For the privative alpha in ἀ-δμητος from **n̥* cf. chapt. 33. Att. ἄδμητος corresponds to Dor. ἄδμᾱτος which shows the reflex of μᾱ < **m̥h*$_2$. Att. μη resulted from vowel raising **ā* > *ę̄*. The PIE root **demh*$_2$*-* 'to tame' does not have cognate forms in Lat.
L24: Old Lat. *gnātus* retained the initial *g* which was lost in Lat. *nātus*. For PIE **ĝ* > Skr. *j* cf. L54/55.
L25: Skr. *stīrṇá-* goes back to **str̥h*$_3$*nó-* instead of **str̥h*$_3$*tó-*. Skr. *ṇ* comes from *n* if *r* precedes in the same word.
L26: The initial laryngeal of PIE **h*$_2$*u̯l̥H-neh*$_2$ is preserved in Het. *ḫulana* 'wool'. After the loss of the laryngeal and the loss of initial **u̯* in Greek, the vowel **ā* was raised to *ę̄*: **u̯lānos* > **lānos* > λῆνος which corresponds to Dor. λᾶνος. In Att., the word was transferred into the *o*-decelension.

6. Nonsyllabic Resonants, Semivowels and the Fricative *s

The Nasals *m*, *n* and liquids *r*, *l* are continued without changes in the compared languages, only *l* changes to Skr. *r* in the most cases. In Att., the semivowel *i̯* caused many combinatory sound changes (cf. SC x19) and remained only as the second element of the diphthongs αι [ai̯] and οι [oi̯] as well as in the groups *σι̯ [si̯] and *ϝι̯ [u̯i̯]. Initial *i̯* became Att. ζ [zd] while initial *Hi̯* led to Att. *h* and intervocalic *i̯* was lost. The semivowel *u̯* was lost in many position and remained as the second element of the Att. diphthongs αυ [au̯] and ευ [eu̯]. In the initial position, *u̯* became *h* or was lost (cf. SC x21). In Skr., the semivowels *i̯* and *u̯* stayed intact if they were not the second element of the diphthongs *ai̯* and *au̯*, which monophthongized to *ē* and *ō*. Intervocalic *i̯* was lost in Latin as well as *u̯* between alike vowels or before a velar vowel. The fricative *s* took part in many combinatory processes and became Att. *h* in the initial position.

	Compared Languages			**Preform and Meaning**		**Sound Correspondences**			
	Sanskrit	**Attic**	**Latin**	**PIE**	**Meaning**	**Skr.**	**Att.**	**Lat.**	**PIE**
27	~*māṃsá-*	μηρός	~*membrum*	**mē(m)srós*	'meat'	*m*	*m*	*m*	***m**
28	*sána-*	ἕνος	~*senex*	**sénos*	'year'	*n*	*n*	*n*	***n**
29	*bhárati*	φέρει	*fert*	**bʰereti*	'he caries'	*r*	*r*	*r*	***r**
30	~*lasati*	λασκή	~*lascīvus*	**las-kéh$_2$*	'to desire'	*l*	*l*	*l*	***l**
31	*pravanta*	πλέω	~*pluit*	**pléu̯-ō*	'to swim'	*r*	*l*	*l*	***l**
32	*yúdhyati*	ὑσμίνη	*iubere*	√**Hi̯eu̯dʰ-*	'to start to move'	*i̯*	*h*	*i̯*	***Hi̯**
33	~*yūṣán-*	ζύμη	~*iūs*	**i̯ūs-meh$_2$*	'broth'	*i̯*	*zd*	*i̯*	***i̯**
34	*vŕ̥ṣan-*	ἄρρην	*verrēs*	**h$_2$u̯ŕ̥sen-*	'male animal'	*u̯*	Ø	*u̯*	***u̯**
35	~*súvar-*	~ἥλιος	~*sōl*	**seh$_2$u̯el*	'sun'	*s*	*h*	*s*	***s**

L27: PIE *m* remains *m* in all three languages. Att. μηρός 'thigh' < *mēsrós* through loss of sigma according to SC 2.2. Skr. *māṃsá-* nt. 'meat' < *mēmsó-*. Lat. *membrum* 'limb, part' < *mēmsrom*. In Lat., vowel shortening according to SC 1.1, *sr* > *br*, and *o* > *u*: *mēmsrom* > *memsrom* > *membrom* > Lat. *membrum*.
L28: PIE *n* remains *n* in all three languages. Skr. *sána-* and Gr. ἕνος go back to *sénos* 'year'. For *s* > Att. *h* cf. SC x13.1 and L35. Lat. *senex* < *sén-ek-s* was enlargend through a *k*-element.
L29: PIE *r* remains *r* in all three languages. For Gr. *bʰ* > *pʰ* cf. L41/42.
L30: PIE *l* remains Skr., Gr., Lat *l*. In Skr., PIE *l* is usually continued by *r* as it is shown in the next line. Skr. *lasati* < *las-e-ti* 'he desires' is one of the rare examples which show the preservation of PIE *l* in Skr. Att. λασκή 'whore' is attested in a gloss. Lat. *lascīvus* 'wanton, lustful'.
L31: PIE *l* remains Gr., Lat. *l* and results in Skr. *r*. The Ved. 3. pl. aor. midd. *pravanta* 'they swim' exhibits the sound change *l* > *r* in contrast to the Classical Skr. root *plu-* 'to swim' in which *l* was preserved. For loss of intervocalic *u̯* in Att. cf. SC x21.2. Lat. *pluit* 'it rains' shows a semantic development.
L32: The initial correspondence Skr. *i̯*, Gr. *h*, Lat. *i̯* goes back to *Hi̯* (cf. chap. 27). Skr. *yúdhyati* 'he fights' < *Hi̯údʰ-i̯e-ti*. In Gr. ὑσμίνη [hysmī́nę̄], the root *Hi̯udʰ-* was enlarged by a suffix *-smīnā*. Old Lat. *ioubēre* 'to command' should have become Lat. *iūbēre** according to regular sound changes but short *u* of Lat. *iubēre* orginated in analogy to the regular forms of the perf. *iussī*, *iussum*.
L33: The initial correspondence Skr. *i̯*, Gr. *zd*, Lat. *i̯* goes back to *i̯*. Skr. *yūṣán-* 'meat broth' < *i̯ūs-én-*, Lat. *iūs* 'broth', Att. ζύμη 'leaven' < *i̯ūs-meh$_2$*. For Skr. *ṣ* < *s* cf. L3.
L34: PIE *u̯* remains Skr., Gr., Lat. *u̯* and is lost in Att. Skr. *vŕ̥ṣan-* preserves the PIE accentuated syllabic resonant *r̥* in the preform *h$_2$u̯ŕ̥sen-*. Hom. ἄρσην is the unassimilated preform of Att. ἄρρην 'male'. Lat. *verrēs* 'boar' comes from *u̯ersēs*, which goes back to *u̯orsēs* and ultimately to *h$_2$u̯ŕ̥sē(n)*.

37 **L35:** Initial PIE **s* remains Skr., Lat. *s* and becomes Att. *h*. The individual developments of this word are very complex.

7. Labial and Dental Stops

Labial and dental stops correspond very exactly. The correspondences for **g* and **k* are dealt with together with the other dorsal stops starting at L48. The so-called "thorn-cluster" **tk̂* becomes Att. *kt* and is simplified differently in Skr. and Lat.

	Compared Languages			Preform and Meaning		Sound Correspondences			
	San-skrit	Attic	Latin	PIE	Meaning	Skr.	Att.	Lat.	PIE
36	*bála-*	βελτίων	*dē-**bilis***	√***bel-***	'strong'	*b*	*b*	*b*	***b***
37	*páti-*	πόσις	*potis*	**pótis*	'husband'	*p*	*p*	*p*	***p***
38	*dáma-*	δόμος	*domus*	**dóm*(h_2)*os*	'house'	*d*	*d*	*d*	***d***
39	*stánati*	στένω	~*tonāre*	*(*s*)*ténh*$_2$-*ō*	'I thunder'	*t*	*t*	*t*	***t***
40	*kṣeti*	κτίζω	*situs*	√***tk̂ei̯-***	'to settle'	*kṣ*	*kt*	*s*	***tk̂***

L36: PIE **b* remains *b* in all three languages. Correspondences which support the reconstruction of PIE **b* are very rare. Skr. *bála-* nt. 'strength', Att. βελτίων 'stronger', Lat. *dēbilis* 'weak' with vowel weakening **dēbelis* > *dēbilis*.
L37: PIE **p* remains *p* in all three languages. Skr. *páti-* 'husband', Att. πόσις 'husband', Lat. *potis* 'able, capable'. The Lat. syntagm *potis est* 'is capable' resulted in the verb *posse* 'can, be able to'. For τι > σι cf. SC x22.1.
L38: PIE **d* remains *d* in all three languages.
L39: PIE **t* remains *t* in all three languages. Skr. *stánati* 'he thunders', Att. στένω 'I moan, I groan', Lat. *tōnāre* 'to thunder'. The phenomenon that languages sometimes exhibit an initial *s* is known as "*s*-mobile".
L40: This line gives an example for the correspondences of the so-called "thorn-cluster" whose name stems from the hypothesis that PIE **t* had an allophone [θ] next to velar stops. This assumption gives an better explanation of the Skr. development **tk̂* > **θk̂* > **k̂θ* > **k̂s* > *kṣ*. Thorn is the name of the old Germanic þ-rune, which can phonetically be interpreted as [θ]. In Gr., metathesis of **tk* > *kt* according to SC 42.1. Lat. *situs* 'situated' exhibits the strongest simplification of the sequence **tk* > *s*.

8. Voiced Aspirated Stops (Mediae Aspiratae)

The PIE voiced aspirated stops usually remained in Skr. if they were not deaspirated due to Grassmann's law. In all Greek dialects, the PIE voiced aspirated stops were devoiced and became Tenuis Aspiratae. Latin exhibits voiceless correspondences in the initial position and voiced correspondences in the medial position. PIE *d^h is continued as Latin *f*.

	Compared Languages			Preform and Meaning		Sound Correspondences			
	Sanskrit	**Attic**	**Latin**	**PIE**	**Meaning**	**Skr.**	**Att.**	**Lat.**	**PIE**
41	~babhrú-	φρῦνος	~fiber	*b^{h}rūnos	'brown animal'	b	p^h	f	*b^h
42	babhrú-	(φρῦνος)	fiber	*b^{h}eb^{h}ro/us-	'brown animal'	b	(p^h)	b	*b^h
43	~dádhāti	τίθησι	~fēcī	*d^{h}i-d^{h}eh$_1$-mi	'to set'	d^h	t^h	f	*d^h
44	édhas-	αἶθος	~aedēs	*h$_2$éi̯d^h-os	'burning'	d^h	*t^h	d	*d^h
45	~ū́dhar-	οὖθαρ	ūber	*Hóu̯d^{h}r̥	'udder'	d^h	t^h	b	*d^h
46	~saṃ-díh-	τεῖχος	~fingō	*d^{h}éi̯ĝ^{h}os	'wall'	h	k^h	g	*ĝ^h
47	śaṅkhá-	κόγχος	(congius)	*k̂onk^{h}os	'shell'	k^h	k^h	-	*k^h

L41/42: PIE *b^h remains Skr. *bh*, becomes Gr. p^h and results in Lat. *f* in the medial position. The unreduplicated formation Gr. φρῦνος < *b^{h}rūnos is related to the English word *brown*. Grassmann's law in Skr. *babhrú-* 'brown' < *b^{h}e-b^{h}rú-. For *-er* < *-ro* in Lat. *fiber* < *b^{h}e-b^{h}ró-s cf. L48. PIE *b^h becomes Lat. *b* in the medial position.
L43: PIE *d^h remains Skr. d^h, becomes Gr. p^h and results in Lat. *f* in the initial position. Skr. *dádhāti* < *dé-d^{h}eh$_1$-ti and Att. τίθησι < *d^{h}i-d^{h}eh$_1$-ti exhibit Grassmann's law (cf. chap. 22). Lat. *fēcī* < *d^{h}ē-k-ī is an unreduplicated formation. The origin of the element *k* has not been found.
L44: PIE *d^h remains Skr. d^h, becomes Gr. t^h and results in Lat. *d* in the medial position (cf. L13).
L45: PIE *d^h remains Skr. d^h, becomes Gr. t^h and results in Lat. *b* in the medial position next to *u̯*. PIE *d^h and *b^h merge in Latin *b* next to *u*. Att. οὖθαρ [ūt^{h}ar] and Lat. *ūber* go back to *(H)ou̯d^{h}r̥ via the development *ou̯ > ǭ > ū (cf. L18). Skr. *ū́dhar* goes back to *(H)uHd^{h}er but the details of the ablaut behavior of this word are very complicated.
L46: PIE *ĝ^h results in Skr. *h*, Gr. k^h and Lat. *g* in the medial position. Skr. (*saṃ*)-*díh-* 'wall' orginated from *d^{h}iĝ^h- > *dhih- > *dih-* through Grassmann's law. Att. τεῖχος 'wall' orginated from *d^{h}ei̯ĝ^{h}os > (x1.2) *d^{h}ei̯g^{h}os > (x9) *t^{h}ei̯k^{h}os > (39.10) *tei̯k^{h}os > (14.2) τεῖχος [tẹ̄k^{h}os] also through Grassmann's law and *ei̯* > *ẹ̄*. In this case, ει goes back to an original diphthong *ei̯*. In Lat. *fingō* 'I form', PIE *ĝ^h remained after nasal as *g*. For lat. *f* < *d^h cf. L43.
L47: Skr. *śaṅkhá-* 'seashell' corresponds exactly to Att. κόγχος 'seashell' so that both forms go back to the reconstruction *k̂onk^{h}os with tenuis aspirata *k^h. Lat *congius* 'an ancient liquid measure' seems to be a borrowing from Att. κόγχος and is therefore not relevant for the reconstruction. Based mainly on the Sanskrit phoneme system of Sanskrit, IE studies in its early days reconstructed tenuis aspiratae for PIE, which was mainly based on the Sanskrit phoneme system which has tenuis aspiratae. This is not done anymore except for forms like *k̂onk^{h}os in which tenuis aspiratae must be reconstructed. In many cases, aspirated voiceless stops in Skr. are nowadays explained through secondary developments such as the aspiration through laryngeal *h$_2$ (cf. L2/3/22). Words with voiceless aspirated stops such as *kak^h- > καχ-άζω 'I laugh', which is related to Skr. *kákhati* and Lat. *cachinnō* and, are mostly onomatopoetic formations and therefore not relevant for reconstruction because onomatopoetic formations often resemble each other due to iconicity. Other cases such as σφαραγέομαι 'I hiss' and Skr. *sphū́rjati* 'I roar', which hint to a common root *sp^{h}erh$_2$g-, as well as Gr. σφάλλω 'I let fall' and Skr. *skhalate* 'I stumble', which hint to a root *sk^{wh}al-, can be explained by assuming an assimilation of voice through initial *s, which enables to reconstruct original voiced aspirated stops for the relevant rules. This assimilation is known as Siebs' law and enables to trace the mentioned roots *sp^{h}erh$_2$g- and *sk^{wh}al- back to *(s)b^{h}erh$_2$g- and *(s)g^{wh}al-.

	Compared Languages			Preform and Meaning		Sound Correspondences			
	Sanskrit	**Attic**	**Latin**	**PIE**	**Meaning**	**Skr.**	**Att.**	**Lat.**	**PIE**
48	*~káp̥rth-*	κάπρος	*caper*	***kápros*	'male animal'	*k*	*k*	*k*	***k**
49	*~kaví-*	κοέω	*~caueō*	**(s)kéu̯h$_1$-ō*	'to look'	*k*	*k*	*k*	***k**
50	*kákṣā-*	-	*coxa*	***kókseh$_2$*	'curve'	*k*	-	*k*	***k**
51	*yugá-*	ζυγόν	*iugum*	**i̯ugóm*	'yoke'	*g*	*g*	*g*	***g**
52	*árśas-*	ἕλκος	*ulcus*	**h$_1$él**k̂**os*	'wound'	*ʃ*	*k*	*k*	***k̂**
53	*śáṃsati*	Κασσ-άν-δρα	*cēnseō*	√***k̂eNs-*	'to proclaim'	*ʃ*	*k*	*k*	***k̂**
54	*~jóṣa-*	γεύω	*~gustō*	***ĝéu̯s-ō*	'to try'	*ʤ*	*g*	*g*	***ĝ**
55	*~jñāti*	γιγνώσκω	*~(g)nōscō*	***ĝi-ĝnéh$_3$-sk̂-ō*	'to know'	*ʤ*	*g*	*g*	***ĝ**

L48: PIE **k* remains *k* in all three languages. Skr. *káp̥rth-* 'penis' has a *th*-enlargement, Att. κάπρος 'boar', Lat. *caper* 'he-goat'. The reconstruction **kápros* 'male animal' subsumes the meanings of the individual languages. In Lat., loss of the final syllable through syncope which led to the formation of syllabic *r̥* which was resolved to *-er*: **kápros* > **kapr̥s* > **kápers*. The sequence *-rs* subsequently assimilated to *-rr* and simplified to *-r*: **kápers* > **káperr* > Lat. *caper*.
L49: PIE **k* remains *k* in all three languages. Skr. *kaví-* 'wise, poet, visionary', Att. κοέω 'I perceive' < *κοϝέω, Lat. *caveō* 'I beware'. For the loss of intervocalic **u̯* in Att. cf. SC x21.2.
L50: PIE **k* remains *k* in all three languages. Skr. *kákṣā* 'armpit', Lat. *coxa* 'hipbone', no Att. cognate form. The meaning 'bending, curvature' of PIE **kókseh$_2$* was applied to the upper extremities in Skr. and to the lower extremeties in Lat.
L51: PIE **g* remains *g* in all three languages. All words share the meaning 'yoke' and are exact phonological cognates. Due to the Att. development, an initial laryngeal is reconstructed (cf. L33, chap. 27).
L52: PIE **k̂* results in Att., Lat. *k* and becomes Skr. *ʃ* which was spelled <ś>. Skr. *árśas-* 'haemorrhoids', Att. ἕλκος 'wound', Lat. *ulcus* 'ulcer' go back to PIE **h$_1$élk̂os* whose initial laryngeal was lost without a trace. For Skr. **l* > *r* cf. L31. The Att. aspiration is secondary and probably in analogy to ἕλκω 'I drag'. In Lat. *ulcus* [uɫkus], the lateral /l/ of the preform **élkos* was allophonically articulated as velar [ɫ] which caused initial **e* to become first *o* and then *u*.
L53: PIE **k̂* results in Att., Lat. *k* and becomes Skr. *ʃ* which was spelled <ś>. Skr. *śáṃsati* 'he praises, he proclaims', Lat. *cēnseō* 'I suppose, I think'. The nasal of the root cannot be determined with certainty is is therefore reconstructed as *N*. Zero-grade in Att. **k̂n̥s-* > κασ-.
L54: PIE **ĝ* results in Att., Lat. *g* and becomes Skr. *ʤ* which is transcribed <j>. Skr. *jóṣa-* 'liking, pleasure' < **ĝéu̯so-*, Att. γεύω 'I taste' < *γεύσω, Lat. *gustō* 'I taste' is a derivation of the zero-grade **ĝus-* in **ĝus-tó-* > **gusto-*. In Skr., **ĝ* became *ʤ* and **s* became *ṣ* according to the *ruki*-rule before **e* and **o* became **a* and **au̯* became *ō*: **ĝéu̯so-* > **ʤéu̯so-* > **ʤéu̯ṣo-* > **ʤáu̯ṣa-* > Skr. *jóṣa-* [ʤóṣa].
L55: PIE **ĝ* results in Att., Lat. *g* and becomes Skr. *ʤ* which is transcribed <j>. Skr. *jñāti* < *ĝnéh$_3$ti*, Att. γιγνώσκω < **ĝi-ĝnéh$_3$-sk̂-ō* is a reduplicated formation with the suffix *-sk̂-* which is also found in Old Latin *gnōscō*. Classical Lat. exhibits the loss of the initial *g* in *nōscō*.

9.2 Labiovelars

PIE had velar stops which were articulated with the additional feature of lip rounding which was the reason for their naming as labiovelars. In the so-called satem-languages (cf. part 9.3), the feature of lip rounding was lost completely. The labiovelars are preserved in Myc., Arc. and Cyp. as individual phonemes with individual spelling. Dialectal differences such as Att. θήρ ~ Aeol. φήρ or Att. δελφῡς ~ Aeol. βελφῡς also rely on different developments of the labiovelars (cf. chap. 30).

	Compared Languages			Preform and Meaning		Sound Correspondences			
	Sanskrit	**Att.**	**Latin**	**PIE**	**Meaning**	**Skr.**	**Att.**	**Lat.**	**PIE**
56	*riṇákti*	λείπω	*re-lin**qu**ō*	**lei̯**k**^{w}-*	‘to leave’	*k*	*p*	*ku̯*	****k**^{w}
57	*vṛ́**k**a-*	λύκος	*(lupus)*	**u̯ĺ̥**k**^{w}os*	‘wolf’	*k*	*k*	*(p)*	****k**^{w}
58	*pa**k**vá-*	πεπτός	*co**c**tus*	**pe**k**^{w}-to/u̯o-*	‘cooked, ripe’	*k*	*t*	*k*	****k**^{w}
59	*pá**ñc**a*	πέντε	*quī**nqu**e*	**pén**k**^{w}e*	‘five’	*ʧ*	*t*	*ku̯*	****k**^{w}
60	***g**atá-*	βατός	***v**entus*	*****g**^{w}m̥tós*	‘come’	*g*	*b*	*u̯*	****g**^{w}
61	***j**īvá-*	~βίος	***v**īvus*	*****g**^{w}iHu̯ós*	‘life’	*ʤ*	*b*	*u̯*	****g**^{w}
62	*tyá**j**ati*	σέβομαι	-	**ti̯e**g**^{w}-*	‘to withdraw’	*ʤ*	*b*	-	****g**^{w}
63	*~u**k**ṣáti*	ὑγρός	*~ū**v**idus*	**ú**g**^{w}-ro-s*	‘to moisten‘	*k*	*g*	*u̯*	****g**^{w}
64	*ó**h**ate*	εὔχομαι	*vo**v**ēre*	**h$_1$u̯e**g**^{wh}-*	‘to utter’	*h*	*k^h*	*u̯*	****g**^{wh}
65	*á**h**i-*	ὄφις	*(an**gu**is)*	**h$_3$e**g**^{wh}is*	‘snake’	*h*	*p^h*	*gu*	****g**^{wh}
66	*ra**gh**ú-*	ἐλαχύς	*le**v**is*	**h$_1$ln̥**g**^{wh}us*	‘light, few’	*gh*	*k^h*	*u̯*	****g**^{wh}
67	*á**śv**a-*	ἵππος	*e**qu**us*	**h$_1$e**k̂u̯**os*	‘horse’	*ʃu̯*	*p(p)*	*ku̯*	****k̂u̯***
68	*~**hv**árate*	θήρ	*~**f**erus*	*****ĝ**^{h}**u̯**ér-s*	‘wild animal’	*h*	*t^h*	*f*	****ĝ**^{h}**u̯***

L56: PIE **k*^{w} results in Skr. *k*, Att. *p* before *o* and remains after as Lat. *ku̯* after a nasal consonant. Skr. *riṇákti* < **linék*^{w}*ti* and Lat. *re-linquō* are nasal-infix formations. Skr. *ṇ* is due to the preceding *r*. Att. λείπω < **léi̯k*^{w}*ō*. Analogical levelling of the other forms of the paradigm e.g. in the 3. sg. λείπει instead of regular λείτει* (cf. chap. 36).

L57: PIE **k*^{w} results in Skr., Att. *k*. The Attic result is due to delabialization next to *u*. For Skr. *ṛ* < **l̥* cf. L21. Metathesis of **u̯r̥* > *lu* in Lat. and Gr. Lat. *lupus* is a borrowing from the Sabellic languages in which **k*^{w} is regularly continued as *p*. In Lat. *vulpēs* ‘fox’, the PIE initial sequence was retained without metathesis.

L58: PIE **k*^{w} results in Skr. *k*, Lat. *k* before consonant, and Gr. *p* before consonant. Att. πεπτός comes from **pek*^{w}*tós* and is derived from the root **pek*^{w}- ‘to cook, to ripe’ which is also the derivation base of **pék*^{w}*i̯ō* > (x11.1) > *πέκι̯ω > (x19.4) πέσσω ‘koche’. In Lat.. the labial element of the labiovelar was lost before a consonant.

L59: PIE **k*^{w} remains in Lat. *ku̯* and results in Att. *t* before *e*. In Skr., delabialization of **k*^{w} > *k* with subsequent secondary palatalization *k* > *ʧ*. In Lat., the initial **p* of the preform **peŋk*^{w}*e* assimilated to **k*^{w}*eŋk*^{w}*e* which resulted in *quīnque*, before vowel raising *e* > *i* and lengthening *i* > *ī* before *ŋ* took place **k*^{w}*eŋk*^{w}*e* > **k*^{w}*iŋk*^{w}*e*.

L60: PIE **g*^{w} results in Skr. *g*, Att. *b* before *a* and Lat. *v* in the initial position. The syllabic resonant **n̥* resulted in Skr. and Att. *a* as well as Lat. *en* (cf. L19). Loss of initial *g* before *u̯* in Lat.: **gu̯entus* > *u̯entus*.

L61: PIE **g*^{w} results in Skr. *g* which was palatalized to *ʤ*. PIE **g*^{w} results in Att. *b* before *i* and Lat. v in the initial position. The sequence**iH* results in *ī* which was continued in Skr. and Lat., and was shortened in Att. before a vowel following.

L62: PIE **g*^{w} results in Skr. *g* which was palatalized to *ʤ*. PIE **g*^{w} results in Att. *b* before *o*. In σέβομαι ‘I respect’, initial **ti̯* is continued as *s*. No cognate form in Lat.

L63: PIE *g^w results in Skr. *g* which was devoiced to *k* before *s*. PIE *g^w results in Gr. *g* next to *u*, and intervocalic Lat. *v*. Skr. *ukṣáti* 'makes wet' < *ug^w*séti* from the root *$\underset{\frown}{u}eg^w$-. Retroflex *ṣ* according to the ruki-rule (cf. L12). Att. ὑγρός 'wet' < *ug^w*rós*.
L64: PIE *g^{wh} results at first in Skr. *gh* before it was palatalized to *h*. PIE *g^{wh} became Proto-Greek *k^{wh} which became k^h in the position next to *u*. The Lat. correspondence is intervocalic *v*.
L65: PIE *g^{wh} results at first in Skr. *gh* before it was palatalized to *h*. PIE *g^{wh} became Att. p^h before *i*, and resultes in Lat. *gu̯* after a nasal consonant. Lat. *anguis* continued probably the formation *$h_2eng^{wh}is$ derived from a similar but not the same root. Gr. *o* < *h_3o through laryngeal coloring.
L66: PIE *g^{wh} results in Skr. *gh*, Proto-Greek *k^{wh} which results in Gr. k^h next to *u*, as well as Lat. *v* between vowels. Fr Skr. *r* < **l* cf. L31. For Skr., Att. *a* < *n̥ cf. L20. For Skr. *raghú-* 'light' and Att. ἐλαχύς 'little' cf. L20. Att. initial ε may continue a PIE laryngeal. (cf. chap. 16/34). If Lat. *levis* belongs etymologically to the same root, the medial nasal is absent.
L67: In Lat. and Att., **k̂u̯* developed exactly like *k^w but in Skr. the difference can be seen because **k̂* is continued as *ś* (cf. L52–53). Initial Att. *hi* has not been explained satisfactory. Initial *i* is already attested in Myc. *i-qo*. Medial *pp* could be the regular outcome of **k̂u̯*.
L68: Skr. *hvárate* 'walks crookedly' < *$\hat{g}^h$*u̯éreti* is connected with θήρ/φήρ 'animal' and Lat. *ferus* 'wild' because animals walk crookedly compared to humans.

9.3 Centum-Languages and Satem-Languages

Due to the word correspondences of L49, L52 and L56, three series of dorsal stops must be reconstructed for PIE: velar, palatal and labiovelar stops. Otherwise, it is not possible to connect all the correspondences.

	Compared Languages			**Preform and Meaning**		**Sound Correspondences**			
	Sanskrit	**Att.**	**Latin**	**PIE**	**Meaning**	**Skr.**	**Att.**	**Lat.**	**PIE**
=49	*kaví-*	κοέω	*caueō*	*(s)**k**eu̯h_1-	'to look'	*k*	*k*	*k*	***k**
=52	*árśas-*	ἕλκος	*ulcus*	*h_1*él**k̂**os*	'wound'	*ʃ*	*k*	*k*	***k̂**
=56	*riṇákti*	λείπω	*re-lin**qu**ō*	**lei̯**k^w-	'to leave'	*k*	*p*	*ku̯*	*k^w

The individual IE languages, however, always have only two series of dorsal stops. The so called centum-languages share the same reflex of the velar and palatal series, whereas the so called satem-languages share the same reflex of the velar and labiovelar series, due to the loss of the labial element of the labiovelars. In the satem-languages, the palatal series develops further to *s*-like sibilants or affricates, although divergences to this pattern are found in Slavic and Baltic. The Anatolian language Luwian, which normally would be expected to be classified as a centum-language, even seems to have reflexes of all three series of stops. The examples used for the argumentation are, however, disputed because of alternative etymologies or scant attestation of the words.

10. The laryngeals

The Anatolian language Hittite is attested from 1700 BC on and is therefore the oldest attested IE language. In some positions, Hittite has an aspirate sound *ḫ* which the other IE languages do not have anymore. Therefore, one can assume at least one phoneme in an older state of language, which was lost on the way to the other languages Sanskrit, Greek and Latin. Due to different structural arguments, historical linguistics nowadays normally assumes three of those phonemes, which are called laryngeals and reconstructed for PIE. The exact phonetic value of these laryngeals is unknown.

	Compared Languages				Preform and Meaning		Sound Correspondences				
	Hitt.	**Skr.**	**Att.**	**Lat.**	**PIE**	**Meaning**	**Hitt.**	**Skr.**	**Att.**	**Lat.**	**PIE**
69	***ḫant-***	***anti***	ἀντί	***ante***	****h**$_2$**é**nti*	'at the front'	*ha*	*a*	*a*	*a*	*$^*h_2e$*
70	*pa**ḫ**s-*	***pā-***	-	***pā**stor*	**pe**h**$_2$-(s)-*	'to guard'	*ah*	*ā*	-	*ā*	*$^*eh_2$*
71	***ḫau̯i***	***ávi-***	ὄις	*ovis*	****h**$_2$**ó**u̯is*	'sheep'	*ha*	*a*	*o*	*o*	*$^*h_2o$*

L69: The Hittite word means 'frontside' and reveals the other language forms to be an old locative with the meaning 'at the frontside', which semantically developed to 'in front of'. PIE *$^*h_2$* caused the coloring of PIE **e* to **a*. The laryngeal, which can be still seen in Hittite, was lost afterwards. L**70**: PIE *$^*h_2$* caused the 'coloring' of */e/ to */a/. The larygeal was lost afterwards and caused a compensatory lengthening of the preceding vowel. **L71**: *$^*h_2$* did not alter **o* because the laryngeals only affected PIE **e*. Intervocalic **u̯* was lost in Greek.

	Compared Languages			Preform and Meaning		Sound Correspondences			
	Skr.	**Att.**	**Latin**	**PIE**	**Meaning**	**Skr.**	**Att.**	**Lat.**	**PIE**
72	*hitá-*	θετός	*factus*	*$^*d^h$**h**$_1$tós*	PPP 'done'	*i*	*e*	*a*	***$^*h_1$***
73	*~ ániti*	ἄνεμος	*animus*	*$^*h_2$énh$_1$mos*	'wind'	*i*	*e*	*i*	***$^*h_1$***
74	*sthitá-*	στατός	*status*	**st**h**$_2$tós*	PPP 'put'	*i*	*a*	*a*	***$^*h_2$***
75	*ditá-*	δοτός	*datus*	**d**h**$_3$tos*	PPP 'given'	*i*	*o*	*a*	***$^*h_3$***

L72: Between consonants, all laryngeals are continued as Skr. *i* and Lat. *a*. The Greek vowel color, however, depends on the kind of the laryngeal. In this case, PIE *$^*d^h$* is continued as Skr. *h* (cf. L43/44). The PPP *$^*d^hh_1tós$* from the verbal root *$^*d^heh_1$-* 'to put' is not continued regularly as Lat. *fatus** but was remodeled to *factus* in analogy to *facere* which exhibits a *k*-extension. **L73**: The verbal formation Skr. *aniti* 'he breathes' goes back to *$^*h_2enh_1ti$*. Lat. *animus* < **anamos* exhibits weakening of interior syllables whereas Oscan *anams* retaines Proto-Italic **a*. **L74**: In Skr., aspiration of **t* through *$^*h_2$*. **L75**: Cf. L72.

RECONSTRUCTION

Key to Exercises

Chapter 2: Spelling and Transcription

E1 Easy Transcriptions

A λόγος [lógos] 'word' **B** πόνος [pónos] 'effort' **C** τόνος [tónos] 'tension' **D** κλΐνω [klī́nǭ] 'I lean' **E** κλέπτω [kléptǭ] 'I steal' **F** μῑκρός [mīkrós] 'small'

E2 Transcription of φ, θ, χ as [p^h], [t^h], [k^h]

A τίθημι [tít^{h}ę̄mi] 'I put' **B** φημί [p^{h}ę̄mí] 'I say' **C** χώρᾱ [k^{h}ǭ́rā] 'space' **D** συμφορά́ [symp^{h}orā́] 'occurence' **E** συχνός [syk^{h}nós] 'frequently' **F** λόχος [lók^{h}os] 'ambush'

E3 Transcription of ι and υ as [i̯] and [u̯] in Diphthongs

A καυλός [kau̯lós] 'stalk' **B** αἱρέω [hai̯réǭ] 'I take' **C** σπεύδω [spéu̯dǭ] 'I hurry up'

E4 Transcription of ψ, ξ, ζ as [ps], [ks], [zd]

A ξένος [ksénos] 'foreigner' **B** ξύλον [ksýlon] 'wood' **C** ψεύδειν [pséu̯dẹ̄n] 'I lie' **D** ψυχή [psyk^{h}ę̄́] 'soul' **E** ψέγειν [pségẹ̄n] 'to criticize' **F** νίζω [nízdǭ] 'I wash'

E5 Transcription of Inital ῥ as [r^h]. Transcription of Iota-Subscript as [i̯]:

A ῥῆμα [r^{h}ę̄̂ma] 'word' **B** ῥίπτειν [r^{h}íptẹ̄n] 'to throw' **C** ῥήτωρ [r^{h}ę̄́tǭr] 'speaker' **D** dat. λόγῳ [lógǭi̯] 'word' **E** dat. τῑμῇ [tīmę̄̂i̯] 'honor' **F** dat. θεᾷ [t^{h}eā̂i̯] 'goddess'

E6 Transcription of γ [ŋ] Before γ, κ, χ, μ, ν

A ἄγγελος [áŋgelos] 'messenger' **B** ἀγμός [aŋmós] 'abyss' **C** ὄγμος [óŋmos] 'furrow'

E7 The Symbols *ϝ and *ϳ Can Be Used for [u̯] and [i̯]:

A *κλέϝος [kléu̯os] 'honor' **B** *ὄϝις [óu̯is] 'sheep' **C** *καλϝός [kalu̯ós] 'beautiful' **D** *τένι̯ω [téni̯ǭ] 'I stretch' **E** *μάνι̯ω [máni̯ǭ] 'I am furious' **F** *δαι̯ϝήρ [dai̯u̯ę̄́r] 'brother-in-law'

Chapter 4: Defining Attic Consonant and Vowel Phonemes

Consonant Phonemes

Opposition	Minimal Pairs
p :: *b*	πάθος 'misery' :: βάθος 'depth'
p :: *t*	ἔπος 'word' :: ἔτος 'year'
p :: *m*	ὕπνος 'sleep' :: ὕμνος 'song'
p :: *h*	πόλος 'pole' :: ὅλος 'whole'
p^h :: *k^h*	φόρτος 'burden' :: χόρτος 'fodder'
p^h :: *m*	τρέφω 'I nourish' :: τρέμω 'I tremble'
b :: *d*	βόλος 'throw' :: δόλος 'trick'
b :: *m*	βαίνω 'I go' :: μαίνω 'I am furious'
t :: *k*	τέρας 'omen' :: κέρας 'horn'
n :: *m*	τόνος 'tension' :: τόμος 'a piece cut off'
n :: *l*	νεώς 'temple' :: λεώς 'people'
r :: *l*	ῥύμη 'force' :: λύμη 'insult'
s :: *l*	πόσις 'husband' :: πόλις 'city'
s :: *t*	σορός 'urn' :: τορός 'piercing'
s :: *d*	σῶμα 'body' :: δῶμα 'house'

Vowel Phonemes

Opposition	Minimal Pairs
a :: *ā*	ἄκων 'spear' :: ἄκων 'involuntary'
a :: *e*	δασμός 'Steuer' :: δεσμός 'Fessel'
a :: *o*	ἄχος 'pain' :: ὄχος 'carriage'
ā :: *ę̄*	acc. pl. νίκᾱς 'victories' :: gen. sg. νίκης 'of the victory'
ā :: *ǭ*	inf. prs. νικᾶν 'to win' :: ptc. prs. νικῶν 'winning'
e :: *ę̄*	λέγω 'I speak' :: λήγω 'I stop'
e :: *ẹ̄*	1. pl. prs. ἔχομεν 'we have' :: 1. pl. ipf. εἴχομεν 'we had'
e :: *o*	λέχος 'bed' :: λόχος 'hideout'
e :: *i*	3. sg. imp. ἔστω 'he shall be' :: 3. sg. imp. ἴστω 'he shall know'
ę̄ :: *ẹ̄*	λύπη 'a mourning' :: λύπει 'mourn!'
ę̄ :: *ǭ*	ἦμος 'when' :: ὦμος 'shoulder'
ẹ̄ :: *ū*	inf. prs. λῡπεῖν 'to mourn' :: ptc. prs. nt. λῡποῦν 'mourning'
i :: *u*	πίστις 'trust' :: πύστις 'investigation'
i :: *ī*	1. pl. prs. ἱκετεύομεν 'we beg' :: 1. pl. ipf. ῑ̔κετεύομεν 'we begged'
o :: *u*	τόκος 'birth' :: τύκος 'mallet'

Chapter 6: Exercises of Chapters 5 and 6

E1 Complete the Feature Structures of the Following Sounds:

r^h [trill, aspirated, alveolar]

n [nasal, voiced, alveolar]

h [glottal, fricative]

i [close, unrounded, front, short]

y [close, rounded, front, short]

ę [open-mid, unrounded, front]

ẹ [close-mid, unrounded, front]

ǫ [open-mid, rounded, back]

ȳ [close, rounded, front, long]

E2 Which Feature Separates the Following Minimal Pairs?

p ~ p^h : Aspiration   ŋ ~ n : Place of Articulation

g ~ k : Voice   r ~ r^h : Aspiration / Voice

E3 Complete the Binary Features of the Following Consonants

	Labial				Alveolar								Velar				Glottal
	p	**p^h**	**b**	**m**	**s**	**t**	**t^h**	**d**	**n**	**l**	**r**	**[r^h]**	**k**	**k^h**	**g**	**[ŋ]**	**h**
Stop	+	+	+	-	-	+	+	+	-	-	-	-	+	+	+	-	-
Nasal	-	-	-	+	-	-	-	-	+	-	-	-	-	-	-	+	-
Fricative	-	-	-	-	+	-	-	-	-	-	-	-	-	-	-	-	+
Lateral	-	-	-	-	-	-	-	-	-	+	-	-	-	-	-	-	-
Voiced	-	-	+	+	-	-	-	+	+	+	+	-	-	-	+	+	-
Aspirated	-	+	-	-	-	-	+	-	-	-	-	+	-	+	-	-	+
Approximant	-	-	-	-	-	-	-	-	-	-	-	-	-	-	-	-	-
Trill	-	-	-	-	-	-	-	-	-	-	+	+	-	-	-	-	-

Chapter 7: Methodology of Historical Comparative Linguistics

E1 Complete the Missing Formula or Description:

SC	Formula		Description
25.3	*p^h > p / _m*	*φμ > πμ	*p^h* becomes *p* before *m*.
29.2	*b > p / _t*	*βτ > πτ	*b* becomes *p* before *t*.
31.1	*p > b / _m*	*πμ > βμ	*p* becomes *b* before *m*.
32.2	*b > m / _m*	*βμ > μμ	*b* becomes *m* before *m*.
35.1	*n > r / _r*	νϱ > ϱϱ	*n* becomes *r* before *r*.
35.2	**u̯ > r / _r*	*ϝϱ > ϱϱ	**u̯* becomes *r* before *r*.
42.1	**tk > kt*	*τκ > κτ	**tk* becomes *kt*.
47.4	*Ø > b / m_l*	*μλ > μβλ	*b* is inserted between *m* and *l*.
x16.1	**i̯ > Ø / V_V*	*ι̯ > Ø / V_V	**i̯* is lost between vowels.

E2 Fill in the Sound Change Formula According to the Sound Change Number:

A *πάλϝᾱ > (13) *πάλϝη > (x21.3) πάλη 'flour'

*πάλϝᾱ > (*ā > e*) *πάλϝη > (**u̯ > Ø / C_*) πάλη 'flour'

B **ág^{w}nos* > (x24.3) *ἄβνος > (32.1) ἄμνος 'lamb'

**ág^{w}nos* > (**g^w > b / _C*) *ἄβνος > (*b > m / _n*) ἄμνος 'lamb'

C *Δι̯ηύς > (1.3) *Δι̯εύς > (x18.2) Ζεύς 'Zeus'

*Δι̯ηύς > (*V̄ > V̆ / _RC*) *Δι̯εύς > (**di̯ > zd*) Ζεύς 'Zeus'

E3 Complete the Gap:

A ἁγνός 'holy' :: prs. *ἅγι̯ω > (x18.1) ἅζω 'I revere'

B λέγω 'I speak' :: perf. *λέλεγται > (29.10) λέλεκται 'has spoken'

C κῆρυξ, κήρυκος 'herald' :: aor. pass. *ἐκηρύκθη > (26.3) ἐκηρύχθη 'was proclaimed'

D φλέγω 'I burn' :: nom. sg. *φλόγ-ς > (29.9) φλόξ 'flame'

Chapter 8: Accentuation of Attic Words

E1 Fill in the Table:

	Antepenultimate Syllable	Penultimate Syllable	Last Syllable
Oxytona			θήρ / κρατήρ / ἀνήρ
Paroxytona		ῥήτωρ / θυγάτηρ / δαίμων	
Proparoxytona	φερόμενος / θήρατρον		
Perispomena			ἰχθῦς / Περικλῆς / ναῦς
Properispomena		δοῦλος / δῶρον / πτῶμα	

KEY

E2 Accentuate the Word Forms:

Nominative	δοῦλος	δῆμος	δῶρον	πόλεμος	ἄνθρωπος	υἱός
Genitive	δούλου	δήμου	δώρου	πολέμου	ἀνθρώπου	υἱοῦ
Dative	δούλῳ	δήμου	δώρῳ	πολέμῳ	ἀνθρώπῳ	υἱῷ
Accusative	δοῦλον	δῆμου	δῶρον	πόλεμος	ἄνθρωπον	υἱόν

Chapter 9: Apophony in Greek

e-grade	*o*-grade	*ē*-grade	*ō*-grade	zero-grade
δέρκομαι	δέδορκα	-	-	δρακεῖν
πείθω	πέποιθα	-	-	ἔπιθον
-	κύον	-	κύων	κυνός
πατέρες	εὐπάτορες	πατήρ	ἀπάτωρ	πατράσιν
τρέπειν	τρόπος	-	τρωπάω	ἔτραπον
ἐγενόμην	γέγονα	-	-	γίγνομαι
ἔθος	-	ἦθος	εἴ-ωθα	-
εἰδέναι	οἶδα	-	-	ἰδεῖν
λείπω	λοιπός	-	-	λιπεῖν
στέλλω	στόλος	-	-	ἔσταλκα
σπεύδω	σπουδή	-	-	-
φέρω	φόρος	-	φώρ	δίφρος
πέτομαι	ποτέομαι	-	πωτήεις	πτέσθαι
τίθεμεν	-	τίθημι	-	-
ἐλεύθερος	ἐλήλουθα	-	-	ἔλυθον
φεύγω	-	-	-	φυγεῖν

Chapter 10: Vowel Shortening

E1 Vowel Before Vowel is Shortened

A aor. ἔδρᾱσα 'I did' :: prs. *δρᾱ́ω > (1.1) δράω 'I do' **B** Hom. ζωή :: *ζωή > (1.1) ζοή 'life' **C** fut. δῡ́σομαι 'I will immerse' :: *δῡ́ομαι > (1.1) δύομαι 'I immerse' **D** nom. sg. σῦς 'pig' :: gen. sg. *σῡός > (1.1) συός 'of the pig' **E** nom. sg. ἰχθῦς 'fish' :: gen. sg. *ἰχθῡ́ος > (1.1) ἰχθύος 'of the fish' **F** ναῦς 'ship' :: gen. pl. *νᾱϝῶν > (13) *νηϝῶν > (x21.2) *νηῶν > (1.1) νεῶν 'of the ships' **G** gen. pl. Hom. βασιλήων :: *βασιλήϝων > (x21.2) *βασιλήων > (1.1) βασιλέων 'of the kings' **H** Hom. αἰετός :: ᾱ̓ετός > (1.1) ἀετός 'eagle' **I** Hom. αἰεί :: ᾱ̓εί > (1.1) ἀεί 'always'

E2 Quantitative Methesis

A ἄστυ 'city' :: gen. sg. *ἄστηϝος > (x21.2) *ἄστηος > (1.2) ἄστεως 'of the city' **B** Hom. νηός :: gen. sg. *νᾱϝός > (13) *νηϝός > (x21.2) *νηός > (1.2) νεώς 'of the ship' **C** βασιλεύς 'king' :: gen. sg. βασιλῆϝος > (x21.2) Hom. βασιλῆος > (1.2) βασιλέως 'of the king'

E2 Osthoff's Law

A √βᾱ- 'to go one step' :: ptc. aor.*βᾱ́ντες > (1.3) βάντες 'going' **B** √στᾱ- 'to stand' :: ptc. aor. *στᾱ́-ντ-ες > (1.3) στάντες 'standing' **C** √φῡ- 'to become' :: ptc. aor. *φῡ́-ντ-ες > (1.3) φύντες 'being' **D** φαίνω 'I shine' :: ptc. aor. *φανή-ντ-ες > (1.3) φανέντες 'shining' **E** Ion. Πήρσαι :: *Πᾱ́ρσαι > (13) *Πήρσαι > (1.3) Πέρσαι 'Persians' **F** nom. sg. *βασιληύς > (1.3) βασιλεύς 'king' **G** Skr. *dyaús* 'sky' :: *Ζηύς > (1.3) Ζεύς 'Zeus' **H** Av. *snāvarə* :: *νηῦρον > (1.3) νεῦρον 'tendon' **I** Av. *dāiš* :: *ἔδηιξα [édēi̯ksa] > (1.3) [édei̯ksa] > (14.2) ἔδειξα [édẹ̄ksa] 'I showed'

Chapter 11: Compensatory Lengthening I

E1 Resonant plus Fricative *σ

A prs. κραίνω 'I finish' :: aor. *ἔκρανσα > (2.1) ἔκρᾱνα 'I finished' **B** prs. περαίνω 'I finish' :: *ἐπέρανσα > (2.1) ἐπέρᾱνα 'I finished' **C** καθαρός 'pure' :: *ἐκάθαρσα > (2.1) *ἐκάθᾱρα > (13) ἐκάθηρα 'I cleaned' **D** prs. γαμέω 'I marry' :: aor. *ἔγαμσα > (2.1) *ἔγᾱμα > (13) ἔγημα 'I married' **E** σφάλμα 'fall' :: *ἔσφαλσα > (2.1) *ἔσφᾱλα > (13) ἔσφηλα 'I deceived' **F** fut. κλινῶ 'I will lean' :: aor. *ἔκλινσα > (2.1) ἔκλῑνα 'I leaned' **G** prs. ἀγγέλλω 'I proclaim' :: aor. *ἤγγελσα > (2.1) ἤγγειλα 'I proclaimed' **H** fut. κρινῶ 'werde I will judge' :: aor. *ἔκρινσα > (2.1) ἔκρῑνα 'I judged' **I** fut. κτενῶ 'I will kill' :: aor. *ἔκτενσα > (2.1) ἔκτεινα 'I killed' **J** prs. δέρω 'I skin' :: aor. *ἔδερσα > (2.1) ἔδειρα 'I skinned' **K** fut. σπερῶ 'I will sow' :: aor. *ἔσπερσα > (2.1) ἔσπειρα 'I sowed' **L** fut. φθερῶ 'I will destroy' :: aor. *ἔφθερσα > (2.1) ἔφθειρα 'I destroyed'

E2 Fricative *σ plus Resonant

A κάρᾱ 'head' :: *κάρασνος > (2.2) κάρᾱνος 'chief' **B** 2. pl. ἐστέ 'you are' :: 1. sg. *ἐσμί > (2.2) εἰμί 'I am' **C** ναῦς 'ship' :: *ναύ-κρασρος > (2.2) ναύκρᾱρος 'captain' **D** κρύσταλλος 'ice' :: *κρυσμός > (2.2) κρῡμός 'frost'

E3 Loss of Resonant in the Final Position

A nom. sg. nt. μέλαν :: nom. sg. m. *μέλανς > (4.2) μέλᾱς 'black' **B** acc. pl. f. *τάνς > (4.2) τᾱ́ς 'those' **C** Lat. *sim-plex* 'simple' :: *σένς > (x13.1) *ἕνς > (4.2) εἷς 'one' **D** Skr. *mā́s-* :: *μήνς > (1.3) *μένς > (4.2) Ion. μείς 'month' **E** φίλος 'friend' :: acc. pl. *φίλονς > (4.2) *φίλο̄ς > (15) φίλους 'friends'

Chapter 12: Compensatory Lengthening II

E1 Compensatory Lengthening or Assimilation

A φόνος 'murder' :: *θένι̯ω > (3.1) θείνω 'I kill' **B** aor. ἔκτεινα 'I killed' :: prs. *κτένι̯ω > (3.1) κτείνω 'I kill' **C** ἀμεύομαι 'I cross' :: *ἀμύνι̯ω > (3.3) ἀμῡ́νω 'I repel' **D** ἡδύς :: f. sg. *ἡδέϝι̯α > (3.1) *ἡδεῖϝα > (x21.2) ἡδεῖα 'sweet' **E** aor. ἤγγειλα 'I proclaimed' :: prs. *ἀγγέλι̯ω > (36.4) ἀγγέλλω 'I proclaim' **F** perf. πέπαλμαι 'I have shaken' :: prs. *πάλι̯ω > (36.4) πάλλω 'I shake' **G** ἀγερμός 'the collecting' :: *ἀγέρι̯ω > (36.4) ἀγείρω 'I collect' **H** σπέρμα 'seed' :: prs. *σπέρι̯ω > (3.1) σπείρω 'I sow' **I** Lat. *sterilis* :: *στέρι̯α > (3.1) στεῖρα 'infertile' **J** aor. ἔβαλον 'I threw' :: prs. *βάλι̯ω > (36.4) βάλλω 'I throw'

E2 Iota-Epenthesis

A μέλαν :: f. sg. *μέλανι̯α > (x17) μέλαινα 'black' **B** aor. ἐπέρᾱνα 'I finished' :: prs. *περάνι̯ω > (x17) περαίνω 'I finish' **C** μανίᾱ 'fury' :: prs. *μάνι̯ω > (x17) μαίνω 'I am furious' **D** μαχή 'fight' :: *μάχαρι̯α > (x17) μάχαιρα 'butcher's knife' **E** χάρις 'happiness' :: *χάρι̯ω > (x17) χαίρω 'I am happy' **F** Lat. *cum* :: *κομι̯ός > (24.4) *κονι̯ός > (x17) κοινός 'together' **G** fut. κρανῶ 'I will finish' :: prs. *κράνι̯ω > (x17) κραίνω 'I finish' **H** aor. ἔκλαυσα 'I closed' :: prs. *κλάϝι̯ω > (x17) *κλάι̯ϝω > (x21.3) κλαίω 'I close' **I** Hom. δαΐς 'torch' :: *δάϝι̯ω > (x17) *δάι̯ϝω > (x21.3) δαίω 'I ignite'

E3 Compensatory Lengthening after Loss of *ν

A Att. εἵλλω :: *ϝέλνω > (5) *ϝείλω > (x21.1) Ion. εἵλω 'I urge' **B** Lesb. ὀφέλλω :: *ὀφέλνω > (5) Att.-Ion. ὀφείλω 'I must' **C** ἀολλίζω 'I gather' :: *ἀϝελνής > (5) *ἀϝειλής > (x21.2) Hom. ἀειλής [haẹ̄lḗs] > (9.1) Att. ἁλής 'gathered'

Chapter 13: Vowel Contraction I

E1 Contraction of Alike Vowels

A 3. pl. perf. Hom. βεβάᾱσι :: *βεβά-ᾱσι > (7.1) βεβᾶσι 'they have gone' **B** ποιεῖν 'to do' :: 2. pl. *ποιέ-ετε > (7.2) ποιεῖτε 'you do' **C** κέρας 'horn' :: pl. *κέρασα > (x15.1) *κέραα > (7.1) κέρᾱ 'horns' **D** ὄφις 'snake' :: *ὀφι-ίδιον > (7.4) ὀφῑ́διον 'little snake' **E** λαγώς 'rabbit' :: gen. pl. *λαγώ-ων > (7.7) λαγῶν 'of the rabbits'

E2 Contraction of Unlike Vowels

A1 θηρᾶν 'to chase' :: 1. pl. *θηρά-ομεν > (10.1) θηρῶμεν 'we chase' **A2** 3. sg. ipf. *ἐθήρα-ον > (10.1) ἐθήρων 'he chased' **A3** 3. sg. imp. *θηρα-έτω > (9.1) θηράτω 'he shall chase!' **A4** ptc. prs. m. *θηρά-ων > (10.1) θηρῶν 'chasing' **A5** ptc. prs. f. *θηρά-ǭσα > (10.1) θηρῶσα **A6** 2. pl. imp. *θηρά-ετε > (9.1) θηρᾶτε 'chase!' **B** σῦκον 'fig' :: pl. *συκέ-ᾱ > (9.2) συκῆ 'figs' **C** inf. *ῥῑγώειν > (10.2) ῥῑγῶν 'to freeze' :: 2. pl. subj. *ῥῑγώητε > (10.2) ῥῑγῶτε **D** Hom. φάος :: *φάος > (10.1) φῶς 'light' **E** ὁρᾶν 'to see' :: 3. pl. *ὁρά-ǭσι > (10.1) ὁρῶσι **F** ἐστί 'he is' :: 3. sg. ipf. *ἦ-εν > (8.2) ἦν 'he was'

E3 Contraction after Loss of *σ, *i̯ and *ϝ

A πόλις 'city' :: pl. *πόλει̯ες > (x16.1) *πόλεες > (7.1) πόλεις 'cities' **B** Hom. σάος > (10.1) Att. σῶς :: nt. pl. *σάϝα > (x21.2) *σάα > (7.1) σᾶ 'unhurt' **C** γένος 'kin' :: pl. *γένεσα > (x15.1) *γένεα > (9.2) γένη **D** κλέος 'fame' :: *κλεϝεσνός > (2.2) *κλεϝεινός > (x21.2) *κλεεινός > (7.2) κλεινός [klẹ̄nós] 'famous'

Chapter 14: Vowel Contraction II

E1 Hiatus is Resolved by Diphthongization

A ὄρος 'mountain' :: dat. sg. *ὄρεσι [óresi] > (x15.1) Hom. ὄρεϊ [órei] > (23.1) Att. ὄρει [órei̯] **B** κέρας 'horn' :: dat. sg. *κέρασι [kérasi] > (x15.1) Hom. κέραϊ [kérai] > (23.1) Att. κέραι [kérai̯] **C** Lat. *puer* :: *πάϝις [páu̯is] > (x21.2) Hom. πάϊς [páis] > (23.1) Att. παῖς [pāi̯s] 'child'

E2 Long Diphthongs

A λύω 'I release' :: 2. sg. pass. *λύεσαι [lýesai̯] > (x15.1) *λύεαι [lýeai̯] > (9.2) λύῃ [lýę̄i̯] 'you are released' **B1** ζῆν 'to live' :: 2. sg. *ζήεις [zdę̄ei̯s] > (8.2) ζῇς [zdę̄i̯s] **B2** 3. sg. *ζήει [zdę̄ei̯] > (8.2) ζῇ [zdę̄i̯] **B3** 2. sg. subj. *ζήῃς [zdÐÐi̯s] > (7.6) ζῇς [zdę̄i̯s] **C1** φιλεῖν 'to love' :: 2. sg. subj. *φιλέ-ῃς [p^hiléę̄i̯s] > (8.1) φιλῇς [p^hilę̄i̯s] **C2** 3. sg. subj. *φιλέ-ῃ [p^hiléę̄i̯] > (8.1) φιλῇ [p^hilę̄i̯] **E1** τῑμᾶν 'to revere' :: 2. pl. opt. *τῑμάοιτε > (10.1) τῑμῷτε [tīmǭi̯te] **E2** 3. sg. opt. *τῑμαοίη > (10.1) τῑμῴη [tīmǭi̯ę̄]

E3 Crasis

A τὸ ὄπισθεν > (7.3) *τǭπισθεν > (15) τοὔπισθεν **B** τὸ ὀπίσω > (7.3) *τǭπίσω > (15) τοὐπίσω **C** τὰ ἄλλα > (7.1) τἆλλα **D** ἃ ἐγώ > (9.1) ἅγώ **E** προ-έλεγον > (10.4) *πρǭλεγον > (15) προὔλεγον **F** τὸ ἐπέκεινα > (10.4) *τǭπέκεινα > (15) τοὐπέκεινα **G** τὸ ἐλάχιστον > (10.4) *τǭλάχιστον > (15) τοὐλάχιστον **H** τὸ ἔμπαλιν > (10.4) *τǭμπαλιν (15) τοὔμπαλιν **I** τὸ ἐναντίον > (10.4) τοὐναντίον **J** τὸ ἔργον > (10.4) *τǭργον (15) τοὔργον **K** τὸ ἐντεῦθεν > (10.4) *τǭντεῦθεν > (15) τοὐντεῦθεν

Chapter 16: Qualitative Vowel Changes

E1 Cowgill's Law

A Lat. *folium* :: *p^hóli̯on* > (36.4) *p^hóllon* > (11) *p^húllon* > (12.1) φύλλον 'leaf' **B** Lat. *mola* 'millstone' :: *mólā* > (11) *múlā* > (12.1) *mýlā* > (13) μύλη 'mill' **C** Skr. *nakhá-* :: gen. sg. *ónok^{wh}os* > (11) *ónuk^{wh}os* > (x10.3) *ónukhos* > (12.1) ὄνυχος 'of the nail' **D** Lat. *formīca* :: *mórmēks* > (11) *múrmēks* > (12.1) μύρμηξ 'ant' **E** Lat. *nox* :: *nók^{w}s* > (11) *núk^{w}s* > (x10.1) *núks* > (12.1) νύξ 'night' **F** *smṓnok^{wh}es* > (11) *smṓnuk^{wh}es* > (x10.3) *smṓnuk^{h}es* > (12.1) *smṓnyk^{h}es* > (x15.3) Hom. μώνυχες 'solid-hoofed'

KEY

E2 The Development *ā > ę̄

A παλῡ́νω 'to sprinkle' :: *πάλϝᾱ > (13) *πάλϝη > (x21.3) πάλη 'flour' **B** Lat. *dūdum* :: *δϝᾱ́ν > (13) *δϝήν > (x21.3) δήν 'a long time' **C** δαῆναι 'to learn' :: *δάνσος > (2.1) *δᾶνος > (13) δῆνος 'plan' **D** Skr. *tāvat-* :: *τᾱ́ϝος > (13) *τήϝος > (x21.2) *τήος > (1.2) τέως 'as long as' **E** Dor. μᾱ́τηρ :: *μᾱ́τηρ > (13) Att. μήτηρ 'mother' **F** Lat. *fārī* :: *φᾱμί > (13) φημί 'I speak' **G** aor. Dor. ἐκάθᾱρα :: *ἐκάθᾱρα > (13) Att. ἐκάθηρα 'I cleaned' **H** aor. Dor. ἐπέρᾱνα :: *ἐπέρᾱνα > (13) Att. ἐπέρηνα 'I finished' **I** Dor. διαφορᾱ́ :: *διαφορᾱ́ > (13) Ion. διαφορή 'difference' **J** Dor. σᾶμα :: *σᾶμα > (13) Att. σῆμα 'sign' **K** Arc. κόρϝᾱ :: *κόρϝᾱ > (13) *κόρϝη > (x21.3) κόρη 'girl'

E3 Intermediate Steps of the Development *ā > ę̄

A Myc. *pa-ra-wo-jo* 'two cheeks' :: *παράϝσᾱ > (2.1) *παρᾱ́ϝᾱ > (13.1) *παρǣ́ϝǣ > (x21.2) *παρǣ́ǣ > (1.1) *παρέǣ > (13.2) παρέᾱ 'cheek' **B** Dor. ἁ̄μέρᾱ :: **hāmérā* > (13.1) **hǣmérǣ* > (13.2) **hǣmérā* > (13.3) ἡμέρᾱ [hę̄mérā] 'day'

Chapter 17: Vowel Assimilation / Anaptyxis / Syncope / Hyphaeresis / Elision / Prothetic Vowels

E1 Assimilate the bold marked vowels regressively or progessively

A Skr. *jihmá-* :: *δ**α**χμ**ό**ς > (21.2) δ**ο**χμ**ό**ς 'sloping' **B** λοξός 'sloping' :: λ**ε**κ**ά**νη > (21.2) λ**α**κ**ά**νη 'bowl' **C** ψ**ε**κ**ά**ς > (21.2) ψ**α**κ**ά**ς 'drop' **D** Skr. *prathimán-* 'width' :: *πλ**ε**τ**α**μών > (21.2) Hom. πλ**α**τ**α**μών 'even place' **E** **ὀ**στ**α**φίς > (21.2) **ἀ**στ**α**φίς 'raisin' **F** ἥμ**ι**σ**υ**ς > (21.2) ἥμ**υ**σ**υ**ς 'half' **G** β**υ**βλ**ί**ον > (21.2) β**ι**βλ**ί**ον 'book' **H** Dor. κρᾱ́νᾱ :: *κρ**ᾱ́**ν**ᾱ** > (13) *κρᾱ́νη > (21.2) κρήνη 'well' **I** ἐστί 'is' :: 2. sg. imp. *ἔσθ**ι** > (21.2) ἴσθ**ι** 'be!' **J** Arc. ὀδελός :: Att. **ὀ**β**ε**λός > (21.1) **ὀ**β**ο**λος 'obol' **K** Lat. *collis* 'hill' :: *κ**ο**λ**α**φών > (21.1) κ**ο**λ**ο**φών 'summit' **L** τέμαχος 'piece' :: *τ**έ**μ**α**νος > (21.1) τέμενος 'piece of land' **M** Ion. χείλιοι :: *χέσλιοι > (2.2) *χείλιοι > (21.2) χῑ́λιοι 'thousand'

E2 Pretonic or Posttonic syncope

A οἴομαι > (16.1) οἶμαι 'I believe' **B** σκόροδον > (16.1) σκόρδον 'garlic' **C** 2. pl. imp. φέρετε > (16.1) φέρτε 'carry!' **D** πέρυσι > (16.1) πέρσι 'last year' **E** γέμω 'I am full' :: aor. *γέμετο > (16.1) *γέμτο > (24.3) Hom. γέντο 'he grasped' **F** Φερενῑ́κη > (16.2) Φερνῑ́κη 'bringing victory' **G** 2. sg. imp. *ἐλυθέ > (16.2) ἐλθέ 'come!'

E3 Add the SC-number into the brackets:

A Ἑρμῆς > (19) Ἑρεμῆς 'the God Hermes' **B** κλέος 'glory' :: *εὐκλεέος > (18) εὐκλέος 'glorious' **C** βράγχος > (19) βαράγχος 'hoarseness' **D** γοάω 'I lament' :: aor. Hom. γόεον > (18) γόον 'I lamented'

E4 Elision with Possible Aspiration of a Final Tenuis

A ἀπὸ ἐμοῦ > (17) ἀπ' ἐμοῦ **B** ἀντὶ ὧν > (17) ἀντ' ὧν > (28.2) ἀνθ' ὧν **C** ἀπὸ οὗ > (17) ἀπ' οὗ > (28.1) ἀφ' οὗ **D** ἐπὶ αὐτῷ > (17) ἐπ' αὐτῷ **E** ἐπὶ ἐμοί > (17) ἐπ' ἐμοί

Chapter 18: Assimilation of Consonants I: Voice and Aspiration

E1 Loss of the Feature Voice

A λαμβάνω 'I seize' :: *ληβ-τός > (29.2) ληπτός 'seized' **B** νίζω 'I wash' :: *νιβ-τός > (29.2) νιπτός 'washed' **C** τρῑ́βω 'I rub' :: perf. *τέτριβ-ται > (29.2) τέτριπται 'I have rubbed' **D** φλέβιον 'small vein' :: *φλέβ-ς > (29.1) φλέψ 'vein' **E** στίγμα 'stitch' :: *στιγ-τός > (29.10) στικτός 'stitched' **F** τρῑ́βω 'I rub' :: fut. *τρίβ-σω > (29.1) τρίψω 'I will rub' **G** φλέγω 'I burn' :: *φλόγ-ς > (29.9) φλόξ 'flame' **H** λήγω 'I stop' :: fut. *λήγ-σω > (29.9) λήξω 'I will stop' **I** λέγω 'I speak' :: perf. *λέλεγ-ται > (29.10) λέλεκται 'he has spoken'

E2 Assimilation of Voiceless and Voiced Consonants

A ἑπτά 'seven' :: *ἕπ-δομος > (30.1) ἕβδομος 'seventh' **B** κρύπτω 'I hide' :: *κρύφδην > (25.4) *κρύπδην > (30.1) κρύβδην 'hidden' **C** ὀκτώ 'eight' :: *ὄκ-δοος > (30.2) ὄγδοος 'eighth' **D** σπέρχω 'I urge' :: *σπέρχδην > (25.13) *σπέρκδην > (30.2) σπέργδην 'urgent'

E3 Loss or Assimilation of Aspiration

A διώκω 'I follow' :: aor. pass. *ἐδιώκ-θην > (26.3) ἐδιώχθην 'I was followed' **B** ἔχω 'I hold' :: *ἑχ-τός > (25.11) ἑκτός 'held' **C** πλέκω 'I twine' :: aor. pass. *ἐπλέκ-θην > (26.3) ἐπλέχθην 'was twined' **D** βρέχω 'I get wet' :: perf. *βέβρεχ-ται > (25.11) βέβρεκται 'he is wet' **E** τρῑ́βω 'I rub' :: aor. pass. *ἐτρῑ́β-θην > (29.3) *ἐτρῑ́πθην > (26.1) ἐτρῑ́φθην 'was rubbed' **F** διορύττω 'I dig out' :: *διῶρυχ-σ > (25.10) διώρυξ 'complete puncture' **G** τρέφω 'I nourish' :: fut. *θρέφ-σω > (25.1) θρέψω 'I will nourish' **H** prs. γράφω 'I write' :: perf. *γέγραφ-ται > (25.2) γέγραπται 'he has written' **I** εὔχομαι 'I pledge' :: fut. *εὔχ-σομαι > (25.10) εὔξομαι 'I will pledge' **J** πέμπω 'I send' :: aor. pass. *ἐπέμπ-θην > (26.1) ἐπέμφθην 'was sent' **K** κῆρυξ 'herald' :: perf. pass. *κεκήρυκ-θαι > (19.3) κεκήρυχθαι 'it has been proclaimed'

Chapter 19: Assimilation of Consonants II: Dental Sequences

E1 Simplification of Geminate σσ

A χάρις 'favor' :: dat. pl. *χάριτσιν > (33) *χάρισσιν > (45.1) χάρισιν **B** δατέομαι 'I distribute' :: fut. *δάτσομαι > (33) *δάσσομαι > (45.1) δάσομαι 'I will distribute' **C** πείθω 'I persuade' :: fut. *πείθσω > (25.6) *πείτσω > (33) *πείσσω > (45.1) πείσω 'I will persuade' **D** ἐρείδω 'I support' :: fut. *ἐρείδ-σω > (29.4) *ἐρείτσω > (33) *ἐρείσσω > (45.1) ἐρείσω 'I will support' **E** μυδάω 'I rot' :: *μύδσος > (29.4) *μύτσος > (33) *μύσσος > (45.1) μύσος 'disgust' **F** σπεύδω 'eile' :: aor. *ἔσπευδσα > (29.4) *ἔσπευτσα > (33) *ἔσπευσσα > (45.1) ἔσπευσα 'I hurried' **G** λύω 'I loosen' :: ptc. aor. f. *λύσαντι̯α > (x19.2) *λύσανσσα > (45.4) *λύσανσα > (4.1) λύσᾱσα 'loosened' **H** prs. σπένδω 'I pour' :: fut. *σπένδσω > (29.4) *σπέντσω > (33) *σπένσσω > (45.4) *σπένσω > (4.1) σπείσω 'I will pour' **I** τίθημι 'I set' :: ptc. prs. f. *τιθέντι̯α > (x19.2) *τιθένσσα > (45.4) *τιθένσα > (4.1) τιθεῖσα 'setting'

E2 Complex Development of Dental Sequences

A1 πείθω 'I persuade' :: *ἐπείθ-θην > (46.2) *ἐπείθσθην > (43.2) ἐπείσθην 'was persuaded' **A2** *πιθτός > (25.7) *πιττός > (46.1) *πιτστός > (43.1) πιστός 'faithful' **B** σκευάζω 'I equip' :: *ἐσκεύαδ-ται > (29.5) *ἐσκεύατ-ται > (46.1) *ἐσκεύατσται > (43.1) ἐσκεύασται 'he has equipped' **C** ψεύδω 'I lie' :: *ἔψευδ-ται > (29.5) *ἔψευτ-ται > (46.1) *ἔψευτσται > (43.1) ἔψευσται 'he has lied'

E3 Loss of Dental Stop Before Velar Stop

A νομίζω 'I consider' :: perf. *νενόμιδκα > (29.7) *νενόμιτκα > (44) νενόμικα 'I have considered' **B** πείθω 'I persuade' :: perf. *πέπειθ-κα > (25.8) *πέπειτ-κα > (44) πέπεικα 'I have persuaded' **C** σκευάζω 'I equip' :: perf. *ἐσκεύαδ-κα > (29.7) *ἐσκεύατ-κα > (44) ἐσπεύακα 'I have equipped'

Chapter 20: Assimilation of Consonants III: Stop Before Nasal Consonant

E1 Labial Stop before Nasal Consonant

A σέβομαι 'I revere' :: *σεβνός > (32.1) σεμνός 'revered' **B** ἔρεβος 'darkness' :: *ἐρεβνός > (32.1) ἐρεμνός 'dark' **C** φυλάττω 'I guard' :: perf. *πεφύλακ-μαι > (31.2) *πεφύλαγ-μαι > (32.5) πεφύλαγμαι [pepʰy̆laŋmai̯] 'I have guarded' **D** τρῖβω 'I rub' :: *τρῖβμα > (32.2) τρῖμμα 'master' **E** στέφανος 'garland' :: *στέφμα > (25.3) *στέπμα > (31.1) *στέβμα > (32.2) στέμμα 'band' **E** ἅπτω 'I touch' :: *ἅπμα > (31.1) *ἅβμα > (32.2) ἅμμα 'knot'

E2 Velar Stop before Nasal Consonant

A σφίγγω [spʰíŋgɔ̄] 'I string' :: perf. *ἔσφιγγμαι [éspʰiŋgmai̯] > (32.5) *ἔσφιγγμαι [éspʰiŋŋmai̯] > (45.6) ἔσφιγμαι [éspʰiŋmai̯] 'I have stringed' **B** ἐλέγχω [eléŋkʰɔ̄] 'I curse' :: perf. *ἐλήλεγχμαι [elȩ̄leŋkʰmai̯] > (25.12) *ἐλήλεγκμαι [elȩ̄leŋkmai̯] > (31.2) *ἐλήλεγγμαι [elȩ̄leŋgmai̯] > (32.5) *ἐλήλεγγμαι [elȩ̄leŋŋmai̯] > (45.6) ἐλήλεγμαι [elȩ̄leŋmai̯] 'I have cursed' **C** φθόγγος [pʰtʰóŋgos] :: *φθέγγμα [pʰtʰéŋgma] > (32.5) *φθέγγμα [pʰtʰéŋŋma] > (45.6) φθέγμα [pʰtʰéŋma] 'sound' **D** πλέκω 'I twine' :: ptc. perf. midd. *πεπλεκμένος > (31.2) *πεπλεγμένος > (32.5) πεπλεγμένος [pepleŋménos] 'twined'

E3 Dental Stop before Nasal Consonant

A σκευάζω 'I equip' :: perf. *ἐσκεύαδ-μαι > (34.1) ἐσκεύασμαι 'I have equipped' **B** πείθω 'I persuade' :: *πέπειθμαι > (34.2) πέπεισμαι 'I am persuaded' **C** δατέομαι 'I distribute' :: *δατ-μός > (34.3) δασμός 'piece' **E** φράζω 'I speak' :: Hes. πεφραδμένος > (34.1) Att. πεφρασμένος 'proclaiming' **F** κόρυς, κόρυθος 'helmet' :: Hom. κεκορυθμένος > (34.2) Att. κεκορυσμένος 'having a helmet' **G** καίνυμαι 'to distinguish' :: Pind. κεκαδμένος > (34.1) Att. κεκασμένος 'distinguished'

Chapter 21: Assimilation of Consonants IV: Resonants

E1 Assimilation of *νρ, ρσ and *σν

A ῥάπτω 'I sew' :: *συνράπτω > (35.1) συρράπτω 'I sew together' **B** παλίν 'again' + ῥοά 'flowing' :: *παλίν-ροια > (35.1) παλίρροια 'flowing back and forth' **C** German *Arsch* 'ass' :: *ὄρσος > (35.3) ὄρρος 'buttocks' **D** δέρω 'I skin' :: *δέρσις > (35.3) Att. δέρρις 'furr' **E** ἐραστός :: *ἐρασνός > (37.1) ἐραννός 'lovely' **F** ἀργεστής 'illuminating' ::*ἀργεσνός > (37.1) ἀργεννός 'radiant' **G** ἔρεβος 'evening' :: *ἐρεβεσνός > (37.1) ἐρεβεννός 'in the evening' **H** Aeol. κλεεννός :: *κλεϝεσνός > (37.1) *κλεϝεννός > (x21.2) *κλεεννός [kleennós] > (7.2) *κλειννός [klȩ̄nnós] > (Simplification the of double consonant) Att.-Ion. κλεινός [klȩ̄nós] 'famous'

E2 Development of Initial *ϝρ

A ῥήτρᾱ 'statute' :: *ἄϝρητος > (35.2) ἄρρητος 'unspeakable' **B** ῥάπτω 'I sew' :: *πολύϝραφος > (35.2) πολύρραφος 'strongly sewed' **C** Myc. *wi-ri-za* = ῥίζα 'root' :: *πολύ-ϝριζος > (35.2) πολύρριζος 'having many roots' **D** Att.-Ion. ῥίπτω 'I throw' :: *ἀναϝρίπτω > (35.2) ἀναρρίπτω 'I throw upwards'

E3 Assimilation of Nasal Consonants

A μένω 'I stay' :: ἐνμένω > (24.1) ἐμμένω 'I stay within' **B** πάλιν 'again' :: παλιν-μήκης > (24.11) παλιμ-μήκης 'twice as long' **C** φαίνω 'I seem' :: *πέφανκα > (24.2) πέφαγκα 'I seemed' **D** κλείω 'I close' :: *ἐνκλείω > (24.2) ἐγκλείω 'I enclose' **E** πάλιν 'again' :: παλίν-κοτος > (24.2) παλίγ-κοτος 'recidivist' **F** παροξύνω 'I excite' :: *παρώξυνμαι > (24.1) παρώξυμμαι 'I have excited'

Chapter 22: Dissimilation / Dissimilatory Deletion / Haplology / Metathesis

E1 Dissimilation and Dissimilatory Loss

A θηράω 'I hunt' :: θηρητήρ > (39.1) θηλητήρ 'hunter' **B** ναῦς 'ship' :: *ναύ-κρασρος > (2.2) *ναύκρᾱρος > (39.1) *ναύκλᾱρος > (13) ναύκληρος 'captain' **C** Ion. τέρας :: Hom. Aeol. *πέρωρ > (39.1) πέλωρ 'monster' **D** παλύνω 'to sprinkle' :: *παλ-πάλη > (39.5) παιπάλη 'flour' **E** δέλτος 'writing tablet' :: *δάλ-δαλον > (39.5) δαίδαλον 'artwork' **F** νάρναξ > (39.7) λάρναξ 'container' **G** πνέω 'I breathe' :: *πον-πνύω > (39.8) ποιπνύω 'I gasp' **H** Skr. *grás-ati* 'eats' :: *γρασ-τήρ > (41.2) γαστήρ 'stomach' **I** κλῖβανος > (39.6) κρῖβανος 'oven' **J** νίτρον > (39.9) λίτρον 'natron' **K** Lat. *Cerberus* :: Κέρβερος > (40.1) Κέρβελος 'hellhound' **L** ἄλγος 'pain' :: *ἀλγαλέος > (39.3) ἀργαλέος 'difficult'

E2 Loss of One Syllable through Haplology

A κελαινός 'black' + νέφος 'cloud' :: *κελαι**νονε**φής > κελαινεφής 'of black clouds' **B** Lat. *pōtus* 'drinking' :: *πο**τοτής** > ποτής 'drink' **C** ποινή 'fine' :: *ἀ**πόποι**να > *ἀποῖνα > (Vendryes' law, cf. chap. 8) ἄποινα 'ransom' **D** τετρα- 'four' + δραχμή 'drachma' :: *τέ**τρα-δρα**χμον > τέτραχμον 'four drachmas' **E** κάλαμος 'shaft' + μίνθη 'mint' :: *κα**λαμο-μίν**θη > καλαμίνθη 'peppermint' **F** ἀρήν 'sheep' + νάκη 'fur' :: *ἀ**ρνο-νακ**ίς > ἀρνακίς 'sheepskin' **G** ὄπισθεν 'behind' + θέναρ 'hand' :: *ὀπισ**θο-θέ**ναρ > ὀπισθέναρ 'back of the hand'

E3 Metathesis

A Lat. *quippe* :: *k^w*ídpe* > (29.8) *k^w*ítpe* > (x23.1) *τίτπε > (42.3) τίπτε 'why then?' **B1** PIE *tken-* 'to injure' :: 1. pl. aor. *ἔτκαμεν > (42.1) Hom. ἔκταμεν 'we slayed' **B2** 3. sg. aor. pass. *ἔτκατο > (42.1) Hom. ἔκτατο 'he was slayed' **C** PIE *t̂kei̯-* 'to settle' :: *τκίζω > (42.1) κτίζω 'I found' **D** Ved. *ṛ́kṣa-* :: *ἄρτκος > (42.1) ἄρκτος 'bear'

Chapter 23: Grassmann's Law

E1 Loss of Aspiration

A1 θάπτω 'I bury' :: nom. sg. *θάφος > (39.10) τάφος 'grave' **A2** aor. pass. *ἐθάφην > (39.10) ἐτάφην 'I was buried' **B** θάττων 'faster' :: *θαχύς > (39.10) ταχύς 'fast' **C** ἅπτω 'I touch' :: prs. *ἁφάσσω [hap^hássǭ] > (39.10) Ion. ἀφάσσω [ap^hássǭ] 'I feel' **D** aor. ἔθρεξα 'I ran' :: prs. *θρέχω > (39.10) τρέχω 'I run' **E** θρύπτω 'I rub' :: *θρυφή > (39.10) τρυφή 'debauchery' **F1** θρίξ 'hair' :: nom. pl. *θρίχες > (39.10) τρίχες 'hairs' **F2** gen. sg. *θριχός > (39.10) τριχός 'of the hair' **H** nom. sg. *φάϝος > (x21.2) φάος 'light' :: prs. *φιφαύσκω > (39.10) πιφαύσκω 'I let appear' **I** θύω 'I sacrifice' :: aor. pass. *ἐθύθην > (39.10) ἐτύθην 'I was sacrificed' **J** τίθημι 'I set' :: aor. pass. *ἐθέθην > (39.10) ἐτέθην 'was set' **K** θεσμός :: *θεθμός > (39.10) Dor. τεθμός 'statute' **L** χείρ 'hand' + ἔχω 'I hold' :: *ἐχε-χειρίᾱ > (39.10) ἐκεχειρίᾱ 'ceasefire'

E2 Reconstruct the Preforms:

A φιλέω 'I love' :: perf. *φεφίληκα > (39.10) πεφίληκα 'I have loved' **B** χράομαι 'I need' :: perf. *χέχρημαι > (39.10) κέχρημαι 'I needed' **C** φύω 'I become' :: perf. *φέφῡκα > (39.10) πέφῡκα 'I have become' **D** Lat. *fīdō* 'I trust' :: *φείθω > (39.10) πείθω 'I persuade' **E** *χιχάνω > (39.10) κιχάνω 'I achieve' **F** χέω 'I pour' :: perf. *χέχυμαι > (39.10) κέχυμαι 'I have poured'

E3 Which of the Following Forms is an Analogical Formation?

Answer: τεθράφθαι is an analogical formation to τέθραμμαι because Grassmann' law did not deaspirate the first aspirate.

E4 Why is it Difficult to Trace φάτνη 'Manger' back to *φάθνη?

Answer: In this case, the second aspirate was deaspirated which is a very rare development. This etymology is, however, very probably because the preform *φάθνη can be explained as PIE *b^h*n̥*d^h*nā* from the root *b^h*end*^{h}- which can be connected to English to bind.

Chapter 24: Loss and Re-Emergence of the Fricative σ

E1 Development of *σ in the Initial and Medial Position

A Lat. *sāl* :: *σάλς > (x13.1) ἅλς 'salt' **B** Lat. *sulcus* 'plow' :: *σέλκω > (x13.1) ἕλκω 'I drag' **C** Lat. *sēmi* :: *σημι- > (x13.1) ἡμι- 'half' **D** γένος 'kin' :: gen. sg. *γένεσος > (x15.1) *γένεος > (10.3) *γένǭς > (15) γένους **E** Skr. *trásāmi* :: *τρέσω > (x15.1) τρέω 'I tremble' **F** μένω 'I stay' :: fut. *μενέσω > (x15.1) *μενέω > (10.1) μενῶ 'I will stay'

E2 Transposition of the Glottal Fricative *h*

A Lat. *ūrō* 'I burn' :: *εὔσω > (x13.2) *εὔhω > (x14.2) εὕω 'I singe' **B** ὁράω 'I see' :: *προ-ὁρά [prohorá] > (x14.2) *φροορά [p^hroorá] > (7.3) *φρǭρά > (15) φρουρά [p^hrūrá] 'guard' **C** ὁδός 'way' :: *πρό-ὁδος [próhodos] > (x14.2) *φρόοδός [p^hróodos] > (7.3) *φρǭδος > (15) φροῦδος [p^hrū̂dos] 'vanished' **D** Skr. *iṣirá-* 'agile' :: *ἰσερός > (x13.2) *ἰhερός > (x14.2) ἱερός 'strong'

E3 Re-emergence of Initial σ from *τϝ

A1 Skr. *tavás-* 'strong, brave' :: *τϝάϝος > (x21.2) *τϝάος > (x21.5) σάος 'healthy' **A2** *τϝῶκος > (x21.5) σῶκος 'strong' **B** Skr. *tveṣá-* 'vehement' :: *τϝείσω > (x15.1) *τϝείω > (x21.5) σείω 'I shake' **C1** Lith. *tveriù* 'to grasp' :: *τϝωρός > (x21.5) σωρός 'heap' **C2** *τϝορός > (x21.5) σορός 'urn' **C3** *τϝερι̯ᾱ́ > (3) *τϝειρᾱ́ > (x21.5) Att. *σειρᾱ́ > (13) Ion. σειρή 'rope' **E** aor. ἔσαξα 'I crammed' :: prs. *τϝάκι̯ω > (x21.5) *σάκι̯ω > (x19.4) Att. σάττω 'I cram' **F** Skr. *tváṣṭar-* 'name of a creator deity' :: *tu̯r̥ks* > (x25.1) *τϝάρξ > (x21.5) σάρξ 'meat'

Chapter 25: Consonant Sequences Containing the Fricative σ

E1 *σ plus Resonant in the Initial and Medial Position

A OHG *snuor* 'string' :: prs. *σνήι̯ω > (x16.1) *σνήω > (x15.3) *νήω > (1.1) νέω 'I spin' **B** prs. *σνέϝω > (x16.1) *σνέω > (x15.3) νέω 'I swim' :: ipf. *ἔσνεον > (x15.2) ἔννεον 'I swam' **C** prs. *σρέϝω > (x13.3) *ῥέϝω > (x21.2) ῥέω 'I flow' :: ipf. *ἔσρεϝον > (x15.2) *ἔρρεϝον > (x21.2) ἔρρεον 'I flowed' **D** prs. *σλήγω > (x15.3) λήγω 'höre I stop' :: aor. *ἔσληγσα > (x15.2) ἔλληξα 'I stopped' **E** Lith. *smagus* 'heavy' :: *σμόγος > (x15.3) μόγος 'effort' **F** Skr. *smárati* 'he thinks of' :: *σμέριμνα > (x15.3) μέριμνα 'sorrow' **G** Latv. *smaida* 'smile' :: *φιλο-σμειδής > (x15.2) φιλομμειδής 'loving to smile' **H** Lat. *frīgus* 'coldness' :: prs. *σρῑγέω > (x13.3) ῥῑγέω 'I shudder' **I** λαμβάνω 'I grasp' :: ipf. *ἔσλαβον > (x15.2) ἔλλαβον 'I grasped' **J** *σμικρός > (x15.2) μικρός 'small' **L** Av. *snāvarə* :: *σνηῦρον > (x15.2) *νηῦρον > (1.3) νεῦρον 'tendom'

E2 Aspiration of κ by *σ

A Lat. *texō* 'I weave' :: *τέκσνᾱ > (x13.5) *τέκhνᾱ > (27.2) *τέχνᾱ > (13) τέχνη 'art' **B** λευκός 'shining' :: *λύκσνος > (x13.5) *λύκhνος > (27.2) λύχνος 'lamp' **C** Lat. *arānea* :: *ἀράκσνᾱ > (x13.5) *ἀράκhνᾱ > (27.2) *ἀράχνᾱ > (13) ἀράχνη 'spider' **D** ἀκίς 'pointed object' :: *ἄκσνᾱ > (x13.5) *ἄκhνᾱ > (27.2) *ἄχνᾱ > (13) ἄχνη 'chaff'

E3 Loss or Preservation of σ in Consonant Sequences

A aor. ἔλακον 'I cried' :: prs. *λάκ-σκω > (43.3) λάσκω 'I cry' **B** βλαβή 'damage' :: perf. inf. midd. *βέβλαπσθαι > (43.6) *βέβλαπθαι > (26.1) βεβλάφθαι 'having damaged' **C** τρίβω 'I rub' :: perf. inf. midd. *τετρίβσθαι > (29.1) *τετρίπσθαι > (43.6) *τετρίπθαι > (26.1) τετρίφθαι 'having rubbed' **D** Skr. *pārṣṇi-* :: *πάρσνᾱ > (43.6) *πάρνᾱ > (13) *πήρνη > (1.3) *πέρνη > (x20) πτέρνη 'heel' **E** Lat. *cēnseō* 'I estimate' :: *κόνσμος > (43.7) κόσμος 'jewellery' **F** πάλιν 'again' :: *παλίνσκιος > (43.7) παλίσκιος 'shadowed again and again' **G** Skr. *dámpati-* :: *δεμσπότης > (24.3) *δενσπότης > (43.7) δεσπότης 'male head of a household'

Chapter 26: The Semivowel *ϝ

E1 Loss and Debuccalization of Initial *ϝ

A Skr. *vidmá* :: 1. pl. *ϝίδμεν > (x21.1) ἴδμεν 'we know' **B** Lat. *vīnum* :: *ϝοῖνος > (x21.1) οἶνος 'wine' **C** Lat. *vīs* :: *ϝίς > (x21.1) ἴς 'force' **C** Lat. *Vesta* 'goddess of the hearth' :: *ϝεστίᾱ > (x21.4) ἑστίᾱ 'hearth' **D** Lat. *lāna* :: *ϝλᾶνος > (13) *ϝλῆνος > (x21.1) λῆνος 'wool' **E** German *Werk* :: *ϝέργον > (x21.1) ἔργον 'work' **F** Skr. *vácas-* 'word' :: *$u̯ék^w$os > (x24.2) *ϝέπος > (x21.1) ἔπος 'speech'

E2 Loss of Intervocalic *ϝ

A Myc. *di-wo* :: gen. sg. *Διϝός > (x21.2) Διός 'of Zeus' **B** aor. ἔπνευσα 'I breathed' :: *πνέϝω > (x21.2) πνέω 'I breath' **C** Skr. *kravíṣ-* 'raw meat' :: *κρέϝας > (x21.2) κρέας 'meat' **D** Skr. *avidam* 'I found' :: aor. *ἔϝιδον [éu̯idon] > (x21.2) *ἔϊδον [éidon] > (23.1) *[éi̯don] > (14.2) εἶδον [ẹ̄don] 'I saw' **E** ἀπο-λαύω 'I benefit' :: *λᾱϝίς > (13) *ληϝίς > (x21.2) Hom. ληίς 'prey' **F** ἀήρ 'wind' :: *ἄϝελι̯α > (36.4) *ἄϝελλα > (x21.2) ἄελλα 'storm' **J** Lat. *ventus* 'wind' :: *ἄϝητι > (x22.1) *ἄϝησι > (x21.2) ἄησι 'it blows'

E3 Loss of *ϝ After Consonant. Compensatory Lengthening in Ionic:

A Myc. *wo-wo* :: *ϝόρϝος > (x21.4) *ὄρϝος > (x21.3) Att. ὅρος / Ion. οὖρος 'border' **B** Dor. μῶνος :: *μόνϝος > (x21.3) Att. μόνος / Ion. μοῦνος 'alone' **C** *μάνϝος > (x21.3) Att. μανός / Ion. μᾱνός 'thin' **D** Skr. *sárva-* :: *σόλϝος > (x13.1) *ὁλϝος > (x21.3) Att. ὅλος / Ion. οὖλος 'whole' **E** Myc. *ke-se-nu-wo* :: *ξένϝος > (x21.3) Att. ξένος / Ion. ξεῖνος 'foreigner' **F** Skr. *dvíṣ* :: *δϝίς > (x21.3) δίς 'twice' **G** *δέρϝᾱ > (13) *δέρϝη > (x21.3) δέρη / Ion. δειρή 'neck' **H** Arc. ὀλοϝά :: *ὀλϝαί > (x21.3) Att. ὀλαί / Ion. οὐλαί 'barley-corns' **I** Skr. *dagh-* 'to reach' :: *φθάνϝω > (x21.3) Att. φθάνω / Ion. φθᾱ́νω 'I come'

Chapter 27: The Semivowel *i̯

E1 Loss of intervocalic *i̯

A1 πειθώ 'persuasion' :: dat. sg. *πειθόι̯ι [pei̯tʰói̯i] > (x16.1) *πειθόι [pei̯tʰói] > (23.1) πειθοῖ [pei̯tʰōi̯] **A2** gen. sg. *πειθόι̯ος > (x16.1) *πειθόος > (7.3) *πειθǭς > (15) πειθοῦς **B** πόλις 'city' :: gen. sg. *πόληι̯ος > (x16.1) *πόληος > (1.2) πόλεως 'of the city' **C** σταῖς 'bread dough' :: *στάι̯αρ > (x16.1) *στάαρ > (13) *στήαρ > (1.1) στέαρ 'hard fat' **D** Skr. *dyati* 'he binds' :: *δέι̯ω > (x16.1) δέω 'I bind' **E** Skr. *dīdāye* 'it shines' :: *δέι̯αται > (x16.1) δέαται 'he seems' **F** Lat. *plēnus* :: *πλήι̯ος > (x16.1) *πλήος > (1.1) πλέος 'full' **G** fut. νήσω 'I will spin' :: prs. *νήι̯ω > (x16.1) *νήω > (1.1) νέω 'I spin' **H** Hitt. *ariyezzi* 'he investigates' :: *ἐρέι̯ω > (x16.1) ἐρέω 'I ask'

E2 Change of *Hi̯ to *h* in the Initial Position

A1 Av. *yārə* :: **Hi̯ō̃rā* > (x16.2) ὥρᾱ 'time' **A2** **Hi̯ō̃ros* > (x16.2) ὧρος 'year' **B** **Hi̯ópʰra* > (x16.2) *ὅφρα > (39.10) Hom. ὄφρα 'as long as' **C** Skr. *yájāmi* :: **Hi̯ági̯ō* > (x16.2) *ἅγι̯ω > (x18.1) ἅζω 'I worship' **D** Skr. *yad* :: nt. sg. **Hi̯ód* > (x16.2) *ὁδ > (x12.2) ὅ 'which'

E3 Loss of *i̯ after α with Compensatory Lengthening

A Lat. *lēvir* :: *δαι̯ϝήρ > (x21.3) *δαι̯ήρ > (6.1) Hom. δᾱήρ 'brother-in-law' **B** ἔλαιον 'oil' :: *ἐλαί̯ϝᾱ > (x21.3) Old Att. ἐλαίᾱ > (6.1) ἐλᾱ́ᾱ 'olive tree' **C** κλαίειν > (6.1) κλάειν 'to cry' **D** Ἀθᾱναίᾱ > (13) Ἀθηναίᾱ > (6.1) Ἀθηνάᾱ > (7.1) Ἀθηνᾶ 'Athena' **E** Lat. *avis* 'bird' :: *ἀϝι̯ετός > (x17) *αἰϝετός > (21.2) Hom. αἰετός 'eagle'

Chapter 28: Palatalization of Voiced Sounds

E1 ζ from the Sound Cluster *γi̯

A ἁγνός 'holy' :: *ἅγι̯ω > (x18.1) ἅζω 'I worship' **B** σταγών 'drop' :: *στάγι̯ω > (x18.1) στάζω 'I drop' **C** μέγα 'big' :: *μέγι̯ων > (x18.1) Ion. μέζων 'bigger' **D** στέναγμα 'roaring, raging' :: *στενάγι̯ω > (x18.1) στενάζω 'I moan' **E** βίος 'life' :: *g^wi̯ēn* > (x11.2) *γι̯ῆν > (x18.1) ζῆν 'to live'

E2 ζ from the Sound Cluster *δi̯

A Lat. *scindō* 'I split' :: *σχίδι̯α > (x18.2) σχίζα 'piece of wood' **B** Skr. *dyāus* 'sky' :: *Δι̯ηύς > (1.3) *Δι̯εύς > (x18.2) Ζεύς 'Zeus' **C** πέδον 'ground' :: *πεδι̯ός > (x18.2) πεζός 'on foot' **D** κομιδή 'transport' :: *κομίδι̯ω > (x18.2) κομίζω 'I transport' **E** κλύδων 'wash of waves' :: *κλύδι̯ω > (x18.2) κλύζω 'I rinse' **F** Hom. ὀδμή 'smell' :: *ὄδι̯ω > (x18.2) ὄζω 'I smell' **G** νόμος 'custom' :: *νομίδι̯ω > (x18.2) νομίζω 'I have in use'

KEY

E3 ζ from Initial *i̯

A Lat. *iūs* 'broth' :: *i̯όσμᾱ > (x16.3) *ζόσμᾱ > (2.2) *ζόμᾱ > (13) ζόμη 'leaven' **B** ζωστός 'girded' :: *i̯ώσνᾱ > (x16.3) *ζώσνᾱ > (2.2) *ζώνᾱ > (13) ζώνη 'belt' **C1** Skr. *yásyati* 'it becomes hot' :: *i̯εστός > (x16.3) ζεστός 'boiling hot' **C2** *i̯έσω > (x16.3) *ζέσω > (x15.1) ζέω 'siede' **D** Skr. *yáva-* 'cereal' :: *i̯εϝi̯αί > (x16.3) *ζεϝi̯αί > (3) *ζειϝαί > (x21.2) ζειαί [zde̯ái̯] 'spelt'

E4 ζ from the Sound Cluster */sd/

A German *Ast* :: *ó-sd-os* > ὄζος 'twig'

B *χαμά 'earth' :: acc. pl. *χαμάσ-δε > χαμᾶζε 'to the ground'

Chapter 29: Palatalization of Voiceless Sounds

E1 πτ from the Sequences *πi̯ and *φi̯

A κλοπή 'theft' :: *κλέπi̯ω > (x19.1) κλέπτω 'I steal' **B** κόπος 'striking' :: *κόπi̯ω > (x19.1) κόπτω 'I hit' **C** τύπος 'hit' :: *τύπi̯ω > (x19.1) τύπτω 'I hit' **D** τάφος 'funeral' :: *θάφi̯ω > (25.5) *θάπi̯ω > (x19.1) θάπτω 'I bury'

E2 The Development τι > σι

A δοτός 'given' :: *δότις > (x22.1) δόσις 'gift' **B** Skr. *sthiti-* :: *στατίς > (x22.1) στασίς 'setting' **C** Skr. *páti-* :: *πότις > (x22.1) πόσις 'husband' **D** ἐσ-τί 'ist' :: *τίθη-τι > (x22.1) τίθησι 'he puts' **E** ἐργάτης 'worker' :: *ἐργατίᾱ > (x22.1) *ἐργασίᾱ 'work' **F** Ved. *-dhiti-* :: *θέτις > (x22.1) θέσις 'setting' **G** ἄμβροτος 'immortal' :: *ἀμβρότιος > (x22.1) ἀμβρόσιος 'divine' **H** Dor. ϝίκατι :: Att. *εἴκοτι > (x22.1) εἴκοσι 'twenty' **I** Dor. διᾱκάτιοι :: Att. *διᾱκότιοι > (x22.1) διᾱκόσιοι 'two hundred'

E3 Attic and Ionic Forms

A φρακτός 'fenced' :: *φράκi̯ω > (x19.4) Att. φράττω / Ion. φράσσω 'I fence' **B** ἐρέτης 'rower' :: *ἐρέτi̯ω > (x19.3) Att. ἐρέττω / Ion. ἐρέσσω 'I row' **C** τάξις 'order' :: *τάκi̯ω > (x19.4) Att. τάττω / Ion. τάσσω 'I arrange' **D** λῑτός :: *λιτi̯ός > (x19.3) Ion. λισσός 'smooth' **E** Lat. *pix* :: *πίκi̯α > (x19.4) Att. πίττα / Ion. πίσσα 'pitch' **F** νακτός 'solid' :: *νάκi̯ω > (x19.4) Ion. νάσσω 'I stamp' **G** aor. ἔμαξα 'I kneaded' :: prs. *μάκi̯ω > (x19.4) Att. μάττω / Ion. μάσσω 'I knead' **H** λευκός 'shining' :: *λεύκi̯ω > (x19.4) Ion. λεύσσω 'I watch' **I** λιτή 'imploration' :: *λίτi̯ομαι > (x19.3) Ion. λίσσομαι 'I implore' **J** ταραχή 'confusion' :: *ταράχi̯ω > (25.14) *ταράκi̯ω > (x19.4) Att. ταράττω / Ion. ταράσσω 'I confuse' **K** βήξ, βηχός 'cough' :: *βήχi̯ω > (25.14) *βήκi̯ω > (x19.4) Att. βήττω / Ion. βήσσω 'I cough' **L** κοροπλάθος 'producer of figurines' :: *πλάθi̯ω > (25.9) *πλάτi̯ω > (x19.3) Att. πλάττω / Ion. πλάσσω 'I produce'

Chapter 30: Development of PIE Labiovelars

E1 Context-Sensitive Development of Labiovelars

A Lat. *vorāre* 'to devour' :: *g^{w}orā́* > (x24.4) βορά 'food' **B** Skr. *carati* 'he walks' :: *k^{w}élos* > (x23.1) τέλος 'end' **C** Lat. *quid* :: *k^{w}id* > (x12.2) *k^{w}í* > (x23.1) τί 'what?' **D** Skr. *páñca* :: *pénk^{w}e* > (x23.1) πέντε 'five' **E** Lat. *oculus* 'eye' :: *ók^{w}setai̯* > (x24.1) fut. ὄψεται 'he will see' **F** Lat. *sequor* :: *sék^{w}omai̯* > (x13.1) *hék^{w}omai̯* > (x24.2) ἕπομαι 'I follow' **G** Lith. *káina* 'price' :: *k^{w}oi̯nā́* > (x24.2) *ποινά > (13) ποινή 'penitence' **H** Myc. *qe-ja-me-no* :: *k^{w}inu̯ō* > (x23.1) *τίνϝω > (x21.3) τίνω 'I pay' **I** πέντε 'five' :: *pénk^{w}tos* > (x24.1) πέμπτος 'the fifth' **J** Skr. *jyā́-* 'bowstring' :: *g^{w}iós* > (x24.4) βιός 'bow' **K** Skr. *paktí-* 'cooked meal' :: *pék^{w}tos* > (x24.1) πεπτός 'cooked'

E2 Loss of Labial Coarticulation next to Velar Vowels

A Lat. *lupus* :: *lúk^{w}os* > (x10.1) λύκος 'wolf' **B** Lat. *nox* :: *nók^{w}ts* > (11) *núk^{w}ts* > (x10.1) *νύκτς > (33) *νύκσς > (45.3) νύξ 'night' **C** βίος 'life' :: *sug^{w}īu̯ḗs* > (x10.2) *sugīu̯ḗs* > (x13.1) *ὑγῑϝής > (x21.2) *ὑγῑής > (1.1) ὑγιής 'healthy'

E3 Loss of Labial Coarticulation with Subsequent Palatalization

A ὄμμα 'eye' :: *ók^{w}i̯omai̯* > (x11.1) *ὄκi̯ομαι > (x19.4) Ion. ὄσσομαι 'I anticipate' **B** acc. *u̯ók^{w}a* > (x24.2) *ϝόπα > (x21.1) Hom. ὄπα 'voice' :: nom. *u̯ók^{w}i̯a* > (x11.1) *ϝόκi̯α > (x19.4) *ϝόσσα > (x21.1) Hom. Ion. ὄσσα 'rumor' **C** Skr. *pácati* :: *pék^{w}i̯ō* > (x11.1) *πέκi̯ω > (x19.4) Att. πέττω 'I cook' **E** χέρ-νιψ 'water for washing the hands' :: *níg^{w}-i̯ō* > (x11.2) *νίγi̯ω > (x18.1) νίζω 'I wash'

Chapter 31: Development of PIE Mediae Aspiratae

E1 Standard Development

A Skr. *dhūmá-* :: *d^{h}ūmós* > (x9.2) θῡμός 'courage' **B** Skr. *prá dhanvati* 'he dies' :: *d^{h}nātós* > (x9.2) *θνᾱτός > (13) θνητός 'dead' **C** Skr. *dádhāmi* :: *d^{h}í-d^{h}ē-mi*> (x9.2) *θίθημι > (39.10) τίθημι 'I put' **D** Lat. *ānser* :: gen. sg. *ĝ^{h}ansós* > (x1.3) *g^{h}ansós* > (x9.3) *χανσός > (2.1) *χᾱνός > (13) χηνός 'of the goose' **E** θύρᾱ 'door' :: *d^{h}ur̥-i̯ó-s* > (x9.2) *t^{h}ur̥i̯ós* > (x25.1) *θϝαρi̯ός > (x17) *θϝαιρός > (x21.3) θαιρός 'hinge' **F** Skr. *bhāti* 'he speaks' :: *b^{h}āmí* > (x9.1) *φᾱμί > (13) φημί 'I speak' **G** Skr. *bahú-* 'arm' :: *b^{h}n̥ĝ^{h}ús* > (x1.3) *b^{h}n̥g^{h}ús* > (x9.1+x9.3) *p^{h}n̥k^{h}ús* > (x26.1) *φαχύς > (39.10) παχύς 'thick' **H** Goth. *bindan* 'to bind' :: *b^{h}énd^{h}-sma* > (x9.1+x9.2) *p^{h}ént^{h}-sma* > (39.10) *πένθσμα > (25.6) *πέντσμα > (33) *πένσσμα > (45.4) *πένσμα > (4.1) πεῖσμα 'rope'

E2 Context-Sensitive Development of *g^{wh}*

A Skr. *gharmá-* 'burning heat' :: *g^{wh}ermós* > (x9.4) *k^{wh}ermós* > (x23.3) θερμός 'warm' **B** θείνω 'I kill' :: *g^{wh}ónos* > (x9.4) *k^{wh}ónos* > (x24.6) φόνος 'murder' **C** Skr. *áhi-* :: *óg^{wh}is* > (x9.4) *ók^{wh}is* > (x24.6) ὄφις 'snake' **D** Lat. *nix* :: acc. *níg^{wh}m̥* > (x9.4) *ník^{wh}m̥* > (x26.3) *ník^{wh}a* > (x24.6) νίφα 'snow' **E** Goth. *bidjan* 'to ask for' :: *g^{wh}od^{h}éi̯ō* > (x9.2+x9.4) *k^{wh}ot^{h}éi̯ō* > (x16.1) *k^{wh}ot^{h}éō* > (39.10) *k^{w}ot^{h}éō* > (x24.2) Hom. ποθέω 'I desire' **F** Hom. ποθέω 'I desire' :: *k^{wh}ét^{h}i̯est^{h}ai̯* > (25.9) *k^{wh}éti̯est^{h}ai̯* > (x23.3) *θέτi̯εσθαι > (x19.3) Ion. θέσσεσθαι 'to implore' **G** Lat. *voveō* 'I promise' :: *éu̯g^{wh}omai̯* > (x9.4) *éu̯k^{wh}omai̯* > (x10.3) εὔχομαι 'I pray'

Chapter 32: Epenthetic and Final Consonants

E1 Epenthetic Consonants in the Initial and Medial Position

A1 μορμύρω :: *μρέμω > (47.1) βρέμω 'I roar' **A2** *μρόμος > (47.1) βρόμος 'roaring' **A3** *μρομτή > (24.4) *μροντή > (47.1) βροντή 'thunder' **B** aor. ἔμολον 'I came' :: prs. *μλώσκω > (47.3) βλώσκω 'I come' **C** μέλδομαι 'I melt' :: *μλαδύς > (47.3) βλαδύς 'smooth' **D** μαλακός 'smooth' :: *μλάξ > (47.3) βλᾱ́ξ 'limp' **E** Skr. _marcáyati_ :: *μλάπτω > (47.3) βλάπτω 'I harm' **F** βλώσκω 'I come' :: perf. *μέ-μλω-κα > (47.4) μέμβλωκα 'I have come' **G** ἀμαλός 'smooth' :: *ἀμλύς > (47.4) ἀμβλύς 'weak' **H** Av. _mərəzu-_ :: *_mr̥ĝʰús_ > (x1.3) *_mr̥gʰús_ > (x9.3) *_mr̥kʰús_ > (x25.2) *μραχύς > (47.1) βραχύς 'short' **I** Russ. _morozgá_ 'drizzling rain' :: *μρέχω > (47.1) βρέχω 'I make wet' **J** Skr. _mūrtá-_ 'coagulated' :: *μρότος > (47.1) βρότος 'coagulated blood' **K** Skr. _amŕ̥ta-_ :: *ἄμροτος > (47.2) ἄμβροτος 'immortal'

E2 Loss of Final Consonants Except for ν, ϱ, σ

A gen. ἑκόντος :: nom. nt. *ἑκόντ > (x12.3) ἑκόν 'voluntary' **B** gen. γυναικός :: voc. *γύναικ > (x12.2) γύναι 'woman!' **C** gen. μέλιτος :: nom. *μέλιτ > (x12.2) μέλι 'honey' **D** gen. γάλακτος :: nom. *γάλακτ > (x12.2) γάλα 'milk' **E** gen. Hom. ἄνακτος :: voc. *ἄνακτ > (x12.2) ἄνα 'master!' **F** κρῑθή :: nom.-acc. *κρῖθ > (x12.2) Hom. κρῖ 'barley' **G** Hom. πόρσω :: *πόρσωδ > (x12.2) *πόρσω > (35.3) πόρρω 'forward' **H** δέρκομαι 'I see' :: *ὑπόδρακ > (x12.2) ὑπόδρα 'glowering' **I** Skr. _yákr̥t_ :: *_Hi̯ēkʷr̥t_ > (x16.2) *_hēkʷr̥t_ > (x24.1) *_hēpr̥t_ > (x25.1) *ἧπαρτ > (x12.3) ἧπαρ 'liver' **J** Skr. _abharant_ :: 3. pl. ipf. *ἔφεροντ > (x12.3) ἔφερον 'they carried' **K** Skr. _abharat_ :: 3. sg. ipf. *ἔφερετ > (x12.2) ἔφερε 'he carried'

Chapter 33: Development of PIE Syllabic Resonants *m̥, *n̥, *r̥, *l̥

E1 Development of *r̥ and *l̥

A σπείρω 'I sow' :: *_spr̥tós_ > (x25.1) σπαρτός 'sowed' **B** Skr. _pr̥thú-_ :: *_pl̥tús_ > (x25.4) πλατύς 'flat' **C** Lat. _saliō_ :: *_sĺ̥i̯omai̯_ > (x25.3) *σάλι̯ομαι > (36.4) *σάλλομαι > (x13.1) ἅλλομαι 'I jump' **D** τρέπω 'I turn' :: perf. *_té-tr̥p-mai̯_ > (x25.2) *τέτραπμαι > (31.1) *τέτραβμαι > (32.2) τέτραμμαι 'I have turned' **E** Lat. _porrum_ :: *_pŕ̥son_ > (x25.2) πράσον 'leek' **F** boiot. πέτταρες :: *_kʷétu̯r̥es_ > (x25.1) *_kʷétu̯ares_ > (x21.6) *_kʷéttares_ > (x23.1) Att. τέτταρες 'four' **G** βέλος 'missile' :: *_bĺ̥i̯ō_ > (x25.3) *βάλι̯ω > (36.4) βάλλω 'I throw'

E2 Development of *n̥ and *m̥

A Lat. _inguen_ abdomen' :: *_n̥gʷḗn_ > (x26.1) *_agʷḗn_ > (x23.2) ἀδήν 'gland' **B** δόμος 'house' :: *_dḿ̥pedom_ > (x26.3) *δάπεδομ > (x12.1) δάπεδον 'ground' **C** λανχάνω 'I draw lots' :: *_lń̥̥kʰos_ > (x26.1) λάχος 'alloted portion' **D** Hom. βένθος :: *_bń̥tʰos_ > (x26.1) βάθος 'depth' **E** πένθος 'grief' :: *_pń̥tʰos_ > (x26.1) πάθος 'suffering' **F** βαίνω 'gehe' :: *_gʷm̥tós_ > (x26.3) *_gʷatós_ > (x24.4) βατός 'gone' **G** βατός 'gone' :: *_gʷḿ̥-i̯ō_ > (x26.4) *_gʷámi̯ō_ > (24.3) *_gʷáni̯ō_ > (x24.4) *βάνι̯ω > (x17) βαίνω 'I go' **H** Skr. _sanitúr_ 'without' :: *_sń̥ter_ > (x13.1) *_hń̥ter_ > (loss of aspiration) *_ń̥ter_ > (x26.1) ἄτερ 'fern far from' **I** νόστος 'return' :: *_ń̥smenos_ > (x26.1) ἄσμενος 'saved' **J** χανδόν 'with open mouth' :: *_kʰń̥u̯os_ > (x26.1) *χάϝος > (x21.2) χάος 'airspace' **K** Skr. _dáṃśati_ 'he bites' :: *_é-dn̥kon_ > (x26.1) ἔδακον 'biss' **L** Lat. _densus_ :: *_dn̥sús_ > (x26.1) δασύς 'thick' **M** Skr. _ánudra-_ :: *_ń̥-udro-s_ > (x26.2) ἄνυδρος 'without water'

Chapter 34: Development of PIE Laryngeals I

E1 Laryngeals Become Vowels

A Lat. _līber_ :: *_$h_1$léu̯dʰeros_ > (x5.1) *_eléu̯dʰeros_ > (x9.2) ἐλεύθερος 'free' **B** Skr. _urú-_ :: *_$h_1$urús_ > (x5.1) εὐρύς 'broad' **C** Skr. _úkṣati_ :: *_$h_2$uks-ō_ > (x5.2) αὔξω 'I grow' **D** Lat. _migrāre_ 'to wander' :: *_$h_2$méi̯gʷō_ > (x5.2) *_améi̯gʷō_ > (x24.4) ἀμείβω 'I change' **E** Skr. _óhate_ 'he praises' :: *_h_1u̯gʷʰomai̯_ > (x5.1) *_éu̯gʷʰomai̯_ > (x9.4) *_éu̯kʷʰomai̯_ > (x10.3) εὔχομαι 'I pray' **F** Skr. _rákṣati_ :: *_$h_2$léksō_ > (x5.2) ἀλέξω 'I repel' **G** Skr. _patnī́-_ :: *_pótnih_2_ > (x6.4) πότνια 'mistress' **H** Skr. _máhi-_ :: *_méĝh_2_ > (x1.2) *_mégh_2_ > (x6.4) μέγα 'big' **I** Lat. _pater_ :: *_ph_2tḗr_ > (x6.2) πατήρ 'father' **J** Hom. ὄπα 'voice' :: *_u̯ókʷih_2_ > (x6.5) *_u̯ókʷi̯a_ > (x11.1) *ϝόκι̯α > (x19.4) Ion. *ϝόσσα > (x21.1) Ion. ὄσσα 'rumor' **K** Skr. _hitá-_ :: *_dʰ$h_1$tós_ > (x6.1) *_dʰetós_ > (x9.2) θετός 'set' **L** Lat. _fānum_ :: *_dʰh_1s-bʰ$h_2$tos_ > (x6.1+x6.2) *_dʰés-bʰatos_ > (x9.1+x9.2) θέσ-φατος 'said by a deity' **M** Skr. _jánitar-_ :: *_ĝenh_1tōr_ > (x1.2)*_genh_1tōr_ > (x6.1) γενέτωρ 'creator' **N** τέρω 'I drill' :: *_térh$_1$trom_ > (x6.1) *τέρετρομ > (x12.1) τέρετρον 'drill'

E2 Coloring and Non-Coloring of Initial Vowels

A Lat. _aevum_ :: *_$h_2$ei̯u̯esí_ > (x2.1) *_$h_2$ai̯u̯esí_ > (x3.2) *αἰϝεσί > (x15.1) *αἰϝεί > (x21.2) Hom. Ion. αἰεί 'eternal' **C** Skr. _édhas-_ 'firewood' :: *_$h_2$ei̯dʰos_ > (x2.1) *_$h_2$ai̯dʰos_ > (x3.2) *_ai̯dʰos_ > (x9.2) αἶθος 'embers' **D** Hitt. _ḫanti_ :: *_$h_2$entí_ > (x2.1) *_$h_2$antí_ > (x3.2) ἀντί 'before' **E** Skr. _ásmi_ :: *_$h_1$ésmi_ > (x3.1) *ἐσμί > (2.2) εἰμί 'I am' **F** Lat. _ite_ :: 2. pl. imp. *_$h_1$íte_ > (x3.1) ἴτε 'go!' **G** Lat. _uncus_ :: *_h_2óŋkos_ > (x3.3) ὄγκος 'barb' **H** Lat. _animus_ :: *_$h_2$én$h_1$mos_ > (x2.1) *_$h_2$án$h_1$mos_ > (x3.2) *_án$h_1$mos_ > (x6.1) ἄνεμος 'wind'

Chapter 35: Development of PIE Laryngeals II

E1 Unaccented Syllabic Resonant Plus Laryngeal Before Consonant or Vowel

A στόρνῡμι 'I spread out' :: *_str̥h_3-tós_ > (x7.4) στρωτός 'spread out' **B** ἁμαρτάνω 'I miss' :: *_n̥-$h_2$mertēs_ > (x7.11) *_nāmertḗs_ > (13) νημερτής 'unfailing' **C** πίμπλημι 'I fill' :: 3. sg. aor. midd. *_pl̥h_1-to_ > (x7.5) Hom. πλῆτο 'it became full' **D** Skr. _ā́śīrta-_ :: *_ń̥-k̂r̥h_2-tos_> (x1.1) *_ń̥kr̥$h_2$tos_ > (x7.2) *_ń̥krātos_ > (x26.1) ἄκρᾱτος 'unmixed' **E** Myc. _no-pe-ra-ha_ :: *_n̥-h_3bʰelḗs_ > (x7.13) *_nōbʰelḗs_ > (x9.1) *νωφελής > (+privative alpha) ἀνωφελής 'useless' **F** Dor. λᾶνος :: *_u̯l̥$h_2$nos_ > (x7.6) *ϝλᾶνος > (x21.1) *λᾶνος > (13) λῆνος 'wool' **G** aor. ἔμολον 'I came' :: *_ml̥$h_3$sk̂ō_ > (x1.1) *_ml̥$h_3$skō_ > (x7.8) *μλώσκω > (47.4) βλώσκω 'I come' **H** Dor. ἄδμᾱτος :: *_ń̥-dm̥$h_2$tos_ > (x7.15) *_ń̥dmātos_ > (x26.1) *ἄδμᾱτος > (13) ἄδμητος 'untamed' **I** δέμω 'I build' :: *_neu̯ó-dm̥$h_2$tos_ > (x7.15) *_neu̯ódmātos_ > (x21.2) *νεόδμᾱτος > (13)

*νεόδμητος ‘newly built’ **J** κάμνω ‘I become tired’ :: **k̂e-k̂m̥h$_2$-u̯ōs* > (x1.1) **ke-km̥h$_2$-u̯ōs* > (x7.15) *κεκμᾱϝώς > (13) *κεκμηϝώς > (x21.2) Hom. κεκμηώς ‘tired’ **K** aor. ἔγρετο ‘woke up’ :: **n̥h$_1$gretos* > (x7.9) νήγρετος ‘without waking up’ **L** κάμνω ‘I am tired’ :: aor. **k̂ḿ̥h$_2$om* > (x1.1) **kḿ̥h$_2$om* > (x8.3) *κάμομ > (x12.1) *κάμον > (+accentuated augment) ἔκαμον ‘I became tired’

E2 Accented Syllabic Resonant Plus Laryngeal Before Consonant

A Skr. *adāṃta-* :: **n̥-dḿ̥h$_2$tos* > (x7.16) **n̥-dámatos* > (x26.1) ἀδάματος ‘untamed’ **B** Skr. *śīrṣán-* :: **k̂ŕ̥h$_2$sn̥h$_2$* > (x1.1) **kŕ̥h$_2$snh$_2$* > (x6.5) **kŕ̥h$_2$sna* > (x7.3) *κάρασνα > (2.2) *κάρᾱνα > (13) Hom. κάρηνα ‘head’ **C** Lat. *palma* :: **pĺ̥h$_2$meh$_2$* > (x2.2) **pĺ̥h$_2$mah$_2$* > (x4.2) **pĺ̥h$_2$mā* > (x7.7) *παλάμᾱ > (13) παλάμη ‘palm of the hand’

Chapter 36: Analogical Changes

E1 The *s*-stem ἔπος, ἔπους, ἔπει goes back to the preforms **u̯ék^{w}os*, **u̯ék^{w}esos*, **u̯ék^{w}esi*. Is this the regular result? Where did analogy take place?

Answer: The regular development would have been **u̯ek^{w}os* > ἔπος, **u̯ek^{w}esos* > ἔτους*, **u̯ek^{w}esi* > ἔτει*. In forms like ἔπους and ἔπει, τ was analogically replaced by π.

E2 Why is the difference of the paradigmatic forms prs. θείνω ‘I kill’ :: aor. ἔπεφνε ‘I killed’ a peculiarity?

Answer: In this case, no levelling took place but the regular forms were maintained.

E3 Is the nom. pl. ὀστᾶ of ὀστοῦν ‘bone’ regular if it goes back to *ὀστέα?

Answer: The nom. pl. of ὀστοῦν should have been ὀστῆ* because the contraction ε+α normally yielded η. The form ὀστᾶ can be explained in analogy to neuter nouns such as δῶρα which end in final α.

E4 Seen in relation to ἅπτω ‘I touch’, why is ἀφάσσω ‘I touch’ a regular form and ἁφάω ‘I touch’ not?

Answer: The verb ἀφάσσω lost its initial aspiration due to Grassmann’s law. In ἁφάω, the initial aspiration was reintroduced in analogy to ἅπτω.

E5 The numeral διᾱκόσιοι ‘two hundred’ should be διᾱκασιοι* with *α* instead of *o*, because the second element -κασι- goes back to *κατι which is a variant of ἑκατόν ‘hundred’. What is the origin of the analogical formation?

Answer: In this case, the *o* of εἴκοσι ‘20’, τριάκοντα ‘30’, τετταράκοντα ‘40’ was the origin of the analogical formation.

E6 The paradigms of the contracted verbs τῑμάω, ποιέω, δουλόω with their future forms τῑμήσω, ποιήσω, δουλώσω were analogically leveled. While ποιέω < *ποιέ-ω and δουλόω < *δουλό-ω are nominal derivations with short vowel ε/ο, verbs like τῑμάω < *τῑμᾱ-ω are derivations from ᾱ-stems. Where did analogy take place if one assumes that rule SC 1.1 “a vowel before a vowel was shortened” took place in a relatively recent period of time and definitively after the vowel raising ᾱ > η?

Answer: *τῑμᾱω was shortened very early to *τῑμάω in analogy to the short vowel of ποιέω and δουλόω. After that it was contracted to *τῑμάω > (10.1) τῑμῶ. Otherwise, *τῑμᾱω would have become ^{x}τῑμηω and subsequently ^{x}τῑμεω or ^{x}τῑμη. The long vowel of the future formations did, however, originate from formations such as *τῑμᾱω because its long vowel stayed intact before a consonant in future forms like *τῑμᾱσω before ᾱ became η except before ε, ι, ρ producing τῑμήσω. This long vowel was subsequently taken over by formations like ποιήσω and δουλώσω, which originally had a short vowel.

Overview of Sound Change Rules

Vowel Changes

1	Vowel Shortening
2–6	Vowel Lengthening
7–10	Vowel Contraction
11–15	Vowel Raising and Monophthongization
16–23	Syncope / Elision / Hyphaeresis / Anaptyxis / Prothetic Vowels / Vowel Assimilation / Diphthongization

Consonant Changes

24	Assimilation of Place of Articulation
25–34	Assimilation of Manner of Articulation
35–37	Assimilation of Place and Manner of Articulation
38–42	Distant Assimilation / Dissimilation / Metathesis
43–47	Loss and Emergence of Consonants

From Proto-Indo-European to Attic

x1	Merger of PIE Palatals and PIE Velars
x2–x8	Development of Laryngeals
x9	Mediae Aspiratae Become Tenuis Aspiratae
x10–x11	Loss of Labial Coarticulation of Labiovelars
x12	Loss of Final Consonants
x13–x15	Development of *σ and Therefrom Resulting *h*
x16	Loss and Strengthening of Semivocalic *ι̯
x17	Iota-Epenthesis
x18	Palatalization of Voiced Consonants
x19	Palatalization of Voiceless Consonants
x20	The Initial Sequence πτ
x21	The Semivowel *ϝ and Its Combination *τϝ
x22	Assibilation of *τι and *τυ
x23–24	Development of the Labiovelars
x25–x26	Development of Syllabic Resonants

INDEX

Vowel Changes[1]

Vowel Shortening

Long Vowels Were Shortened Before Vowels and Before Resonant plus Consonant

SC	Rule	Example	
1.1	*V̄ > V̆ / _V*[2]	ωη > οη	Hom. ζωή :: *ζωή > (1.1) Att. ζοή 'life'
1.2	*V̄V̆ > V̆V̄*[3]	ηο > εω	πόλις 'city' :: gen. sg. *πόληι̯ος > (x16.1) *πόληος > (1.2) πόλεως 'of the city'
1.3	*V̄ > V̆ / _RC*	ηϱν > εϱν	Skr. *pā́rṣṇi-* :: *πήϱσνη > (x20) *πτήϱσνη > (43.6) *πτήϱνη > (1.3) πτέϱνη 'heel'

Vowel Lengthening

Compensatory Lengthening After "Sigma-Loss"[4]

SC	Rule	Example	
2.1	**VRs > V̄R*[5]	*εμσ > ειμ	νέμω 'I attribute' :: aor. *ἔνεμσα [énemsa] > (2.1) ἔνειμα [énẹ̄ma] 'I attributed'
2.2	**VsR > V̄R*	*υσμ > ῡμ	κϱύσταλλος 'ice' :: *κϱυσμός [krysmós] > (2.2) κϱῡμός [krȳmós] 'frost'

Compensatory Lengthening After "Iota-Loss"[6]

SC	Rule	Example	
3.1	**VRi̯ > V̄R*	*ενι̯ > ειν	√τεν- 'to stretch' :: *τένι̯ω [téni̯ǭ] > (3.1) τείνω [tẹ̄́nǭ] 'I stretch'
3.2		*ινι̯ > ῑν	√κλιν- 'to incline' :: *κλίνι̯ω [klíni̯ǭ] > (3.2) κλῑ́νω [klī́nǭ] 'I incline'
3.3		*υνι̯ > ῡν	ἀμεύομαι 'I transgress' :: *ἀμύνι̯ω [amýni̯ǭ] > (3.3) ἀμῡ́νω [amȳ́nǭ] 'I repel'

1 The sound change rules are not strictly chronologically ordered but in a mixture of chronologic and thematic order. The x-rules, which begin after sound change 47.6, usually present an older chronological layer of developments.

2 In cases such as *h_3b^hruHs* > ὀφϱῦς 'eyebrow' :: gen.. sg. *h_3b^hruHos* > ὀφϱύος, the synchronic shortening can be regarded as a different treatment of original PIE laryngeals. In the nom. *h_3b^hruHs*, the laryngeal caused the lengthening of the preceding vowel and in the gen. *h_3b^hruHos* the intervocalic laryngeal was lost and caused vowel hiatus (cf. Rix §81).

3 This sound change only affected Attic words and was the reason for the formation of the so-called "Attic declension" of the kind λεώς 'people', νεώς 'temple' in contrast to Dor. λᾱός, νᾱός. Speakers of the Koine language did not use these forms anymore because they were thought to be too specifically Attic (cf. Horrocks 1997:36).

4 There are two phonetic explanations of this sound change. The starting point is in both cases the development *σ > *h*, which caused a preform such as *σελάσνα to become *σελάhνα. At this stage, the fricative *h* disappeared with compensatory lenghtening of the foregoing vowel. This led to *σελᾱ́να which is preserved in Dor. σελᾱ́να and is also the preform of Att.-Ion. σελήνη. In Aeol. σελάννα, however, the sequence *σν developed to geminate νν which is an argument that in the preform *σελάhνα, the fricative h first assimilated to the ν following so that *σελάhνα became σελάννα, which is preserved in Aeol. and became Dor. σελᾱ́να and Att.-Ion. σελήνα by degemination of νν with compensatory lenghtening of the preceding vowel. This second development is very probable because one finds gemination of sequences **sR* and **Rs* at morpheme boundaries if preverb and verb in forms like *ἐπισϱέϝει > ἐπειϱϱέει or *ἄσληκτον > ἄλληκτον in Attic, too.

5 As the sequences **VRs* and **VsR* exhibit exactly the same phonological development, one often finds the assumption that they had merged by metathesis (which was either **VRs* > **VsR* or **VsR* > **VRs*) before *σ was lost and the vowel was lengthened.

6 The problem of Proto-Greek palatalizations: In many languages of the world, one can observe the phenomenon that the palatal semivowel ι̯ = i̯ = IPA [j] causes the palatalization of adjacent sounds as well as combinatoric sound changes. One can therefore assume that Proto-Greek *ι̯ also had a palatalizing effect on adjacent sounds. As Attic does not exhibit any palatalized consonants but only indirect effects of former palatalized consonants, one must assume the after the period of palatalizations caused by Proto-Greek *ι̯ the palatalized consonants were depalatalized again. A preform such as *τένι̯ω would therefore have first become *τένι̯ω with palatalized νι̯. As one finds that the Attic sequence of a long vowel plus a single consonant in τείνω corresponds to a sequence of a short vowel and a geminate consonant in Aeol. τέννω (like in SC 2), the questions arises whether the Attic long lowels were caused directly by the loss of Proto-Greek *ι̯ or by the degemination of former geminate resonants which caused a compensatory lengthening of the preceding vowel. In this case *τένι̯ω would have become *τέννι̯ω before depalatalization led to Aeol. τέννω and further degemination with compensatory lenghtening led to Att. τείνω. Cf. also SC x17.

Compensatory Lengthening After Nasal-Loss in the Sound Cluster *νσ

SC	Rule		Example
4.1	**VnsV > V̄sV*	*υνσ > ῡσ	δύω ‘I immerse’ :: ptc. prs. f. *δύντι̯α > (x19.2) *δύνσσα > (45.4) *δύνσα > (4.1) δῦσα ‘immersing’
4.2	**Vns# > V̄s#*	*ανς > ᾱς	nom. sg. nt. μέλαν :: nom. sg. m. *μέλανς > (4.2) μέλᾱς ‘black’

Compensatory Lengthening after Nasal-Loss in the Sound Cluster *λν[7]

SC	Rule		Example
5	? **Vln > V̄l*	*αλν > ᾱλ	στέλλω ‘I arrange’ :: *στάλνᾱ > (5) *στᾱ́λᾱ > (13) ion-Att. στήλη ‘pillar’

Compensatory Lengthening after Iota-Loss[8]

SC	Rule		Example
6.1	*ai̯ > ā / _V*	αι > ᾱ	ἐλαίᾱ > (6.1) ἐλᾱ́ᾱ ‘olive tree’
6.2	*yi̯ > ȳ / _V*	υι > ῡ	υἱός [hyi̯ós] > ῡ̔ός [hȳós] ‘son’ ‘son’
6.3	*yi̯ > ȳ / _C*	υι > ῡ	ἰχθῡ́ς ‘fish’ :: *ἰχθυ-ίδιον > (6.3) ἰχθῡ́διον ‘little fish’

Vowel Contractions

Contractions of Alike Vowels

SC	Rule		$\breve{\bar{V}}_1 + \breve{\bar{V}}_1 = \bar{V}_1$
7.1	*a/ā + a/ā > ā*	α/ᾱ + α/ᾱ > ᾱ	καίω ‘I burn’ :: *κάϝαλον > (x21.2) *κάαλον > (7.1) κᾶλον ‘fire wood’
7.2	*e/ẹ̄ + e/ ẹ̄ > ẹ̄*	ε/ει + ε/ει > ει	ποιέω ‘I do’ :: 2. pl. *ποιέ-ετε > (7.2) ποιεῖτε ‘you do’
7.3	*o/ọ̄ + o/ọ̄ > ọ̄*	ο/ọ̄ + ο/ọ̄ > ọ̄	δηλόω ‘I show’ :: 1. pl. *δηλό-ομεν > (7.3) *δηλọ̄̃μεν > (15) δηλοῦμεν
7.4	*ĭ̄ + ĭ̄ > ī*[9]	ῐ̄ + ῐ̄ > ῑ	φθίνω ‘I vanish’ :: 3. sg. opt. *φθί-ῑ-το > (7.4) Hom. φθῖτο ‘he shall vanish’
7.5	*ŭ̄ + ŭ̄ > ū*	ῠ̄ + ῠ̄ > ῡ	Att. υἱός [hyi̯ós] :: inscrip. hυυς > (7.5) hῡς [hȳs] ‘son’
7.6	*ę̄ + ę̄ > ę̄*	η + η > η	παιδεύω ‘I educate’ :: 2. pl. subj. *παιδευθή-ητε > (7.6) παιδευθῆτε
7.7	*ǭ + ǭ > ǭ*	ω + ω > ω	γιγνώσκω ‘I recognize’ :: 1. sg. subj. Hom. γνώω > (7.7) Att. γνῶ

Contractions of Similar Vowels[10]

SC	Rule		Example
8.1	*e/ ẹ̄ + ę̄ > ę̄*	ε/ει + η > η	ποιέω ‘I do’ :: 2. pl. subj. *ποιέ-ητε > (8.1) ποιῆτε
8.2	*ę̄ + e/ẹ̄ > ę̄*	η + ε/ει > η	εἰμί ‘I am’ :: *ἦεν > (8.2) ἦν ‘I was’
8.3	*o/ọ̄ + ǭ > ǭ*	ο/ọ̄ + ω > ω	δοῦλος ‘slave’ :: *δουλό-ω > (8.3) δουλῶ ‘I am a slave’
8.4	*ǭ + o/ọ̄ > ǭ*	ω + ο/ọ̄ > ω	Hom. λαγωός :: *λαγωός > (8.4) Att. λαγῶς ‘hare’

7 This rule is often posed to explain a certain set of words although their etymology is far from clear. Cf. SI §224.

8 This rule is disputed and other explanations are possible. In many cases, one finds vowel shortening according to SC 1.1. after the compensatory lenghtening. This sound change is sometimes labeled as a monophthongization. Cf. Rix §73; LJ §264; Allen 1974:78; Aitchison 1976:188–189.

9 It is very hard to find examples for contractions of ῐ + ῐ and ῠ + ῠ.

10 The similar vowels ε/ει/η as well as ο/ου/ω differ only slightly in their quality disregarding their length.

Contractions of A-Sound (α/ᾱ) and E-Sound (ε/ει/η)[11]

SC	Rule		Example
9.1	*a* + *e*/*ẹ̄*/*ę̄* > *ā*[12]	α + ε/ει > ᾱ	τῑμάω 'I honor' :: 2. sg. imp. *τῑ́μα-ε > (9.1) τῑ́μᾱ 'honor!'
9.2	*e*/*ē*[13] + *a* > *ę̄*	ε + α > η	ὄρος 'mountain' :: nom.-acc. pl. *ὄρεα > (9.2) ὄρη 'mountains'

Contractions of A-Sound (α/ᾱ) and O-Sound (ο/ου/ω)

SC	Rule		Example
10.1	*a* + *o*/*ọ̄*/*ǭ* > *ǭ*	α + ο/ọ̄/ω > ω	τῑμάω 'I honor' :: 1. pl. *τῑμά-ομεν > (10.1) τῑμῶμεν 'we honor'
10.2	*o*/*ọ̄*/*ǭ* + *a* > *ǭ*	ο/ọ̄/ω + α > ω	αἰδώς 'shame' :: acc. sg. Hom. αἰδό-α > (10.2) Att. αἰδῶ

Contractions of E-Sound (ε/ει/η) and O-Sound (ο/ου/ω)

SC	Rule		Example
10.3	*e*/*ẹ̄* + *o*/*ọ̄* > *ọ̄*	ε/ει + ο/ọ̄ > ọ̄	ποιέω 'I do' :: 1. pl. *ποιέ-ομεν > (10.3) *ποιọ̄̃μεν > (15) ποιοῦμεν
10.4	*o*/*ọ̄* + *e*/*ẹ̄* > *ọ̄*	ο/ọ̄ + ε/ει > ọ̄	δηλόω 'I show' :: 2. pl. *δηλό-ετε > (10.4) *δηλọ̄̃τε > (15) *δηλοῦτε
10.5	*e*/*ẹ̄* + *ǭ* > *ǭ*	ε/ει + ω > ω	φίλος 'friend' :: *φιλέ-ω > (10.5) φιλῶ 'I love'
10.6	*ǭ* + *e*/*ẹ̄* > *ǭ*	ω + ε/ει > ω	ῥῑγέω 'I shudder' :: 2. pl. subj. *ῥῑγώετε > (10.6) ῥῑγῶτε
10.7	*ę̄* + *o*/*ọ̄* > *ǭ*	η + ο/ọ̄ > ω	τίθημι 'I put' :: 1. pl. subj. aor. *θήωμεν > (10.7) θῶμεν

Qualitative Vowel Changes

Cowgill's Law

SC	Rule	Example
11	**o* > *u* / *B_R* oder *R_B* *B* = (*m*, *b*, *p*, *p*^{h}, **u̯*, **k*^{w}, **g*^{w}, **k*^{wh})	Lat. *folium* :: **p*^{h}*óli̯on* > (36.4) **p*^{h}*óllon* > (11) **p*^{h}*úllon* > (12.1) φύλλον 'leaf'

Palatalization of [u] > [y][14]

SC	Rule	Example
12	**u* > υ [y]	κύβος [kúbos] > (12) κύβος [kýbos] 'cube'
12.2	**ū* > ῡ [ȳ]	Skr. *dhūma-* 'smoke' :: **d*^{h}*ūmós* > (x9.2) **t*^{h}*ūmós* > (12.2) θῡμός 'courage'

Backing of *e to *o next to Labial Sounds[15]

SC	Rule	Example
12.3	? **e* > **o*	Skr. *cakrá-* 'wheel' :: **k*^{w}*é-k*^{w}*lh*$_1$*os* > (x3.1) **k*^{w}*é-k*^{w}*los* > (12.3) **k*^{w}*ó-k*^{w}*los* > (11) **k*^{w}*ú-k*^{w}*los* > (x10.1) **kúklos* > (12.1) κύκλος 'circle'

The Attic- Ionic Raising ᾱ > η and the Attic Reversion η > ᾱ after ε, ι, ρ

SC	Rule	Example
13	*ᾱ > η	παλΰνω 'to spinkle' :: *πάλϝᾱ > (13) *πάλϝη > (x21.3) πάλη 'flour'
13.1	*ᾱ > *ǣ[16]	Dor. ἁμέρᾱ :: **hāmérā* > (13.1) **hǣmérǣ* > (13.2)
13.2	*ǣ > ᾱ / (ε, ι, ρ)_	(13.1) > **hǣmérǣ* > (13.2) **hǣmérā* > (13.3)
13.3	*ǣ > η	(13.2) > **hǣmérā* > (13.3) ἡμέρᾱ [hę̄mérā] 'day'

11 In contractions of A-sound plus E-sound, always the first sound prevails over the second.

12 The contraction of α+ε happened after the vowel raising of ᾱ > (13) η because forms like τῑ́μᾱ 'honor!' were not further changed to ^{x}τῑ́μη.

13 I did not find examples for *ę̄*.

14 The sound change was not reflected in spelling.

15 Very rare sound change which is needed to bring the acc. κύκλον back to its prestage **k*^{w}*é-k*^{w}*lh*$_1$*om*, which is indicated by Skr. *cakrá-*. Another example is the development of **g*^{w}*enā* > (12.3) **g*^{w}*onā́* > (11) **g*^{w}*unā́* > (x10.2) **gunā́* > (12.1) **gynā́* > (13) γυνή 'woman'. Sound change 12.3 is followed by sound change 11 in both cases (cf. Rix §97a; SI §40a).

16 The result of the vowel shortening of the intermediate step [ǣ] of the development ᾱ > η was ε. An example is: Myc. *pa-ra-wo-jo* :: *παράϝσᾱ > (2.1) *παρᾱ́ϝᾱ > (13.1) *παρǣϝǣ > (x21.2) *παρǣǣ > (1.1) *παρεǣ > (13.2) παρέᾱ 'cheek'.

Monophthongizations

SC	Rule	Example
14.1	**o̯u > *ọ̄*[17]	Att. ἐλήλυθα :: **elḗlou̯tʰe* > (14.1) *ελήλọ̄θε > (15) Hom. εἰλήλουθα 'I have come'
14.2	**ei̯ > ẹ̄*	Av. dāiš :: **édēi̯ksa* > (1.3) **édei̯ksa* > (14.2) ἔδειξα [édẹ̄ksa] 'I showed'

Vowel Raising

SC	Rule	Example
15	**ọ̄ > ū*	δηλόω 'I show' :: 1. pl. *δηλό-ομεν > (73) *δηλọ̄͂μεν > (15) δηλοῦμεν

Vowel Loss / Prothetic Vowels / Vowel Assimilation / Synizesis

Syncope

SC	Rule	Example
16.1	*V > Ø / ′C_C*	οἴομαι > (16.1) οἶμαι 'I believe'
16.2	*V > Ø / C_C ′*	Βερενίκη > (16.2) Βερνίκη : a proper name which literally means 'bringing victory'

Elision

SC	Rule	Example
17	*V > Ø / C_#V*	ἀλλὰ ἐγώ > (17) ἀλλ' ἐγώ 'but I'

Hyphaeresis

SC	Rule	Example
18	*V > Ø / V_V*	Dor. βοᾱθέω :: *βοᾱθοέω > (18) *βοᾱθόω > (8.3) *βοᾱθῶ > (13) βοηθῶ 'I help'

Anaptyxis / Vowel Insertion

SC	Rule	Example
19	*Ø > V / C_C*	ἄρχων 'leader' :: gen. sg. ἄρχοντος > (19) inscrip. ἄραχοντος

Prothetic Vowels[18]

SC	Rule	Example
20	*Ø > V / #_*	Skr. *nápāt-* 'offspring' :: *νεψιός > (20) ἀ-νεψιός 'nephew'

Vowel Assimilation

SC	Rule	Example	
21.1	$V_1 \ldots V_2 > V_1 \ldots V_1$	ε...α > ε...ε	Ion. μέγαθος :: *μέγαθος > (21.1) μέγεθος 'size'
21.2	$V_1 \ldots V_2 > V_2 \ldots V_2$	ε...α > α...α	ψεκάς > (21.2) ψακάς 'drop'

Consonantification of Semivowels / Synizesis

SC	Rule	Example
22.1	*i > i̯ / _V*	πόλις 'city' :: gen. sg. πόλιος [pólios] > (22.1) Hom. πόλι̯ος [póli̯os]
22.2	*e > i̯ / _V*	Hom. στερεός :: *στερεός > (22.2) *στερι̯ός > (35.4) στερρός 'rigid'

17 Cf. Rix §55, §238. Very few examples can be found for the Greek representation of PIE **o̯u*.
18 Apart from the spontaneous vowel prothesis which is described by SC 20, the PIE laryngeals caused a similar phenomenon (SC x5).

Diphthongization through Resolve of Hiatus[19]

SC	Rule		Example
23.1	*ĭ > i̯ / V_*	οϊ [oi] > οι [oi̯]	Lat. ovis :: *ὄϝις > (x21.2) Hom. ὄϊς [óis] > (23.1) Att. οἶς [ói̯s] 'sheep'
23.2	*ŭ > u̯ / V_*	αϋ [au] > αυ [au̯]	Hom. γρᾱΰς :: *γρᾱι̯ύς > (x16.1) *γρᾱΰς [grāús] > (1.3) *γραΰς > (23.2) Att. γραῦς [grāu̯s] 'aged woman'

Consonant Changes

Assimilation of Place of Articulation

Allophonic Assimilation of Nasal Consonants

SC	Rule		Example
24.1	$n > m$ / _(m, b, p, p^h)	*νμ > μμ	μένω 'I stay' :: ἐνμένω > (24.1) ἐμμένω 'I stay within'[20]
24.2	$n > \eta$ / _(g, k, k^h)	*νκ > γκ	φαίνω 'I show' :: perf. *πέ-φαν-κα > (24.3) πέφαγκα 'I have showed'
24.3	$m > n$ / _(*t, d*, *i̯, *s*)	*μι̯ > νι̯	Lat. *veniō* :: *g^wm̥-i̯ō* > (x26.4) *g^wami̯ō* > (24.3) *g^wani̯ō* > (x24.4) **bani̯ō* > (x17) βαίνω 'I go'

Assimilation of Manner of Articulation

Deaspiration: Aspirated Stop Before Non-Aspirated Stops

SC	Rule		C [+aspirated] > C [-aspirated] / _C [-aspirated]
25.1	$p^h > p$ / _s	*φσ > ψ	τροφή 'nourishment' :: fut. *θρέφ-σω > (25.1) θρέψω 'I nourish'
25.2	$p^h > p$ / _t	*φτ > πτ	γράφω 'I write' :: perf. *γέγραφ-ται > (25.2) γέγραπται 'I have written'
25.3	$p^h > p$ / _N	*φμ > *πμ	γράφω 'I write' :: *γράφμα > (25.3) *γράπμα > (31.1) *γράβμα > (32.2) γράμμα 'letter'
25.4	$p^h > p$ / _d	*φδ > *πδ	κρύφα :: *κρύφδα > (25.4) *κρύπδα > (30.1) κρύβδα 'hidden'
25.5	$p^h > p$ / _i̯	*φι̯ > *πι̯	τάφος 'burial' :: *θάφι̯ω > (25.5) *θάπι̯ω > (x19.1) θάπτω 'I bury'
25.6	$t^h > t$ / _s	*θσ > *τσ	πείθω 'I persuade' :: fut. *πείθ-σω > (25.6) *πείτ-σω > (33) *πείσ-σω > (45.1) πείσω 'I will persuade'
25.7	$t^h > t$ / _t	*θτ > *ττ	πείθω 'I persuade' :: *πιθτός > (25.7) *πιττός > (46.1) *πιτστός > (43.1) πιστός 'loyal to'
25.8	$t^h > t$ / _k	*θκ > *τκ	πείθω 'I persuade' :: *πέπειθ-κα > (25.8) *πέπειτ-κα > (44) πέπεικα 'I have persuaded'
25.9	$t^h > t$ / _i̯	*θι̯ > *τι̯	Skr. *dhyā́-* 'to think' :: *θι̯ᾶμα > (25.9) *τι̯ᾶμα > (x19.2) *σσᾶμα > (45.2) *σᾶμα > (13) σῆμα 'sign'
25.10	$k^h > k$ / _s	*χσ > ξ	εὔχομαι 'I pray' :: fut. *εὔχ-σομαι > (25.10) εὔξομαι 'I will pray'
25.11	$k^h > k$ / _t	*χτ > κτ	ταραχή 'confusion' :: perf. pass. *τετάραχται > (25.11) τετάρακται 'has become troubled'
25.12	$k^h > k$ / _N	*χμ > *κμ	ἐλέγχω 'I insult' :: perf. *ἐλήλεγχμαι [elḗleŋkʰmai̯] > (25.12) *ἐλήλεγκμαι [elḗleŋkmai̯] > (31.2) *ἐλήλεγγμαι [elḗleŋgmai̯] > (32.5) *ἐλήλεγγμαι [elḗleŋŋmai̯] > (45.6) ἐλήλεγμαι [elḗleŋmai̯] 'I have insulted'
25.13	$k^h > k$ / _d	*χδ > *κδ	σπέρχω 'I urge' :: *σπέρχδην > (25.13) *σπέρκδην > (30.2) σπέργδην urgent'
25.14	$k^h > k$ / _i̯	*χι̯ > *κι̯	ταραχή 'confusion' :: *ταράχι̯ω > (25.14) *ταράκι̯ω > (x19.4) Att. ταράττω 'I confuse'

19 The hiat was not resolved by contraction but by the transformation of one element into a semivowel.

20 The sound change *n > m / _m* happens after the prefix ἐν- or in the perf. midd. tense such as in παροξύνω 'I excite' :: *παρώξυνμαι > (24.1) παρώξυμμαι.

Aspiration: Stop Before and After Aspirated Stop

SC	Rule		C [-aspirated] > C [+aspirated] / _C_ [+aspirated]
26.1	$p > p^h / \_t^h$	*πθ > φθ	λαμβάνω ‘I seize’ :: 3. sg. aor. pass. *ἐλήβθη > (29.3) *ἐλήπθη > (26.1) ἐλήφθη ‘was seized’
26.2	$t > t^h / \_t^h$	*τθ > *θθ	οἶδα ‘I know’ :: 2. sg. *οἶδ-θα > (29.6) *οἶτ-θα > (26.2) *οἶθ-θα > (46.2) *οἶθσθα > (43.2) οἶσθα ‘you know’
26.3	$k > k^h / \_t^h$	*κθ > χθ	λέγω ‘I speak’ :: 3. sg. aor. pass. *ἐλέγθη > (29.11) *ἐλέκθη > (26.3) ἐλέχθη ‘was spoken’
26.4	$t > t^h / p^h\_$	*φτ > φθ	ἕψω ‘I cook’ :: **hepstós* > (x13.5) **hephtós* > (27.1) *$hep^htós$ > (26.4) ἑφθός ‘cooked’
26.5	$t > t^h / k^h\_$	*χτ > χθ	ἐξ ‘out’ :: *ἐκστρός > (x13.5) *ἐκhτρός > (27.2) *ἐχτρός > (26.5) ἐχθρός ‘hostile’

Monophonematic Development of Sequences Consisting of Stop Plus *h*

SC	Rule	C+h or C+h > Ch
27.1	$ph > p^h$	ἕψω ‘I cook’ :: **hepstós* > (x13.5) **hephtós* > (27.1) *$hep^htós$ > (26.4) ἑφθός ‘cooked’[21]
27.2	$kh > k^h$	Myc. *ai-ka-sa-ma* [ai̯ksmā] :: **ai̯ksmę̄* > (x13.5)**ai̯khmę̄* > (27.2) Hom. αἰχμή ‘lance’
27.3	$hk > k^h$	Skr. *ṛcháti* :: **érsketai̯* > (x13.5) **érhketai̯* > (27.3) ἔρχεται ‘comes, goes’

Aspiration After Elision

SC	Rule		C [-aspirated] > C [+aspirated] / _C [+aspirated]
28.1	$p\#h > p^h$	π#ό > φο	ἐπὶ ὁδόν > (17) ἐπ’ ὁδόν > (28.1) ἔφοδον
28.2	$t\#h > t^h$	τ#ῶ > θω	ἀντὶ ὧν > (17) ἀντ’ ὧν > (28.2) ἀνθ’ ὧν
28.3	$k\#h > k^h$	κ#οὗ > χου	οὐκ οὗτος > (28.3) οὐχ οὗτος

Desonorization: Stop plus Stop or Fricative /s/

SC	Rule		C [+voiced] > C [-voiced] / _C [-voiced]
29.1	$b > p / \_s$	*βσ > ψ	gen. sg. φλεβός ‘of the eagle’ :: nom. sg. *φλέβ-ς [pʰlébs] > (29.1) φλέψ [pʰléps] ‘eagle’
29.2	$b > p / \_t$	*βτ > πτ	λαμβάνω ‘I seize’ :: *ληβτός > (29.2) ληπτός ‘seized’
29.3	$b > p / \_t^h$	*βθ > *πθ	λαμβάνω ‘I seize’ :: 3. sg. aor. pass. *ἐλήβθη > (29.3) *ἐλήπθη > (26.1) ἐλήφθη ‘was seized’
29.4	$d > t / \_s$	*δσ > *τσ	σπεύδω ‘I hurry’ :: aor. *ἔσπευδ-σα > (29.4) *ἔσπευτσα > (33) *ἔσπευσσα > (45.1) ἔσπευσα ‘I hurried’
29.5	$d > t / \_t$	*δτ > *ττ	ψεύδω ‘I lie’ :: *ἔψευδ-ται > (29.5) *ἔψευτ-ται > (46.1) *ἔψευτσται > (43.1) ἔψευσται ‘has lied’
29.6	$d > t / \_t^h$	*δθ > *τθ	οἶδα ‘I know’ :: 2. sg. *οἶδ-θα > (29.6) *οἶτ-θα > (26.2) *οἶθ-θα > (46.2) *οἶθσθα > (43.2) οἶσθα ‘you know’
29.7	$d > t / \_k$	*δκ > *τκ	σπεύδω ‘I hurry’ :: perf. *ἔσπευδ-κα > (29.7) *ἔσπευτ-κα > (44) ἔσπευκα ‘I have hurried’
29.8	$d > t / \_p$	*δπ > *τπ	Lat. *quippe* :: *k^wídpe > (29.8) *k^wítpe > (x23.1) *τίτπε > (42.3) τίπτε ‘why then?’
29.9	$g > k / \_s$	*γσ > ξ	φλέγω ‘I burn’ :: *φλόγ-ς [pʰlógs] > (29.9) φλόξ [pʰlóks] ‘flame’
29.10	$g > k / \_t$	*γτ > κτ	λέγω ‘I speak’ :: perf. *λέλεγται > (29.10) λέλεκται ‘has spoken’
29.11	$g > k / \_t^h$	*γθ > *κθ	λέγω ‘I speak’ :: 3. sg. aor. pass. *ἐλέγθη > (29.11) *ἐλέκθη > (26.3) ἐλέχθη ‘was spoken’

21 Eventually, *h* between *p* and *t* caused the aspiration of both stops simultaneously.

Sonorization: Voiceless Stop Before Voiced Stop

SC	Rule		C [-voiced] > C [+voiced] / _C [+voiced]
30.1	*p > b / _d*	*πδ > βδ	ἑπτά 'seven' :: *ἕπ-δομος > (30.1) ἕβδομος 'seventh'
30.2	*k > g / _d*	*κδ > γδ	ὀκτώ 'eight' :: *ὄκ-δοος > (30.2) ὄγδοος 'eighth'
30.3	*k > g / _g*	κγ > γγ [gg][22]	ἔκγονος [ékgonos] > (30.3) ἔγγονος [éggonos] 'offspring'

Sonorization: Voiceless Stop Before Nasal

SC	Rule		C [-voiced] > C [+voiced] / _C [+voiced, +nasal]
31.1	*p > b / _N*	*πμ > *βμ	ὄψις 'view' :: *ὄπμα > (31.1) *ὄβμα > (32.2) *ὄμμα 'eye'
31.2	*k > g / _N*	*κμ > *γμ	ἐλέγχω 'I insult' :: 1. sg. perf. *ἐλήλεγχμαι [elę́leŋk^{h}mai̯] > (25.12) *ἐλήλεγκμαι [elę́leŋkmai̯] > (31.2) *ἐλήλεγγμαι [elę́leŋgmai̯] > (32.5) *ἐλήλεγγμαι [elę́leŋŋmai̯] > (45.6) ἐλήλεγμαι [elę́leŋmai̯] 'I have insulted'

Voiced Stop Before Nasal

SC	Rule		C [-nasal] > C [+nasal] / _C [+nasal]
32.1	*b > m / _n*	*βν > μν	σέβομαι 'I honor' :: *σεβνός > (32.1) σεμνός 'honorable'
32.2	*b > m / _m*	*βμ > μμ	τρίβω 'I rub' :: *τέτριβμαι > (32.2) τέτριμμαι 'I have been rubbed'
32.3	*d > n / _m*[23]	δμ > *νμ	Hom. μεσό-δμη :: *μεσό-δμη > (32.3) *μεσόνμη > (42.5) inscrip. μεσομνη 'crossbeam'
32.4	*g > ŋ / _n*[24]	γν [gn] > γν [ŋn]	ἅγιος :: ἅγνος [hágnos] > (32.4) ἅγνος [háŋnos] 'holy'
32.5	*g > ŋ / _m*	*γμ [gm] > *γμ [ŋm]	ἐλέγχω 'I insult' :: 1. sg. perf. *ἐλήλεγχμαι [elę́leŋkhmai̯] > (25.12) *ἐλήλεγκμαι [elę́leŋkmai̯] > (31.2) *ἐλήλεγγμαι [elę́leŋgmai̯] > (32.5) *ἐλήλεγγμαι [elę́leŋŋmai̯] > (45.6) ἐλήλεγμαι [elę́leŋmai̯] 'I have insulted'

Fricativization of τ Before σ

SC	Rule		Example
33	*t > s / _s*	*τσ > *σσ	σπεύδω 'I hurry' :: Aor. *ἔσπευδ-σα > (29.4) *ἔσπευτσα > (33) *ἔσπευσσα > (45.1) ἔσπευσα 'I hurried'

Analogical Assimilations[25]

SC	Rule		C/N [+dental] > s / _C[+labial]
34.1	*d > s / _m*	*δμ > σμ	σκευάζω 'I equip' :: perf. *ἐσκεύαδ-μαι > (34.1) ἐσκεύασμαι 'I have equipped myself'
34.2	*th > s / _m*	*θμ > σμ	πείθω 'I persuade' :: *πέπειθμαι > (34.2) πέπεισμαι 'I am persuaded'
34.3	*t > s / _m*	*τμ > σμ	δατέομαι 'I distribute' :: *δατ-μός > (34.3) δασμός 'part'
34.4	*n > s / _m*	*νμ > σμ	φαίνω 'I appear' :: perf. *πέ-φαν-μαι > (34.4) πέφασμαι 'I have appeared'

22 The spelling γγ was originally used for [gg] and in later times for [ŋg] (cf. Sturtevant 1940 §71a).
23 Substandard language. Normally, δ remains before a nasal. (cf. LJ §153, §66.3).
24 Before the later development of *ŋn* > *nn* and *ŋm* > *mm* (cf. Sturtevant 1940 §71b). The pronunciation of /g/ may have been retained in formal registers.
25 The starting point for this analogical sound change were regular forms such as *οἶδ-θα > οἶσθα.

Assimilation of Place and Manner of Articulation

Sequences Which Assimilate to ρρ

SC	Rule		Example
35.1	*n > r / _r*[26]	νρ > ρρ	ῥέω 'I flow' :: συνρέω > (35.1) συρρέω 'I flow together'
35.2	**u̯ > r / _r*	*ϝρ > ρρ	Lesb. αὔρηκτος :: *ἄ-ϝρηκτος > (35.2) ἄρρηκτος 'tearproof'
35.3	*s > r / r_*[27]	ρσ > ρρ	Hom. ἄρσην :: *ἄρσην > (35.3) ἄρρην 'male'
35.4	**i̯ > r / r_*[28]	*ρι̯ > ρρ	βορέᾱς > (22.2) *βορι̯ᾶς > (35.4) βορρᾶς 'north wind'

Sequences Which Assimilate to λλ

SC	Rule		Example
36.1	*n > l / _l*	νλ > λλ	λέγω 'I speak' :: συνλέγω > (36.1) συλλέγω 'I gather'
36.2	*n > l / l_*[29]	*λν > λλ	ὄλεθρος 'destruction' :: *ἀπόλνῡμι > (36.2) ἀπόλλῡμι 'I destroy'
36.3	*d > l / _l*	*δλ > λλ	Lat. *sella* :: *σέδλᾱ > (36.3) *σέλλᾱ > (x13.1) ἕλλᾱ 'seat'
36.4	**i̯ > l / l_*	*λι̯ > λλ	ἄγγελος 'messenger' :: prs. *ἄγγελι̯ω > (36.4) ἄγγελλω 'I proclaim'

Sequences Consisting of σ and ν

SC	Rule		Example
37.1	*s > n / _n*[30]	σν > νν	*Πέλοπος νῆσος > (37.1) Πελοπόννησος 'Peloponnese'
37.2	*n > s / _sV*[31]	νσ > σσ	σῖτος 'bread' :: *σύν-σῖτος > (37.2) σύσσῖτος 'eating together'

Distant Assimilation / Dissimilation / Dissimilatory Deletion / Metathesis

Distant Assimilation

SC	Rule	Example	
38.1	$C_1...C_2 > C_1...C_1$	χ...κ > χ...χ	λέχος 'bed' :: *λέχ-σκη > (38.1) *λέχ-σχη > (43.4) λέσχη 'couch'
38.2	$C_1...C_2 > C_2...C_2$	π...θ > φ...θ	παρθένος 'girl' :: voc. παρθένε > (38.2) inscrip. φαρθένε

Regressive Dissimilation

SC	Rule	Example
39.1	ρ...ρ > λ...ρ	Ion. τέρας :: Hom. Aeol. *πέρωρ > (39.1) πέλωρ 'monster'
39.2	ρ...ρ > ν...ρ	δόρυ 'wood' :: *δέρ-δρεϝον > (x21.2) *δέρ-δρεον > (39.2) δένδρεον 'tree'
39.3	λ...λ > ρ...λ	ἄλγος 'pain' :: *ἀλγαλέος > (39.3) ἀργαλέος 'difficult'
39.4	λ...λ > ν...λ	*παλ-φαλάω > (39.4) *παν-φαλάω > (24.1) παμφαλάω 'I look around'
39.5	λ...λ > ι...λ	παλύνω 'to sprinkle' :: *παλ-πάλη > (39.5) παιπάλη 'flour'
39.6	λ...ν > ρ...ν	κλίβανος > (39.6) κρίβανος 'oven'
39.7	ν...ν > λ...ν	νάρναξ > (39.7) λάρναξ 'container'
39.8	ν...ν > ι...ν	πνέω 'I breathe' :: *πον-πνύω > (39.8) ποιπνύω 'I gasp'
39.9	ν...ρ > λ...ρ	νίτρον > (39.9) λίτρον 'natron'
39.10	$C^h...C^h > C...C^h$	θάττων 'faster' :: *θαχύς > (39.10) ταχύς 'fast'
39.11	π...τ...π > π...δ...π	ποταπός > (39.11) ποδαπός 'from what country?'[32]

26 In earlier times, the sequence νρ was not resolved by assimilation but by the insertion of an epenthetic consonant (SC 47.5).
27 Via voiced [z]. The Koine language dismissed Attic ρρ in favor of Ionic ρσ.
28 This rule is valid for newly formed ι̯ through synizesis.
29 In earlier times, ν was lost with compensatory lenghtening (SC 5).
30 Via voiced [z].
31 The sound ν is lost without compensatory lenghtening if it is followed by another consonant: *σύν-στασις > (43.7) σύστατις 'arrangement'.
32 This is a unique example in which in a sequence of three voiced stops the medial stops was voiced.

Progressive Dissimilation

SC	Rule	Example
40.1	ϱ...ϱ > ϱ...λ	Lat. *Cerberus* :: Κέϱβεϱος > (40.1) Κέϱβελος 'hellhound'
40.2	λ...λ > λ...ϱ	κεφαλαλγία > (40.2) κεφαλαϱγία 'headache'
40.3	ϝ...ϝ > ϝ...i̯	εἴϱω 'I say' :: perf. *ϝέϝϱηκα > (40.3) *ϝέi̯ϱηκα > (x21.1) εἴϱηκα 'I have said'

Dissimilatory Deletion

SC	Rule	Example
41.1	λ...λ > Ø...λ	ἐκπλαγῆναι 'to frighten' :: *ἔκ-πλαγ-λος > (41.1) Hom. ἔκπαγλος 'frightening'
41.2	ϱ...ϱ > Ø...ϱ	φϱᾱτϱίᾱ > (41.2) φᾱτϱίᾱ 'kin'
41.3	ϱ...ϱ > ϱ... Ø	φϱάττω 'I fence' :: *δϱύφϱακτον > (41.3) δϱύφακτον 'wooden shed'

Metathesis

SC	Rule		Example
42.1	**tk* > *kt*	*τκ > κτ	aor. ἔτεκον 'brought forth' :: prs. *τί-τκ-ω > (42.1) τίκτω 'I bring forth'
42.2	*$t^hk^h > k^ht^h$	*θχ > χθ	Hitt. *tekan* :: *θχών > (42.2) χθών 'earth'
42.3	**tp* > *pt*	*τπ > πτ	Lat. *quippe* :: *k^w*ídpe* > (29.8) *k^w*ítpe* > (x23.1) *τίτπε > (42.3) τίπτε 'why then?'
42.4	**dz* > *zd*	-	Lat. *iugum* :: **i̯ugóm* > (x12.1) **i̯ugón* > (12.1) **i̯ygón* > (x16.2) **dzygón* > (42.4) ζυγόν [zdygón] 'yoke'
42.5	**nm* > *mn*[33]	νμ > μν	Hom. μεσό-δμη :: *μεσό-δμη > (32.3) *μεσόνμη > (42.5) inscrip. μεσομνη 'crossbeam'
42.6	*p…k* > *k…p*	πεκ > κεπ	Lat. *speciō* :: *σπέκi̯ομαι > (42.6) *σκέπi̯ομαι > (x19.1) σπέκτομαι 'I watch'

Loss and Emergence of Consonants

Simplification of Sequences Containing Sigma

SC	Rule		Examples
43.1	*t* > Ø / _*st*	*τστ > στ[34]	ἀνύτω 'I accomplish' :: *ἀνυτ-τός > (46.1) *ἀνυτστός > (43.1) ἀνυστός 'accomplished'
43.2	t^h > Ø / _st^h	*θσθ > σθ[35]	οἶδα 'I know' :: 2.sg. *οἶδ-θα > (29.6) *οἶτ-θα > (26.2) *οἶθ-θα > (46.2) *οἶθσθα > (42.2) οἶσθα 'you know'
43.3	*k* > Ø / _*sk*	*κσκ > σκ	aor. ἔλακον 'I cried' :: prs. *λάκ-σκω > (43.3) λάσκω 'I cry'
43.4	k^h > Ø / _sk^h	*χσχ > σχ	λέχος 'bed' :: *λέχ-σκη > (38.1) *λέχ-σχη > (43.4) λέσχη 'couch'
43.5	*g* > Ø / _*zg*	*γσγ > σγ	μιγῆναι 'to mix' :: *μίγσκω > (38.1) *μίγσγω > (43.5) Hom. μίσγω 'I mix'
43.6	*s* > Ø / C_1_C_2	*πσθ > πθ	τϱίβω 'I rub' :: perf. inf. midd. *τετϱίβσθαι > (29.1) *τετϱίπσθαι > (43.6) *τετϱίπθαι > (26.1) τετϱίφθαι 'having rubbed'
43.7	*n* > Ø / _*sC*[36]	*νσC > σC	συνίστημι 'I put together' :: *σύν-στημα > (43.7) σύστημα 'compound'
43.8	*n* > Ø / _*zd*[37]	*νζ > ζ	aor. ἔπλαγξα 'I hit' :: prs. *πλάγγi̯ω [pláŋgi̯ǭ] > (x18.1) *πλάνζω [plánzdǭ] > (43.8) πλάζω [plázdǭ] 'I hit'

33 Normally, Attic δ remains before ν.
34 Via the intermediate steps *τστ > (33) *σστ > (45.5) στ.
35 Via the intermediate steps *θσθ > (25.6) *τσθ > (33) *σσθ > (45.5) σθ.
36 Cf. SC 3 for the loss of ν before σ with compensatory lenghtening and SC 37.2 for the assimilation of ν to σ.
37 Voiced variant of 43.7.

Loss of Dental Stop Before Velar Stop[38]

SC	Rule		Example
44	*t* > *Ø* / _*k*	*τκ > κ	σπεύδω ‘I hurry’ :: perf. *ἔσπευδ-κα > (29.7) *ἔσπευτ-κα > (44) ἔσπευκα ‘I have hurried’

Simplification of Geminate Consonants

SC	Rule		Example
45.1	**ss* > *s* / *V*_*V*	*σσ > σ	γένος ‘kin’ :: dat. pl. *γένεσ-σι > (45.1) γένεσι
45.2	**ss* > *s* / #_[39]	*σσ > σ / #_	Skr. *dhyā́*- ‘to think’ :: *θι̯ᾶμα > (25.9) *τι̯ᾶμα > (x19.2) *σσᾶμα > (45.2) *σᾶμα > (13) σῆμα ‘sign’
45.3	**ss* > *s* / _#[40]	*σσ > σ / _#	prs. γι-γνώ-σκω ‘to recognize’ :: ptc. aor. m. *γνώντς > (33) *γνώνσς > (45.3) *γνώνς > (1.3) *γνόνς > (4.2) *γνǫ́ς > (15) γνούς ‘recognizing’
45.4	**ss* > *s* / *C*_	*σσ > σ / C_	χείϱ ‘hand’ :: dat. pl. *χεϱσ-σί > (45.4) χεϱσί
45.5	**ss* > *s* / _*C*	*σσ > σ / _C	Skr. *dáṃsa*- ‘miracle’ :: **di-dn̥̄s-skō* > (x26.1) *δι-δάσ-σκω > (45.5) διδάσκω ‘I teach’
45.6	**ŋŋ* > *ŋ*	*γγ > γ	prs. ἐλέγχω ‘I insult’ :: 1. sg. perf. *ἐλήλεγχμαι [elȩ̄leŋkʰmai̯] > (18.12) *ἐλήλεγκμαι [elȩ̄leŋkmai̯] > (23.2) *ἐλήλεγγμαι [elȩ̄leŋgmai̯] > (24.5) *ἐλήλεγγμαι [elȩ̄leŋŋmai̯] > (34.6) ἐλήλεγμαι [elȩ̄leŋmai̯] ‘I have insulted’

Insertion of σ into Dental Clusters

SC	Rule		Example
46.1	Ø > *s* / *t*_*t*	*ττ > *τστ	ἀνύτω ‘I accomplish’ :: *ἀνυτ-τός > (46.1) *ἀνυτστός > (43.1) ἀνυστός ‘accomplished’
46.2	Ø > *s* / t^h_t^h	*θθ > *θσθ	οἶδα ‘I know’ :: 2. sg. *οἶδ-θα > (29.6) *οἶτ-θα > (26.2) *οἶθ-θα > (46.2) *οἶθσθα > (32.2) οἶσθα ‘you know’

Consonant Strengthening and Epenthetic Consonants

SC	Rule		Example
47.1	*m* > *b* / #_*r*	μϱ > βϱ / #_	μοϱμύϱω ‘I roar’ :: *μϱόμος > (47.1) βϱόμος ‘roaring’
47.2	Ø > *b* / *m*_*r*	μϱ > μβϱ	Skr. *amŕ̥ta*- :: **n̥-mr̥tós* > (47.2) ἄμβϱοτος ‘immortal’
47.3	*m* > *b* / #_*l*	μλ > βλ / #_	aor. ἔμολον ‘I came’ :: prs. *μλώσκω > (47.3) βλώσκω ‘I come’
47.4	Ø > *b* / *m*_*l*	μλ > μβλ	prs. βλώσκω ‘I come’ :: perf. *μέ-μλω-κα > (47.4) μέμβλωκα ‘I have come’
47.5	Ø > *d* / *n*_*r*	νϱ > νδϱ	ἀνήϱ ‘man’ :: gen. sg. *ἀνϱός > (47.5) ἀνδϱός ‘of the man’
47.6	? *n* > *d* / #_*r* [41]	νϱ > δϱ / #_	ἀνήϱ ‘man’ :: *νϱώψ > (47.6) Hes. δϱώψ ‘male’

38 Cf. SC 42.1 for the metathesis of *τκ > κτ.
39 Usually, a direct development *θι̯ > σ is assumed. The simplification of the initial double consonants probably happened very fast.
40 A proof for the existence of final geminate consonants is provided by Lat. *mīles* ‘soldier’ whose final syllable often counts long in Plautus, which is an indication of the pronunciation *mīless* < **mīlets*.
41 Unique example.

From PIE to Attic

PIE Palatal Consonants Merge with Velar Consonants[42]

SC	Rule	Example
x1.1	*k̂ > k	Skr. dáśa :: *dék̂m̥ > (x1.1) *dékm̥ > (x26.3) δέκα 'ten'
x1.2	*ĝ > g	Lat. agō :: *h2éĝō > (x1.2) *h$_2$égō > (x2.1) *h$_2$ágō > (x3.2) ἄγω 'I lead'
x1.3	*ĝ^h > g^h	Lat. ānser :: gen. sg. *ĝ^{h}ansós > (x1.3) *g^{h}ansós > (x9.3) *χανσός > (2.1) *χᾱνός > (13) χηνός 'of the goose'[43]

Vowel Coloring of *e next to Laryngeals

SC	Rule	Example
x2.1	*e > a / *h$_2$_	Lat. agō :: *h$_2$éĝō > (x1.2) *h$_2$égō > (x2.1) *h$_2$ágō > (x3.2) ἄγω 'I lead'
x2.2	*e > a / _*h$_2$	Skr. bhā́ti :: *b^{h}eh$_2$mi > (x2.2) *b^{h}ah$_2$mi > (x4.2) *b^{h}āmi > (x9.1) *φᾱμί > (13) φημί 'I speak'
x2.3	*e > o / *h$_3$_	Skr. ákṣan- :: *h$_3$ék^{w}mn̥ > (x2.3) *h$_3$ók^{w}mn̥ > (x3.3) *ók^{w}mn̥ > (x24.1) *ópmn̥ > (x26.1) *ὄπμα > (31.1) *ὄβμα > (32.2) ὄμμα 'eye'
x2.4	*e > o / _*h$_3$	Lat. dōnum :: *déh$_3$rom > (x2.4) *dóh$_3$rom > (x4.3) *δῶϱομ > (x12.1) δῶϱον 'gift'

Loss of Laryngeals Before Vowel

SC	**Rule**	**Example**
x3.1	*h$_1$ > Ø / _V	Skr. ásmi :: *h$_1$ésmi > (x3.1) *ἐσμί > (2.2) εἰμί 'I am'
x3.2	*h$_2$ > Ø / _V	Lat. agō :: *h$_2$eĝō > (x1.2) *h$_2$egō > (x2.1) *h$_2$agō > (x3.2) ἄγω 'I lead'
x3.3	*h$_3$ > Ø / _V	Skr. ákṣan- :: *h$_3$ék^{w}mn̥ > (x2.3) *h$_3$ók^{w}mn̥ > (x3.3) *ók^{w}mn̥ > (x24.1) *ópmn̥ > (x26.1) *ὄπμα > (31.1) *ὄβμα > (32.2) ὄμμα 'eye'

Loss of Laryngeals After Vowel With Compensatory Lengthening

SC	**Rule**	**Example**
x4.1	*eh$_1$ > ę̄	Skr. dádhāti :: *d^{h}í-d^{h}eh$_1$-mi > (x4.1) *d^{h}í-d^{h}ē-mi > (x9.2) *θίθημι > (39.10) τίθημι 'I put'
x4.2	*ah$_2$ > ā	Skr. bhā́ti :: *b^{h}eh$_2$mi > (x2.2) *b^{h}ah$_2$mi > (x4.2) *bhāmi > (x9.1) *φᾱμί > (13) φημί 'I speak'
x4.3	*oh$_3$ > ǭ	Lat. dōnum :: *déh$_3$rom > (x2.4) *dóh$_3$rom > (x4.3) *δῶϱομ > (x12.1) δῶϱον 'gift'
x4.4	*iH > ī	Skr. prátīka- 'face' :: *opi-h$_3$k^w-eh$_2$ > (x2.2+x4.2+x4.4+) *opīkwā > (x24.2) *opīpā > (13) *ὀπῑ́πη 'watching out' in Hom. ὀπῑπεύω 'I scout' (cf.: Rix §81)
x4.5	*uH > ū	Lat. fūmus 'smoke' :: *d^{h}uh$_2$mós > (x4.5) *dhūmós > (x9.2) θῡμός 'courage'

Laryngeals in the Initial Position Before Consonant

SC	**Rule**	**Example**
x5.1	*h$_1$ > e / #_C [44]	Skr. r̥cháti :: *h$_1$r̥sketai̯ > (x5.1) *érsketai̯ > (x13.5) *érhketai̯ > (27.3) ἔϱχεται 'comes, goes'
x5.2	*h$_2$ > a / #_C	Lat. ventus 'wind' :: *h$_2$u̯eh$_1$ti > (x4.1) *h$_2$u̯ę̄ti > (x5.2) *ἄϝητι > (x21.2) *ἄητι > (x22.1) ἄησι 'blows'
x5.3	*h$_3$ > o / #_C	Skr. bhrū́- :: *h$_3$b^{h}ruHs > (x4.5) *h$_3$b^{h}rūs > (x5.3) *obhrūs > (x9.1) ὀφϱῦς 'eyebrow'

42 No further sound changes for illustrating this sound changes can be found in the book. Cf. chap. 38 L46;52–55.

43 The nom. χήν is not regular because the supposed preform χάνς* should have produced χᾱ́ς*. It was reshaped in analogy to cases like the gen. χηνός by taking over the stem element ν.

44 For more details cf. RIX §79.

Laryngeals Between Consonants and in the Final Position

SC	Rule	Example
x6.1	*h$_1$ > e / C_C	Lat. *animus* :: *h$_2$énh$_1$mos > (x2.1) *h$_2$ánh$_1$mos > (x3.2) *ánh$_1$mos > (x6.1) ἄνεμος 'wind'
x6.2	*h$_2$ > a / C_C	Lat. *status* :: *sth$_2$tós > (x6.2) στατός 'put'
x6.3	*h$_3$ > o / C_C	Old Irish *arathar* :: *h$_2$érh$_3$trom > (x2.1) *h$_2$árh$_3$trom > (x3.2) *árh$_3$trom > (x6.3) *árotrom > (x12.1) ἄροτρον 'plow'
x6.4	*h$_1$ > e / C_#	Lith. *akí* :: *okʷi̯h$_1$ > (x6.4) *okʷi̯e > (x11.1) *ὄκι̯ε > (x19.4) Hom. Ion. ὄσσε 'two eyes'
x6.5	*h$_2$ > a / C_#	Skr. *patnī́-* :: *pótnih$_2$ > (x6.5) πότνια 'mistress'

Syllabic Resonant plus Laryngeal plus Consonant

SC	Rule	Example
x7.1	*r̥h$_1$ > ρη	Lat. *trītus* 'used' :: *tr̥h$_1$tós > (x7.1) τρητός 'drilled'
x7.2	*r̥h$_2$ > ρᾱ	Skr. *ā́śīrta-* :: *ń̥-k̂r̥h$_2$-tos > (x1.1) *ń̥-kr̥h$_2$-tos > (x7.2) *ń̥-krātos > (x26.1) ἄκρᾱτος 'unmixed'
x7.3	*ŕ̥h$_2$ > αρα	Skr. *śīrṣán-* :: **k̂ŕ̥h$_2$sn̥h$_2$ > (x1.1) *kŕ̥h$_2$sn̥h$_2$ > (x6.4)*kŕ̥h$_2$sna > (x7.3) *κάρασνα > (2.2) *κάρᾱνα > (13) Hom. κάρηνα 'head'
x7.4	*r̥h$_3$ > ρω	Lat. *strātus* :: *str̥h$_3$-tós > (x7.4) στρωτός 'spread out'
x7.5	*l̥h$_1$ > λη	καλέω 'I call out' :: *kl̥h$_1$tós > (x7.5) κλητός 'called out'
x7.6	*l̥h$_2$ > λᾱ	Dor. τλᾱτός:: *tl̥h$_2$-tós > (x7.6) *τλᾱτός > (13) τλητός 'carried'
x7.7	*ĺ̥h$_2$ > αλα	Lat. *palma* :: *pĺ̥h$_2$meh$_2$ > (x2.2) *pĺ̥h$_2$mah$_2$ > (x4.2) *pĺ̥h$_2$mā > (x7.7) *παλάμᾱ > (13) παλάμη 'palm of the hand'
x7.8	*l̥h$_3$ > λω	aor. ἔμολον 'I came' :: prs. *ml̥h$_3$sk̂ō > (x7.8) *μλώσκω > (x47.3) βλώσκω 'I come'
x7.9	*n̥h$_1$ > νη	Lat. *nātus* 'born' :: *-ĝn̥h$_1$tos > (x7.9) κασί-γνητος 'brother'
x7.10	*ń̥h$_1$ > ενε	Lat. *nātiō* :: *ĝn̥h$_1$tís > (x1.2) *gn̥h$_1$tís > (x7.10) *γενετίς > (x22.1) γένεσις 'origin'[45]
x7.11	*n̥h$_2$ > νᾱ	θάνατος 'death' :: *dʰnh$_2$tós > (x7.11) *dʰnātós > (x9.2) *θνᾱτός > (13) θνητός 'dead'
x7.12	*ń̥h$_2$ > ανα	θνητός 'dead' :: *dʰń̥h$_2$tos > (x7.12) *dʰánatos > (x9.2) θάνατος 'death'
x7.13	*n̥h$_3$ > νω	ἔφελος 'use' :: *n̥-h$_3$bʰel-ḗs > (x7.13) *nōbʰel-ḗs > (x8.1) *νωφελής > (addition of privative alpha) ἀνωφελής 'useless'
x7.14	*m̥h$_1$ > μη	No examples for this context.
x7.15	*m̥h$_2$ > μᾱ	δαμάζω 'I tame' :: *ń̥-dm̥h$_2$tos > (x6.15) *ń̥dmātos > (x26.1) *ἄδμᾱτος > (13) ἄδμητος 'untamed'
x7.16	*ḿ̥h$_2$ > αμα	Skr. *adāṃta-* :: *n̥-dḿ̥h$_2$tos > (x6.16) *n̥-dámatos > (x20.1) ἀδάματος 'untamed'
x7.17	*m̥h$_3$ > μω	ὄνυξ 'hoof' :: *sm̥-h$_3$nogʷʰes > (x6.17) *smṓnogʷʰes > (x9.4) *smṓnokʷʰes > (11)*smṓnukʷʰes > (x10.3) *smṓnukʰes > (12.1) *smṓnykʰes > (x15.3) Hom. μώνυχες 'single-hoofed'

Syllabic Resonant plus Laryngeal plus Vowel

SC	Rule	Example
x8.1	*l̥h$_1$V > αλV	κλητός 'called out' :: *kl̥h$_1$éi̯ō > (x8.1) *kaléi̯ō > (x16.1) καλέω 'I call out'
x8.2	*m̥h$_2$V > αμV	κάμνω 'I am tired' :: *k̂m̥h$_2$om > (x1.1) *km̥h$_2$om > (x8.2) *κάμομ > (x12.1) *κάμον > (plus accentuated augment) ἔ-καμον 'I became tired'
x8.3	*r̥h$_3$V > αρV	Skr. purás :: *pr̥h$_3$os > (x8.3) πάρος 'before'

INDEX

45 With analogical accentuation of the root syllable.

Mediae Aspiratae Become Tenuis Aspiratae

SC	Rule	
x9.1	*b^{h} > p^{h}	Skr. *nábhas-* :: **néb^{h}os* > (x9.1) νέφος ‘cloud’
x9.2	*d^{h} > t^{h}	Av. *miždəm* :: **misd^{h}ós* > (x9.2) μισθός ‘hire’
x9.3	*g^{h} > k^{h}	Skr. *váhati* ‘he drives’ :: **u̯óĝ^{h}os* > (x1.3) **u̯óg^{h}os* > (x9.3) *ϝόχος > (x21.1) ὄχος ‘carriage’
x9.4	*g^{wh} > *k^{wh}	Lat. *formus* :: **g^{wh}ermós* > (x9.4) **k^{wh}ermós* > (x23.3) θερμός ‘warm’

Loss of Labial Coarticulation of Labiovelars Next to Velar Vowel

SC	Rule	Example
x10.1	*k^{w} > k / _(u,u̯)_	Myc. *qo-u-ko-ro* :: **g^{w}ou̯-k^{w}ólos* > (x10.1) **g^{w}ou̯-kólos* > (x24.4) **bou̯-kólos* > (14.1) **bǭkólos* > (15) βουκόλος ‘cowherd’
x10.2	*g^{w} > g / _(u,u̯)_	Ved. *jánī-* :: **g^{w}enā́* > (12.3) **g^{w}onā́* > (11) **g^{w}unā́* > (x10.2) **gunā́* > (12.1) **gynā́* > (13) γυνή ‘woman’[46]
x10.3	*k^{wh} > k^{h} / _(u,u̯)_	Skr. *raghú-* ‘light’ :: **h$_1$l̥ng^{wh}ús* > (x5.1) **el̥ng^{wh}ús* > (x9.4) **el̥nk^{wh}ús* > (x10.3) **el̥nk^{h}ús* > (x26.1) Hom. ἐλαχύς ‘small’

Loss of Labial Coarticulation of Labiovelars Before *i̯[47]

SC	Rule		Example
x11.1	*k^{w} > *k / _*i̯	*k^{w}i̯ > *κι̯	Skr. *pácati* :: **pék^{w}i̯ō* > (x11.1) *πέκι̯ω > (x19.4) Att. πέττω ‘I cook’
x11.2	*g^{w} > *g / _*i̯	*g^{w}i̯ > *γι̯	Skr. *niktá-* ‘washed’ :: **níg^{w}-i̯ō* > (x11.2) **nígi̯ō* > (x18.2) νίζω ‘I wash’
x11.3	*k^{wh} > *k^{h} / _*i̯	*k^{wh}i̯ > *χι̯	Skr. *raghú-* ‘light’ :: **h$_1$l̥ng^{wh}i̯ōn* > (x5.1) **el̥ng^{wh}i̯ōn* > (x11.3) **el̥ng^{h}i̯ōn* > (x9.3) **el̥nk^{h}i̯ōn* > (25.14) **el̥nki̯ōn* > (x19.4) **el̥nssōn* > (x26.1) Ion. ἐλάσσων ‘smaller’

Final Consonants

SC	Rule		Example
x12.1	*m > n / _#	*ομ > ον	Lat. *arātrum* :: *ἄροτρομ > (x12.1) ἄροτρον ‘plow’
x12.2	*VC$_1$(C$_2$)# > V# (C$_1$ ≠n,r,l,s)		gen. Hom. ἄνακτ-ος :: voc. *ἄνακτ > (x12.2) ἄνα ‘master!’
x12.3	*VC$_1$(C$_2$)# > VC$_1$# (C$_1$ = n,r,l,s)		Skr. *járant-* ‘old’ :: voc. *γέροντ > (x12.3) γέρον ‘old man!’

Buccalization of *s

SC	Rule	Example
x13.1	*s > h / #_V[48]	Lat. *serpō* :: *σέρπω > (x13.1) ἕρπω ‘I crawl’
x13.2	*s > h / V_V[49]	νόστος ‘return’ :: *νέσομαι > (x13.2) *νέhομαι > (x14.1) νέομαι ‘I come’
x13.3	*s > h / #_R	Skr. *srávati* ‘he flows’ :: **sréu̯ō* > (x13.3) **hréu̯ō* = **rhéu̯ō* > (x21.2) ῥέω ‘I flow’
x13.4	*s > h / _R	ῥέω ‘I flow’ :: ipf. *ἔ-σρεϝον > (x13.4) *ἔhρεϝον > (x14.3) *ἔρρεϝον > (x21.2) ἔρρεον ‘I flowed’
x13.5	*s > *h / C_C[50]	ὄρνῡμι ‘I impel’ :: *ὀρσμά > (x13.5) *ὀρhμά > (x14.2) *ὁρμά > (13) ὁρμή ‘assault’

46 Other explanations are possible because it is not sure if γυνή goes back to **g^{w}enā*.

47 Followed by the regular development of the sequences *κι̯, *γι̯, *χι̯ according to SC x18 and SC x19.

48 Exceptions are the side-forms σῦς from Hom. ὗς ‘pig’ as well as Attic συβώτης and Myc. *su-qo-ta* ‘swineherd’.

49 In some words, intervocalic σ remained after **n̥* or **r̥*. Lat. *dēnsus* corresponds to **dn̥sús* > δασύς ‘thick’, furthermore **ń̥sis* > ἄσις ‘mud’ as well as **d^{h}r̥sús* > θρασύς ‘bold’ which corresponds to Ved. *dhr̥ṣṇú-* (cf. SI §172a).

50 Cf. SC 43.

Rules Concerning the Fricative *h* < *s

SC	Rule	Example
x14.1	**h* > Ø / *V_V*	νόστος 'return' :: *νέσομαι > (x13.2) *νέhομαι > (x14.1) νέομαι 'I come'
x14.2	*#V..h > #hV...*[51]	Lat. *ūrō* :: *εὔσω [éu̯sǭ] > (x13.2) *εὔhω [éu̯hǭ] > (x14.2) εὕω [héu̯ǭ] 'I singe'
x14.3	**h* > *R* / _*R*	ῥέω 'I flow' :: ipf. *ἔ-σρεϝον > (x13.4) *ἔ-hρεϝον > (x14.3) *ἔρρεϝον > (x21.2) ἔρρεον 'I flowed'
x14.4	**h* > Ø / #_*R*	Lith. *smagus* 'heavy' :: *σμόγος > (x13.3) *hμόγος > (x14.4) μόγος 'toil'
x14.5	Ø > *h* / #_*y*	Lat. *unda* 'wave' :: **údōr* > (12) **ýdōr* > (x14.5) ὕδωρ [hýdǭr] 'water'

Global Sigma-Rules

SC	Rule	Example
x15.1	**s* > Ø / *V_V*[52]	νόστος 'return' :: *νέσομαι > (x15.1) νέομαι 'I come'
x15.2	**s* > *R* / _*R*[53]	ῥέω 'I flow' :: ipf. *ἔ-σρεϝον > (x15.2) *ἔρρεϝον > (x21.2) ἔρρεον 'I flowed'
x15.3	**s* > Ø / #_*R*[54]	Lith. smagus 'heavy' :: *σμόγος > (x15.3) μόγος 'toil'

Loss and Strengthening of Semi-Vocalic *i̯

SC	Rule		Example
x16.1	**i̯* > Ø / *V_V*[55]	*ι̯ > 0 / V_V	πόλις 'city' :: gen. sg. *πόληι̯ος > (x16.1) *πόληος > (1.2) πόλεως 'of the city'
x16.2	**Hi̯* > *h* / #_*V*	-	Skr. *yákr̥t* :: **Hi̯ēkʷr̥t* > (x16.2) **hēkʷr̥t* > (x24.1) **hēpr̥t* > (x25.1) *ἧπαρτ > (x12.2) ἧπαρ 'liver'
x16.3	**i̯* > *zd* / #_[56]	*ι̯ > ζ	Lat. *iugum* :: **i̯ugóm* > (x12.1) **i̯ugón* > (12) **i̯ygón* > (x16.3) ζυγόν [zdygón] 'yoke'

Iota-Epenthesis = Insertion of Palatal Glide after *α* and *o*[57]

SC	Rule	Example	
x17	*(*a,o*)*Ri̯* > (*a,o*)*i̯R*[58]	*αρι̯ > αι̯ρ	καθαρός 'pure' :: *καθάρι̯ω > (x17) καθαίρω 'I clean'

Palatalization of Voiced Consonants

SC	Rule		Example
x18.1	**gi̯* > *zd*[59]	*γι̯ > ζ	μέγα 'big' :: *μέγι̯ων > (x18.1) μέζων [mézdǭn] 'bigger'
x18.2	**di̯* > *zd*[60]	*δι̯ > ζ	κομιδή 'transport' :: *κομίδι̯ω > (x18.2) κομίζω [komízdǭ] 'I transport'

INDEX

51 In some cases, it is not possible to determine whether initial *h* goes back to medial *σ or was caused through analogy. The spiritus asper of ἡμεῖς < **n̥s-me-es* was probably taken over from ὑμεῖς. The aspiration of ἧμαι < *ἠσ-μαι 'I sit' can be explained by analogy to the synonymous ἕζομαι < *σέδι̯ομαι (LJ §114).

52 This rule sums up SC x13.1 and SC x14.1.

53 This rule sums up SC x13.4 and SC x14.3.

54 This rule sums up SC x13.3 and SC x14.4.

55 Medial *i̯* was probably not yet completely effaced in Myc. times which can be deduced from variant spellings with <j> such as *e-re-pa-te-jo* and spellings without <j> such as *e-re-pa-te-o* 'made of ivory'. These spellings might as well reflect the phonetic spelling of a natural transition consonant *i̯* between vowels.

56 Via **i̯* > **di̯* > **dz* > *zd*.

57 According to SI §203: loss of **i̯*, compensatory lenghtening **a* > **ā* with subsequent diphthongization **ā* > *ai̯*. A pure metathesis **Ri̯* > *i̯R* cannot be ruled out completely.

58 For R ≠ l, otherwise SC 36.4. Cf. SC 3 for the sequences *(ε,ι,υ) *Ri̯*.

59 Via **gi̯* > **di̯* > **dz* > *zd*.

60 Via **gi̯* > **di̯* > **dz* > *zd*.

Palatalization of Voiceless Consonants

SC	Rule		Example
x19.1	**pi̯ > pt*	*πι̯ > πτ	κλοπή ‘theft’ :: *κλέπι̯ω > (x19.1) κλέπτω ‘I steal’
x19.2	**ti̯ > *ss / C_C*[61]	*τι̯ > *σσ	Dor. Lesb. τόσσος :: *τότι̯ος > (x19.2) *τόσσος > (45.1) τόσος ‘that many’
x19.3	**ti̯ > Att. tt / Ion. ss*	*τι̯ > ττ / σσ	μέλι ‘honey’ :: *μέλιτι̯α > (x19.3) Att. μέλιττα / Ion. μέλισσα ‘bee’
x19.4	**ki̯ > Att. tt / Ion. ss*	*κι̯ > ττ / σσ	φυλακή ‘protection’ :: φυλάκι̯ω > (x19.4) Att. φυλάττω / Ion. φυλάσσω ‘I protect’
x19.5	**ti̯ > s / #_V*[62]	*τι̯ > σ / #_V	Skr. *tyajate* ‘he leaves’ :: **ti̯égʷomai̯* > (x19.5) **ségʷomai̯* > (x24.4) σέβομαι ‘I honor’

Sporadic Emergence of the Initial Sequence πτ

SC	Rule		Example
x20	*p > pt / #_*	π > πτ	πόλις > (x20) πτόλις ‘city’

The Semivowel *ϝ and the Sequence *τϝ

SC	Rule		Example
x21.1	**u̯ > Ø / #_(V,R)*	*ϝ > Ø / #_(V,R)	German *Werk* :: *ϝέργον > (x21.1) ἔργον ‘work’
x21.2	**u̯ > Ø / V_V*	*ϝ > Ø / V_V	Skr. *śrávas-* :: *κλέϝος > (x21.2) κλέος ‘fame’
x21.3	**u̯ > Ø / C_*[63]	*ϝ > Ø / C_	Skr. *sárva-* :: *σόλϝος > (x13.1) *ὁλϝος > (x21.3) ὅλος ‘complete’
x21.4	**u̯ > h / #_V*	*ϝ > h / #_	Lat. vesper :: *ϝέσπερος > (x21.4) ἕσπερος ‘evening’
x21.5	**tu̯ > s / #_*[64]	*τϝ > σ / _#	Skr. *tveṣá-* ‘vehement’ :: *τϝείσω > (x15.1) *τϝείω > (x21.5) σείω ‘I shake’
x21.6	**tu̯* > att. *tt* / ion. *ss* / *V_V*	*τϝ > att. ττ / ion. σσ	Skr. *catvā́ras* :: *τέτϝαρες > (x21.6) Att. τέτταρες / Ion. τέσσαρες ‘vier’

Assibilation of *ti > si and *ty > sy

SC	Rule		Example
x22.1	**ti > si*	*τι > σι	Lat. *datiō* :: *δότις > (x22.1) δόσις ‘gift’
x22.2	**ty > sy*	*τυ > συ	Lat. *sēmi-* :: *ἥμιτυς > (x22.2) ἥμισυς ‘half’

Labiovelars Become Dental Stops Before a Palatal Vowel

SC	Rule	Example
x23.1	**kʷ > t / _(i,e)*	Lat. *quis* :: **kʷís* > (x23.1) τίς ‘who?’
x23.2	**gʷ > d / _e*	Skr. *sagarbha-* ‘pregnant’ :: **sm̥-gʷelbʰós* > (x9.1) **sm̥gʷelpʰós* > (x13.1) **hm̥gʷelpʰós* > (x23.2) **hm̥delpʰós* > (x26.3) *ἀδελφός > (39.10) ἀδελφός ‘brother’
x23.3	**kʷʰ > tʰ / _e*	Lat. *formus* :: **gʷʰermós* > (x9.4) **kʷʰermós* > (x23.3) θερμός ‘warm’

61 Valid for *ti̯ from *tʰi̯. A typologically paralellel development is seen in the Vulgar Latin palataliziation of *ti̯ and *ki̯. The Romance languages exhibit uniform reflexes for *ti̯ but varying reflexes for *ki̯.

62 Via *τι̯ > *σσ > σ.

63 Compensatory lenghtening in Ionic.

64 Via *τϝ > *σσ > σ. In the initial position, *τϝ exhibits the same phonological behavior like *τι̯, and in the medial position like *κι̯ (cf. SI §190.4).

Labiovelars Become Labial Stops Before Consonant or Velar Vowel

SC	Rule	Example
x24.1	*k^{w} > p / _C	Lat. *quintus* :: *pénk^{w}tos > (x24.1) πέμπτος 'fifth'
x24.2	*k^{w} > p / _ (a,o)	Lat. *relinquō* :: *léi̯k^{w}ō > (x24.2) λείπω 'I leave'
x24.3	*g^{w} > b / _C	Lat. *agnus* :: *ág^{w}nos > (x24.3) *ἄβνος > (32.1) ἄμνος 'lamb'
x24.4	*g^{w} > b / _(a,o,i)	Lat. *veniō* :: *g^{w}m̥-i̯ō > (x26.4) *g^{w}ámi̯ō > (24.3) *g^{w}áni̯ō > (x24.4) *báni̯ō > (x17) βαίνω 'I go'
x24.5	*k^{wh} > p^{h} / _C	Skr. *raghú-* 'fast' :: *h$_{1}$ln̥g^{wh}rós > (x4.1) *eln̥g^{wh}rós > (x20.1) *elag^{wh}rós > (x8.4) *elak^{wh}rós > (x24.5) ἐλαφρός 'fast, little'
x24.6	*k^{wh} > p^{h} / _(a,o,i)	Skr. *hánti* 'he slays' :: *g^{wh}ónos > (x9.4) *k^{wh}ónos > (x24.6) φόνος 'murder'

Development of *r̥ and *l̥

SC	Rule	Example
x25.1	*r̥ > ar	σπείρω 'I sow' :: *spr̥tós > (x25.1) σπαρτός 'sowed'
x25.2	*r̥ > ra	Lat. *porrum* :: *pr̥son > (x25.2) πράσον 'leek'
x25.3	*l̥ > al	στέλλω 'I send' :: *stl̥tós > (x25.3) σταλτός 'sent'
x25.4	*l̥ > la	Skr. *pr̥thú-* :: *pl̥th$_{2}$ús > (x3.4) *pl̥tús > (x25.4) πλατύς 'even'

Development of *n̥ and *m̥

SC	Rule	Example
x26.1	*n̥ > a	Skr. *tatá-* :: *tn̥tós > (x26.1) τατός 'stretched'
x26.2	*n̥ > an / _V	Skr. *ánudra-* :: *ń̥-udro-s > (x26.2) ἄνυδρος 'waterless'
x26.3	*m̥ > a	Lat. *decem* :: *dék̂m̥ > (x1.1) *dékm̥ > (x26.3) δέκα 'ten'
x26.4	*m̥ > am / _V	Lat. *veniō* :: *g^{w}m̥-i̯ō > (x26.4) *g^{w}ami̯ō > (24.3) *g^{w}ani̯ō > (x24.4) *bani̯ō > (x17) βαίνω 'I go'

Assimilation of Consonants

		δ ?	τ	θ	σ	σθ	μ
Labial	β	?	πτ	φθ	ψ	φθ	μμ
	π	βδ	πτ	φθ	ψ	φθ	μμ
	φ	βδ	πτ	φθ	ψ	φθ	μμ
Dental	δ	?	στ	σθ	σ	σθ	σμ
	τ	?	στ	σθ	σ	σθ	σμ
	θ	?	στ	σθ	σ	σθ	σμ
	ζ	?	στ	σθ	σ	σθ	σμ
Velar	γ	?	κτ	χθ	ξ	χθ	γμ
	κ	γδ	κτ	χθ	ξ	χθ	γμ
	χ	?	κτ	χθ	ξ	χθ	γμ

Vowel Contraction[65]

	α	αι	η	ῃ	ε	ει [ei̯]	ι	ω	ῳ	ο	ου [ọ̄]	οι
α	ᾱ	ᾱͅ	ᾱ	ᾱͅ	ᾱ	ᾱͅ	αι	ω	ῳ	ω	ω	ῳ
ε	η	ῃ	η	ῃ	ει [ẹ̄]	ει [ei̯]	ει	ω	ῳ	ου	ου	οι
ο	ω	ῳ	ω	οι	ου	οι	οι	ω	ῳ	ου	ου	οι
ω	ω	ῳ	ω	ῳ	ω	ῳ	ῳ	ω	ῳ	ω	ω	ῳ
η	η	ῃ	η	ῃ	η	ῃ	ῃ	ω	ῳ	?	?	?

Labiovelars in Attic

PIE		*g^{w}	*k^{w}	*g^{wh}
Proto-Greek		*g^{w}	*k^{w}	*k^{wh}
Attic	before ε / η	δ	τ	θ
	before ι	β	τ	φ
	before ο / α / Consonant	β	π	φ
	next to υ	γ	κ	χ
	before *i̯	γ	κ	κ

Intermediate Steps of Palatalization Processes[66]

Preforms	Merger	Palatalization and Affrication	Metathesis	Assimilation	Depalatalization	Simplification
*ti̯, *t^{h}i̯ [67]	*τι̯	*τσ$^{ι̯}$	*στ$^{ι̯}$	*σσ$^{ι̯}$	*σσ	σ
*ti̯, *t^{h}i̯ [68]	*τι̯	*τσ$^{ι̯}$	*στ$^{ι̯}$	*ττ$^{ι̯}$	Att. ττ	
*ki̯, *k^{h}i̯, *k^{w}i̯, *k^{wh}i̯	*κι̯	*τσ$^{ι̯}$				

65 The vertical column is the first element of the contraction.
66 Simplified description. For more information cf. Rix §103; SI §195–199; LJ §93–97.
67 In words which are morphologically opaque.
68 In words which are not morphologically opaque.

From PIE to the Attic Phoneme System of Consonants

PIE

	Labial	Inter-dental	Dental	Alveolar	Palatal	Velar	Labio-velar	Glottal
Stop	*p *(b) *b^{h}		*t *d *d^{h}		*k̂ *ĝ *$ĝ^{h}$	*k *g *g^{h}	*k^{w} *g^{w} *g^{wh}	? *h_1 = ?
Fricative		*[θ]	*s ~ *[z]			? *h_2 = χ ? *h_3 = γ	? *h_3 = $γ^{w}$	
Nasal	*m ~ *[m̥]		*n ~ *[n̥]		*[ɲ]	*[ŋ]		
Lateral				*l ~ *[l̥]				
? Trill				*r ~ *[r̥]				
Approximant	*u̯				*i̯			

LWP x1-x12, LWP x14.2, LWP 6, LWP 36, LWP 37, LWP 40.6

Proto-Greek

	Labial	Inter-dental	Dental	Alveolar	Palatal	Velar	Labio-velar	Glottal
Stop	*p *p^{h} *b		*t *t^{h} *d		*tsi̯ ? *dz^{i} ?	*k *k^{h} *g	*k^{w} *k^{wh} *g^{w}	
Fricative			*s ~ *[z]					*h
Nasal	*m ~ *[m̥]		*n ~ *[n̥]			*[ŋ]		
Lateral				*l ~ *[l̥]				
? Trill				*r ~ *[r̥]				
Approximant	*u̯				*i̯			

LWP x13-x20

Attic (5th century BC)

	Labial	Dental	Alveolar	Palatal	Velar	Glottal
Stop	p p^{h} b	t t^{h} d			k k^{h} g	
Fricative		s ~ [z]				h
Nasal	m	n			[ŋ]	
Lateral			l			
Trill			r ~ [r^{h}]			
Approximant	[u̯]			[i̯]		

Indo-European Languages[69]										
Anatolian	**Centum-Languages**					**Satem-Languages**				
	Tocharian	**Greek**	Celtic	Germanic	Italic	Indo-Iranian	Baltic	Slavic	Albanian	Armenian

Ancient Greek Dialects[70]									
Southern-Greek					**Western-Greek**		**Aeolic**		
Mycenaean	Arcadocypriot		Attic-Ionic		North-Western Greek	Doric			
	Arcadian	Cypriotic	Ionic	Attic	Elean Locrian Delphic	Laconian Argolic Corinthian ?	Lesbian	Boeotian	Thessalic

Koine Language

Modern Greek Dialects				
Northern-Greek	**Southern-Greek**	**Tsakonian**	**Cappadocian**	**Pontic**
Rumelian Epirote Thessalian Macedonian Thracian	Megara Aegina Athens Peloponnese Cyclades and Crete Smyrna Cyprus			

69 Cf. Meiser 1998:25 and Meier-Brügger 2000:18ff. The division of the IE languages in centum-languages and satem-languages is dealt with in paragraph 9. For the special status of Anatolian cf. paragraph 7.3 of unit 37.

70 Classification of ancient Greek dialects according to Kümmel 2007:38.

Bibliography

Adrados, Francisco Rodríguez (2005): *A history of the Greek language: from its origins to the present.* Leiden.

Aitchison, Jean (1976): *The Distinctive Features of Ancient Greek.* In Glotta 54 pp 173–201.

Allen, W. Sidney (1974): *Vox Graeca: the pronunciation of Classical Greek* (3rd ed.), Cambridge: University Press.

Bartoněk, Antonin (2003): *Handbuch of the mykenischen Griechisch.* Heidelberg: Winter.

Blümel, Wolfgang (1982): *The aiolischen Dialekte – Phonologie and Morphologie the inschriftlichen Texte out generativer Sicht.* Göttingen.

Brandenstein, Wilhelm (1954): *Griechische Sprachwissenschaft, Bd. I. Einleitung, Lautlehre, Etymologie.* Berlin: Göschen.

Brixhe, Claude (1996): *Phonétique et phonologie du Grec Ancien.* Leuven: Peeters.

Christidis, A.-F. (et al.) (Eds.) (2007): *A history of ancient Greek: from the beginnings to late Antiquity.* Cambridge.

García-Ramòn, José L. (1975): *Les origines postmycéniennes du groupe dialectal éolien.* Salamanca: Suplementos a MINOS.

Grammont, Maurice (1948): *Phonétique du grec ancien.* Lyon.

Horrocks, Geoffrey (1997): *Greek: A History of the Language and its Speakers.* London and New York: Longmans.

Humbert, Jean (1972): *Histoire de la langue grecque.* Paris

Karvounis, Christos (2008): *Aussprache and Phonologie in Altgriechischen.* Darmstadt: Wissenschaftliche Buchgesellschaft.

Kümmel, Martin J. (2007): *Konsonantenwandel.* Wiesbaden: Reichert.

Lejeune, Michel (1955): *Traité de phonétique grecque.* Paris.

LJ = Lejeune, Michel (1972): *Phonétique historique du mycénien et du grec ancien* (2nd ed.), Paris: Éditions Klincksieck.

Liesner, Malte (2012): *Arbeitsbuch zur Lateinischen Historischen Phonologie.* Wiesbaden: Reichert.

Lupaş, Liana (1972): *Phonologie du grec attique.* The Hague: Mouton.

Meier-Brügger, Michael (1992): *Griechische Sprachwissenschaft, Bd. II. Wortschatz, Formenlehre, Lautlehre, Indizes.* Berlin: Walter de Gruyter.

Meier-Brügger, Michael (2000): *Indogermanische Sprachwissenschaft*: Berlin: Walter de Gruyter.

Meillet, Antoine (1965): *Aperçu d'une histoire de la langue grecque.* Paris.

Meyer, Gustav (1896): *Griechische Grammatik.* Leipzig.

Palmer, Leonard Robert (1986): *The griechische Language: Grundzüge the Sprachgeschichte and the historisch-vergleichenden Grammatik.* Innsbruck.

Pisani, Vittore (1960): *Storia della lingua greca.* Torino.

Rix = Rix, Helmut (1992): *Historische Grammatik of the Griechischen.* Darmstadt: Wissenschaftliche Buchgesellschaft.

Schwyzer, Eduard (1939): *Griechische Grammatik, Bd.I: Allgemeiner Teil, Lautlehre, Wortbildung, FlexIon.* München.

SI = Sihler, Andrew L. (1995): *New Comparative Grammar of Greek and Latin.* New York, Oxford: Oxford University Press.

Sommerstein, Alan H. (1973): *The Sound Pattern of Ancient Greek.* Oxford.

Sturtevant, Edgar H. (1940): *The Pronunciation of Greek and Latin.* Pennsylvania: Linguistic Society.

Teodorsson, Sven-Tage (1974): *The Phonemic System of the Attic Dialect.* Göteburg.

Tichy, Eva (1983): *Onomatopoetische Verbalbildungen of the Griechischen.* SbÖAW 409. Wien: Verlag the Österreichischen Akademie the Wissenschaften.

Vendryes, Joseph. (1938): *Traité d'accentuation grecque.* Paris: Klincksieck.

Wilms, Lothar (2013): *Klassische Philologie and Sprachwissenschaft.* Göttingen.

A5 Abbreviations / Notations / Conventions

1. Languages

Arc.	Arcadian	Hitt.	Hittite	Myc.	Mycenaean
Att.	Attic	Hom.	Homeric	OHG	Old High German
Att.-Ion.	Attic-Ionic	IE	Indo-European	Pamph.	Pamphylian
Cyp.	Cyprian	Ion.	Ionic	PIE	Proto-Indo-European
Dor.	Doric	Lat.	Latin	Pind.	Pindar
Cret.	Cretan	Latv.	Latvian	Russ.	Russian
Gr.	Greek	Lesb.	Lesbian	Skr.	Sanskrit
Hes.	Hesiod	Lith.	Lithuanian	Ved.	Vedic

2. Grammatical Terms

acc.	accusative	inf.	infinitive	opt.	optative
act.	active voice	inscrip.	inscriptional	perf.	perfect tense
aor.	aorist tense	ipf.	imperfective tense	pl.	plural
f.	feminine	subj.	subjunctive	PPP	passive past participle
fut.	future tense	m.	masculine	prs.	present tense
gen.	genitive	midd.	middle voice	ptc.	participle
imp.	imperative	nom.	nominative	sg.	singular
ind.	indicative	n./nt.	neuter	voc.	vocative

3. Notations and Symbols

-	morpheme boundary	*B*	labial consonant	*R*	*r, l, n, m, i̯, u̯*
#	word boundary	*C*	any consonant	$\mathring{R}$	syllabic resonant
_	position of derived sound in sound change	$\hat{C}$	palatal consonant	SC	sound change
		C^h	aspirated consonant	*V*	vowel
<	is derived from	C^w	labialized consonant	$\breve{V}$	short vowel
>	becomes	C^j	palatalized consonant	$\bar{V}$	long vowel
**word*	reconstructed form	*H*	laryngeal	$\breve{\bar{V}}$	long or short vowel
*word**	expected word	L	line	IPA	International Phonetic Alphabet
^{x}*wort*	invented word	*N*	*n, m*		

4. Additional Remarks

a. Greek spelling is not used if the following signs appear in the reconstrcutions: $*b^h$, $*d^h$, $*g^h$, $*\hat{g}^h$, $*\hat{g}$, $*\hat{k}$, $*k^w$, $*g^w$, $*g^{wh}$, $*k^{wh}$, *n̥, *m̥, *r̥, *l̥, $*h_{1/2/3}$. **c.** Attic words are not further indicated. **b.** All sounds which are reconstructed out of an Attic viewpoint (e.g. *σ, *ϝ, *ι̯) have been marked with an asterisk. **c.** A derivation like Hom. ὄρεϊ > (23.1) Att. ὄρει does not state that the Attic word developed from the Homeric word but that one finds a Homeric attestation of the preform of the Attic word.